NEW GEOGRAPHY 1968-69

NEW GEOGRAPHY 1968-69

John Laffin

**Illustrated with
Maps and Diagrams**

ABELARD-SCHUMAN
London   New York   Toronto

By the same author:

War and Military History

Anzacs at War
Boys in Battle
British Campaign Medals
Codes and Ciphers
Digger
(Story of the Australian Soldier)
The Face of War
Jackboot
(Story of the German Soldier)
Links of Leadership

Middle East Journey
One Man's War
Return to Glory
Scotland the Brave
(Story of the Scottish Soldier)
Tommy Atkins
(Story of the English Soldier)
The Walking Wounded
Women in Battle

General Non-Fiction

The Anatomy of Captivity
The Hunger to Come
(The Food and
Population Crises)
New Geography 1966-67

© 1969 John Laffin
Standard Book Number 200.71606.9
L.C.C.C. Number 78-84649.
Printed in England by
John Gardner (Printers) Ltd.,
Liverpool, 20

LONDON
Abelard-Schuman
Limited
8 King Street WC2

NEW YORK
Abelard-Schuman
Limited
6 West 57 Street

TORONTO
Abelard-Schuman
Canada Limited
1680 Midland Avenue

CONTENTS

About this Book	page 15
Afghanistan	17
Agriculture	18
Agronomy	20
Aid	21
Alaska	26
Algeria	26
Aluminium	27
Antarctic	29
Aquaculture	29
Arabia	30
Argentina	30
Artificial Foods	31
Atomic Energy	33
Australia	35
Austria	38
Avalanches	39
Aviation	39
Beef	42
Belgium	43
Biafra	44
Biology, Industrial	44
Bolivia	45
Botswana	46
Brazil	47
Bridges	48
British Honduras	49
British West Indies	50
Bulgaria	51

Contents

Cambodia	*page* 52
Canada	53
Canals	55
Central America	56
Ceylon	56
Chile	57
China	57
Cities	58
Coal	59
Cocoa	61
Coffee	61
Colombia	62
Colonies	63
Copper	64
Costa Rica	65
Cotton	65
Cuba	65
Cyprus	66
Czechoslovakia	66
Dahomey	68
Dams	68
Dead Sea	71
Denmark	71
Disease	73
Drought	73
Earthquakes	74
East African Community	77
East Germany	78
Ecuador	78
Education	80
Eire	80
El Salvador	82
Ethiopia	83
European Economic Community	83
European Free Trade Association	85
Falkland Islands	87
Famine	87

Contents

	page
Faroe Islands	89
Finland	89
Fishing	90
Food	93
France	93
Geology	95
Geophysics	95
Ghana	97
Gibraltar	97
Glaciers	97
Gold	98
Greece	98
Guatemala	99
Guyana	100
Hawaii	101
Heating	101
Honduras	102
Hong Kong	102
Hungary	103
Hunger	104
Hurricanes	105
Hydrology	106
Ice Ages	108
Iceland	109
Illiteracy	109
India	110
Indian Ocean	111
Indonesia	111
Iran	112
Iraq	113
Irrigation	113
Israel	115
Italy	116
Jamaica	118
Japan	118
Jordan	119

Contents

Kenya	page 121
Korea (South)	121
Kuwait	123
Labour	124
Land Resources and Development	124
Latin America	125
Lebanon	126
Leeward Islands	127
Lesotho	127
Libya	129
Malawi	130
Malaysia	130
Malta	131
Maps	131
Mauritius	131
Meteorology	132
Methane	132
Mexico	135
Micronesia	136
Mining	136
Morocco	140
Mosquito Control	141
Muscat and Oman	142
Nagaland	143
Nauru	143
Nepal	144
The Netherlands	144
New Guinea	145
New Zealand	145
Nicaragua	147
Nigeria	147
Norway	148
Oceangraphy	149
Oil	149
Oil Pipelines	150
Olives	152

Contents

Pakistan	page 153
Paleontology	154
Panama	154
Paraguay	155
Peru	156
Philippines	156
Phosphates	157
Plastics	157
Poland	158
Pollution	159
Population	161
Portugal	163
Rainmaking	164
Refugees	164
Rhodesia	165
Rubber	165
Rumania	166
Scandinavia	167
Selenology	167
Shipbuilding	169
Sicily	172
Sierra Leone	173
Singapore	173
Somalia	174
South Africa	174
Southern Yemen	175
Spain	175
Spanish Africa	177
Sudan	177
Swaziland	178
Sweden	179
Switzerland	179
Syria	180
Taiwan	181
Tanzania	182
Tea	182

Contents

Telegraphic Communications	page 183
Textiles	183
Thailand	184
Timber	185
Tourism	185
Trade	188
Transport	189
Trinidad and Tobago	193
Tunisia	194
Turkey	195
Uganda	196
United Arab Republic	196
United Kingdom	197
United Nations	211
United Soviet Socialist Republic	212
United States of America	215
Uranium	221
Urban Development	222
Uruguay	224
Venezuela	225
Vietnam (North)	228
Vietnam (South)	228
Volcanoes	229
Water	231
Weather	231
West Germany	232
Wines and Vines	234
Wool	234
Yugoslavia	236
Zambia	237
Appendix	239
Index	241

LIST OF ILLUSTRATIONS

		page
1.	The West Indies	50
2.	Land Use in Cambodia	52
3.	The Rouse-Bisque Theory of Earthquakes	75
4.	East Germany	79
5.	Prospecting Licence Areas in Eire	81
6.	Intra-EFTA Trade	86
7.	The Libyan Oilfield	128
8.	The Gas Council Natural Gas Transmission System for Britain	133
9.	Rival Schemes for the Distribution of Energy in Canada and the U.S.A.	138
10.	Atomic Mining for Copper	140
11.	New Zealand's External Trade	146
12.	Increase in the World Population from 1830 to 2000	160
13.	Estimated Population Increases in Britain between 1964-1981	162
14.	Diagram of World Shipping Tonnage by Flag	170
15.	Esso Motor Hotels in Europe	187
16.	Major British Commodity Markets in 1967	198-199
17.	Main Economic Activities in Cornwall	201
18.	Strategy for the Development of South-East England	205
19.	Canals in England and Wales	208
20.	Agricultural Areas of the U.S.A.	216
21.	The Venezuelan Oilfields	226-227

ACKNOWLEDGMENTS

Several organizations have been helpful in supplying information and illustrations for this book. My thanks are due to: Barclays Bank Economic Intelligence Department for permission to reproduce maps and diagrams; the European Free Trade Association for the table of intra-EFTA trade; the Westminster Bank for the map of British commodity markets; Shell International Petroleum Ltd.; Standard Oil Company; the *Geographical Magazine*, London, for the map of Cambodia; the Gas Council; Esso Motor Hotels Inc.; the British Waterways Board; the Department of Economic Affairs for the map of South-East England; the FAO for the world population diagram; *Newsweek* for the earthquake diagram; the Institution of Mining and Technology for the map of Eire; the U.S. Department of Agriculture; the Commercial Bank of Australia for the diagram of New Zealand trade; the National Bank of Australasia. Many national information bureaux have been co-operative in verifying information, which came in the first place from a multitude of sources.

I must thank Dr. M. E. Witherick of Southampton University for his suggestions; Mr. and Mrs. C. Laffin for tedious hours of filing; Mrs. F. Penfold for typing and, as always, my wife for typing, indexing and much else besides.

Abbreviations used in this book include:

ACC	Aid Ceylon Consortium—U.K., U.S.A., France, West Germany, Italy, Netherlands
ADB	Asian Development Bank
ADC	Andean Development Corporation
AID	Agency for International Development (U.S.A.)
CACM	Central American Common Market
CARE	Co-operative for American Relief Everywhere
COMECON	Council for Mutual Economic Assistance (East European)
COMIBOL	State Mining Corporation of Bolivia
CSIRO	Commonwealth Scientific and Industrial Research Organization (Australia)
FAO	Food and Agricultural Organization
GATT	General Agreement for Tariffs and Trade
HEP	Hydro-electric Power
IACCP	Inter-American Council of Commerce and Production
IADB	Inter-American Development Bank
IAEA	International Atomic Energy Authority
ICO	International Coffee Organization
IDA	International Development Association
IMF	International Monetary Fund
INCAP	Institute of Nutrition for Central America and Panama
ITC	International Tin Council
m	million
OECD	Organization for Economic Co-operation and Development
OEEC	Organization for European Economic Co-operation
sq. m.	square miles
SST	Supersonic Transport
TAL	Trans-Alpine Pipeline
UNCF	United Nations Children's Fund
UNCTAD	United Nations Conference on Trade and Development
UNDP	United Nations Development Programme
UNESCO	United Nations Educational, Scientific and Cultural Organization
WFP	World Food Programme
WHO	World Health Organization

ABOUT THIS BOOK

This second edition of New Geography supplies information new since the publication of *New Geography 1966-67*. I must stress that no entry has merely been revised; all entries are completely new. To notice just how new, they should be read in conjunction with the first edition. Indeed, I suggest this as a practice in using these books, for obviously, by comparing the two, the rate of development can be assessed. Collectively, these two books and those which will follow them will keep orthodox text books up to date.

The classification is similar to that of the first edition—alphabetical on the basis of countries, commodities and related geographical phenomena, such as geology, irrigation and population. Where necessary, entries suggest cross references to a subject; for instance, CEYLON cross-refers to TEA and RUBBER. HAWAII gives a cross-reference to HYDROLOGY.

The index at the rear of the book gives *all* references to a particular subject, for instance to coal, which might be mentioned in relation to a dozen different countries. As another example, in *New Geography 1966-67* Great Britain was referred to no fewer than eighty times and all are shown in the index.

Unless otherwise stated the population statistics are correct for June 1968, trade figures for the end of 1967.

The author is grateful to those geographers, students and others who wrote, following the publication of the 1966-67 edition, expressing their support for such a book and suggesting future additional entries.

A

AFGHANISTAN

250,000 sq.m. Pop. 15.2m. One of the current problems facing this rapidly developing country is that of its nomad population. About one-sixth of the total is nomadic, yet they produce over half the country's supply of meat and nearly all the wool. The nomads are not always liked in the villages near which they graze their animals. When the weather becomes warmer in the spring they leave their winter quarters and move towards the centre of the country, into the mountains of the Hindu Kush. The journey takes up to three months, the nomads then finding plentiful grazing on slopes too steep to be farmed by villagers. But as the summer draws on and the melting snows cease to feed the streams the nomads are forced to restrict their grazing to areas around permanent water supplies usually near villages. This results in a conflict of interests, as it is common for flocks to trample ripe corn crops. The nomads themselves are bitter for until the closing of borders in mid-1967 they were able to go as far as India or Pakistan to overwinter. With this mass migration blocked, the nomads' fortunes have declined, but the Afghan government has been able to use the set-back to induce many nomads to settle on newly irrigated land. Much further change must come, but the government is unsure of the methods to be used. Some administrators believe that the nomadic habit should be allowed to die a natural death, a victim of development, by a slow and painful process that has already started.

After a decade of rivalry among great powers, Afghanistan has ceased to be an undeveloped buffer state and will soon have a complete girdle of well-surfaced roads round its central massif—and under it; the U.S.S.R. has completed a two-mile tunnel through the snow ridge of the Hindu Kush. Even camel trains use this tunnel. The Soviet Union leads in aid, with the U.S.A. and West Germany following. The third five-year plan, which began in 1967, is rapidly expanding tourism, but in 1968 only 25,000 foreign tourists were expected. Many sites of remarkable interest are being discovered and developed. Prime among them is the valley of Bamian, with its cliff caves, trout streams and its gigantic Buddha statues.

AGRICULTURE

BARLEY. In the past two years a strong overseas demand, mainly in Europe, has developed for British barley; 1m tons were exported from the 1966 crop and rather more than this in 1967 compared with only 0.4m tons in 1963. Much of this barley is finding its way to the heart of the Common Market—to Rotterdam, Antwerp and Hamburg, up the Rhine to Duisburg and to Genoa and Leghorn. Because the livestock population of the EEC is expected to rise over the next ten years the demand for feeding-barley should continue to grow.

COMMODITY AGREEMENTS. Energetic efforts are being made, particularly through the United Nations Conference on Trade and Development (UNCTAD), to promote satisfactory commodity agreements, but there is still a great gulf between the ideas of exporters and importers as to the requirements needed in such pacts; the problem of stabilizing prices is complex. While many commodities, such as coffee and cocoa, are in surplus, there is for the importing countries less incentive for agreement and this points to the greatest need at present— agreement among producers to limit not only exports but also output.

CROP PROTECTION. The growth of the crop protection chemical industry is now extremely rapid both in techniques and in volume of business. In 1950 only 4,200 ground crop-sprayers were in use in the U.K.; by mid-1968 the figure was 60,000. This is significant in view of the loss of 1.5m acres of farming land to building and other development since 1945 and an increase of 8m in the population in the same period. In 1967 British farmers spent £10m on crop protection products.

EEC—BRITAIN. Agriculture has been an obstacle in the path of the EEC's development and progress towards a common farm policy is slow. As the EEC agricultural policy develops the Community will be less inclined to make concessions to British agriculture. Production in the Common Market has been rising by about 3% annually while the numbers working on the land have decreased by 4% a year; productivity in the U.K. has been increasing at a similar pace. However, agricultural prices in Britain and Europe diverge; in the EEC prices paid to farmers have risen in line with the cost of living and farm incomes have increased accordingly, whereas in Britain prices for farm produce have remained steady despite steeply rising costs. In an effort to maintain profitability the British farming industry has had to invest heavily in machinery and buildings and to make full use of advanced scientific techniques. As a result British farming has become more highly efficient and adaptable; the competitive position of U.K. farmers is much stronger than is sometimes thought.

From July 1, 1967 uniform prices for grain took effect in the EEC. In order to compensate farmers in Germany and Italy, where the uniform price level will be considerably lower than prices at present prevailing, direct cash compensation from Community funds will be allotted in descending scale during 1967-70. An intervention price, which is 7% below the target price, also operates and, in each country, an official agency is obliged to purchase at this price all home-grown grain which cannot be sold on better terms.

REVOLUTION IN GRASS GROWING. In the autumn of 1968 British farmers who take grass production seriously were eagerly seeking supplies of the tiny seeds of an Italian ryegrass called Ellesmere. It is estimated that if all British hayfields were sown with it farmers would have an extra 1m tons of hay each season and they would be able to graze cattle on it two extra weeks yearly. The National Institute of Agricultural Botany, Cambridge, endorses "unlimited" use of the grass. Ellesmere was bred as long ago as 1908 and is used in Australia and the U.S.A. (See *Agronomy, Artificial Foods*.)

AGRONOMY

For the agricultural scientist the world's increasing population combined with its inadequate food supply present the twofold problem of how to increase the crop yield on existing farmland and how to make use of acreage previously considered uncultivable. In the Philippines, Rockefeller Foundation scientists have successfully tackled the first part of the problem by developing a short, stiff rice plant that may increase the average yield of each crop as much as 800%. Because it can also produce three crops a year instead of the usual one it has the potential of raising total output as much as 2,600%.

Michigan State University agronomists have attacked both parts of the food problem at once. They have learned to lay down underground strips of asphalt that literally pave the way for richer crops of all varieties. Realizing that certain soils were productive because an underlying layer of clay was trapping rain water instead of allowing it to drain away, the agronomists, after much experimenting, found that "planted" asphalt could achieve the same effect. Trial plantings for cabbage yielded 505 crates per acre compared with 260 crates for untreated areas. Potato yields rose 50% and cucumbers as much as 100%. The cost of laying the asphalt could be recouped with the first harvest. The asphalt is laid by a tractor-pulled device that lifts a two-foot strip of earth, sprays warm liquid asphalt underneath it—this dries immediately— and then allows the soil to settle back into place. It is believed that asphalt layers could double the acreage of rice fields in South-East Asia. Used with the new Rockefeller Foundation strain of rice the undersealing method could have dramatic results.

Rust of cereal crops has long caused great economic loss; currently it runs to hundreds of millions of pounds and in the U.S.A. alone destroys 6% of the crop each year. Every time agronomists breed a resistant strain, within a decade or so a new and devastating rust develops through natural mutation. Financed by a grant from the U.S. Agriculture Department, an Israeli plant pathologist, Isaac Wahl, collected 2,500 samples of wild oats and the most promising 100, together with 4,000 resistant selections from other countries, were subjected to rust. A strain of wild oats found near Mount Carmel, Israel, has resisted all rust attacks and will soon go into large scale production; it could save the U.S. farmer alone up to 26m dollars annually. Wahl is now breeding fungi-resistant grain strains that will, like plasma in a blood bank, be immediately available for sowing in areas hard-hit by rust epidemics. He has also found wheat and barley strains that are apparently resistant to rust.

AID

A distinct new trend is apparent in the "aid" given by the developed to the still developing nations. It consists more than ever of helping the undeveloped countries to help themselves—"aid through trade"—and was apparent in the agenda and decisions taken at the second UNCTAD meeting in New Delhi, 1968. Some progress was made towards stabilizing raw material markets, but more notably it will be easier for the developing nations to export finished and semi-finished goods to the industrial nations; these goods, in March 1968, accounted for only one tenth of total exports, with three-quarters going to the U.S.A., Britain, West Germany and France. During the meeting a "Joint International Trade Centre" was agreed upon and will be operated by UNCTAD and GATT (General Agreement on Tariffs and Trade).

New Geography 1968-69

Britain's aid to developing countries for 1968-69 was fixed at £235m (£205m in 1967-68). There are three reasons for the increase. (1) Aid to Singapore and Malaysia was increased following the acceleration of British military withdrawal. (2) Britain's contribution to IDA rose; however, Britain usually contrives to get 30s worth of orders through the IDA for every £1 it contributes. (3) Under the Kennedy Round agreement Britain undertook to contribute £5m to a food aid programme.

Japan is already the fifth largest supplier of foreign aid and by 1970 is expected to be providing about £370m in economic help to developing countries, mostly in South-East Asia.

Despite the large sums of aid-money listed below it has become clear since 1966 that the confidence of donor countries has been shaken. Generally, the receiving countries must now either earn their aid or do without it. The days of benevolence for its own sake are practically gone. Wars fought for tribal suzerainty, as in Africa, or through deep religious rivalry, as between Pakistan and India, are hardly to be supported even indirectly by financial aid. Some critics say that aid, as administered at present, is having precisely the opposite effect to that intended and question whether the £600m spent by the Western Powers in Africa has added to the stability of the nations of this continent. The donor countries have been faced too often in recent history with violent upheavals in the territories to which their money has been assigned. These upheavals have been followed by revelations of corruption in high places amounting almost to the aid given. Where technical and administrative assistance exists in the fields of welfare, agricultural husbandry, medical treatment and education, the policy of aid is valid. Where the aid is of a purely financial nature it frequently evaporates in corruption. Largely following the U.S.A.'s let's-be-rational policy on aid, all aid is becoming more soundly based.

ALGERIA. Algeria has been allotted £7m from the U.N. Development Fund towards an agricultural development project in one of the poorest mountain areas south of Algiers, and £500,000 towards a National Institute for Production and Industrial Development at Boumaredes.

ARGENTINA. The Inter-American Development Bank provided half the 35m dollars needed for grain silos and another 34m dollars for road improvements. The World Bank has lent 15m dollars for credit and technical services for a 39m dollar livestock project. The U.S.A. Treasury and a group of banks from America, Europe, Japan and Canada provided 275m dollars for stand-by credits.

BOLIVIA. This country badly needs foreign aid for welfare programmes (education and housing) especially among the under-privileged mineworkers. In 1967 U.S. AID and the IADB granted loans of 50m dollars but in 1968 the U.S.A. abolished loans and decided to give money only for specific project assistance. Canada has lent 1.5m dollars for mining services and equipment.

BRAZIL. The World Bank had lent 22m dollars to assist the financing of an aluminium smelter and refinery; Britain £16m to purchase marine equipment, and the IADB 36m dollars for HEP work.

CEYLON. The IDA is helping with credit for raising the level of agricultural production, the World Bank has approved a loan to the Development Finance Corporation of Ceylon and the ADB is financing assistance for the tea industry. The ACC pledged £30m in commodity aid for 1968.

COLOMBIA. Colombia has a 200m-dollar stand-by credit from the IMF, AID and the World Bank; a further 17m dollars from the World Bank for livestock development and 9m dollars for irrigation. Money has been given by IADB for farm mechanization.

ECUADOR. £1m is coming from IADB; and Ecuador has long-term credits for the purchase of capital goods from the Netherlands, Switzerland and Czechoslovakia.

GHANA. 12m dollars is being given by the U.S.A. for agricultural commodities and raw materials; £10m from the UNDP to finance 53 projects; and other money is coming from the IMF, the U.K., West Germany and Denmark.

HONDURAS. The World Bank lent 8.6m dollars for road improvements, mainly for the 154-mile Western Highway, the main link with El Salvador.

INDIA. India is receiving large unspecified amounts from the U.S.S.R. for industry. There was a promise in May 1968 of 1,450m dollars from the AID, including 100m dollars in debt relief; none had been handed over by September 1968. The U.S.A. is providing 225m dollars for agricultural and industrial goods.

IRAN. The World Bank has lent 22m dollars for agricultural development on the Ghazvin Plain, west of Teheran.

IRAQ. Spain has provided 50m dollars for investment.

LEBANON. Lebanon is receiving £1.2m from the Kuwait Fund for Arab Economic Development for grain silos in Beirut and £18m from the World Bank for "various projects" including highways.

MALAYSIA. The World Bank has lent £4.5m for irrigation. Other funds are coming from France, Sweden, the U.S.A. and Japan.

MEXICO. Mexico is receiving 25m dollars from the World Bank for extending irrigation in the Rio Colorado district; and 34m dollars from the IAD Bank towards the cost of a programme of small irrigation works.

MOROCCO. The World Bank has lent £200 for the first stage of the River Sebou irrigation/conservation scheme.

PAKISTAN. Pakistan is receiving many loans or grants, including 35m dollars from the world Bank for private industrial development; 70m dollars from AID for agricultural and industrial materials; 450m dollars from the Aid-Pakistan Consortium; 550m dollars from the World Bank to cover "development requirements" 1969-70.

Aid

PANAMA. Panama is being lent 3.45m dollars by IADB for the extension of water supplies and is receiving three AID loans, totalling 9.3m dollars, for roads and drains.

PARAGUAY. Aid to Paraguay consists of 8m dollars from the IMF for stand-by credit; DM 12m from West Germany for small industries; DM 24m for the construction of a cement factory; 3m dollars from Japan for the manufacture of tung oils and soya.

PERU. Unspecified credits are being provided by the IADB for capital goods; 70m dollars from IADB for electricity and irrigation; 1m dollars from the Netherlands for the promotion of dairy farming.

SIERRA LEONE. The U.K. is providing £560,000 for British goods and services.

SOUTH KOREA. £6m is coming from AID for thermal generating stations; a further £5m AID money for various equipment; £70m in commercial loans from Japan, together with £32m in credits for the fishing industry.

SUDAN. 31m dollars is being lent by the World Bank for railways and rolling stock; 6m dollars from AID for roads and airport runways. Yugoslavia has provided finance for the purchase of Yugoslav-built ships. Extensive but unspecified help from the Kuwait Arab Fund is for the development of new agricultural land.

TANZANIA. Tanzania's loans consist of £10.2m from West Germany for agriculture and housing; £7.5m from the World Bank for roads, schools and agriculture; £16m from Communist China; and £2m from the U.S.A.

THAILAND. 21 nations supply aid to Thailand, largely because it is a sound investment. In 1968 the World Bank approved £8.5m towards the Nan River HEP scheme.

URUGUAY. Uruguay is receiving 20m dollars from AID; 19m dollars in wheat supplies from the U.S.A.; 30m dollars privately from U.S. and Canadian banks; 35m dollars from

Argentina and Brazil, and a stand-by credit of 25m dollars from the IMF.

YUGOSLAVIA. The World Bank is lending 10.5m dollars to assist in the financing of industries dealing with iron and steel, synthetic fibres, paper and plywood; 7m dollars is coming from a consortium of British banks for improvements in the lead and zinc industry.

ALASKA

571,000 sq. m. Pop. 255,000. In 1967-68 the salmon catch was the worst since 1889, with disastrous economic consequences. Sockeye reds and humpback pinks were 71% less than in 1966 and State aid was given to the Indians, Eskimos and Aleuts who do most of the fishing. Alaska's fish experts knew in 1963 and 1965 that bad times were coming. In each of these years disastrous freezes occurred; such streams as the Nass and Skeena froze solid and most of the young salmon that survived the ice were swept away with their gravel nurseries. Japanese fishermen, breaking the international treaty precluding other nations from fishing closer to Alaska than 175° west longitude, have helped to deplete the supply of salmon available in Alaskan rivers. (Bristol Bay red salmon, after a 6,000-mile swim, swim back to mate and die in the same streams where they were born. Japanese depredations prevent this.)

ALGERIA

855,000 sq. m. Pop. 12.5m. Austerity measures and protective tariffs introduced during 1967-68 have dampened economic activity. Petroleum and natural gas now provide the major part of the country's foreign exchange earnings. Output in 1967 amounted to 40m metric tons, about 15% above the

1966 figure, but Algeria is having much trouble in expanding its markets. New customers must be found if a new gas liquefaction plant being built at Skikda is to operate economically. At present the U.K. is the major consumer, taking 1,500m cubic metres a year. Agreements have been reached for sales to Italy and Spain and there is a possibility of exporting to Canada. The estimated 1968 revenue from gas and oil was £100m double the 1965 figure. The threat of nationalization has deterred private investment, though a number of light industries have been developed, mainly to supply the local market. Recently approved schemes include factories making knitwear, batteries, glass, textiles, cheese and shoes. A French firm is building a sugar factory, and a plant for packing and distributing dates will employ 2,000. A steel complex, set up at Annaba with French and Russian assistance, will make, among much else, pipes for a fourth oil pipeline. A German firm is to head a foreign group that will modernize Algerian mining and industrialize the south. A large petro-chemical and fertilizer complex at Arzew began operations late in 1968. A French ban on Algerian wine in 1967 led to a loss of £30m in 1967 and again in 1968; however, wine is now being sold to the Soviet Union and to West Germany. The major problem of soil erosion is being studied by a new commission. It was estimated in 1968 that an annual investment of £10m is needed to ensure long-term supplies of water (the present rate is only £300,000). The Soviet Union has helped to build two dams and to drill many wells. Yugoslavia has financed a tannery at Roinba and Egypt a textile mill at Dar-Ben-Kheda. The European population of 1m in 1960 had dropped to 65,000 by 1968.

ALUMINIUM

(Following the 1966-67 edition of *New Geography* the author received several letters seeking reasons for the rapid development of aluminium.) Although the aluminium ore, bauxite, is the most common metallic mineral—forming 8% of the world's crust—aluminium was the last of the major metals to be produced on a commercial scale. Once the technical problems of extraction had been solved consumption grew rapidly because aluminium has valuable properties. It is much the lightest of the major metals (a third the weight of steel, copper or zinc; a quarter that of lead). It has strong resistance to corrosion. It is second only to copper as a conductor of heat and electricity. It is a good reflector of light and radiant heat. These qualities, coupled with a relatively stable price, have made aluminium the established material for a wide range of uses in the engineering and construction industries.

It seems to be not generally realized that in the last decade the importance of HEP resources as a determinant of bauxite-smelter location has declined. Power usage per unit of output has been reduced while other forms of power generation have become more competitive. In addition, substantial reductions in the cost of transporting bauxite and alumina in bulk have made location of smelters near to large markets more attractive. Add political stability and investment incentives and it makes good sense to build new smelters in many countries.

Substantial variations exist in the levels of aluminium consumption. In 1967 consumption per head in the U.S.A. was 39 lb, more than double the level in the leading Western European countries. In India consumption was less than 1 lb a head. The amount of aluminium used in a country can be related to the purchasing power of the people. On this basis, the future growth in the demand for the metal in less developed countries could be considerable.

Aluminium consumption has been boosted by substitution at the expense of other metals. Notable examples are the displacement of copper in the electric cable, of chrome-plated steel in car trim, of steel and wood in windows, wood in beer barrels and tinplate in canning. But aluminium itself is now under attack from some materials that it has displaced. Thin tinplate and corrosion resistant steels are examples. In the long run plastics present a more serious threat; examples are fibreglass containers and plastic compounds for car trim.

Despite these threats the Institute of Metals predicts that by 1975, in thousand metric tons, Japan's use of aluminium will have increased from 390 to 750, Western Europe's from 1798 to 3000 and the U.S.A.'s from 3274 to 5000. (In 1957 the figures were, respectively, 75, 817 and 1374.)

ANTARCTIC

Members of the British Antarctic Survey base at Halley Bay completed, in 1968, a route to the Shackleton Mountains in British Antarctic Territory. The trip of 1200 miles is the longest made from the base; the route mapped will assist future surveying and geological research. The team reconnoitred beyond the Theron Mountains towards the Shackleton Mountains, finding the Slessor Glacier much further east than expected.

AQUACULTURE

One of the most promising crops for sea farms is giant kelp; off California it grows to 300 feet tall, its surface fronds spreading 200 feet wide. Kelp assimilates and stores iodine, potassium and other nutrients and it attracts many fish. It is the fastest-growing plant on earth, with fronds lengthening two feet a day. Floating reapers are beheading the Californian kelp forests to make cattle cake and large scale experiments are in progress to make kelp culture a thriving branch of marine agriculture. The production of kelp has increased in the last two years, especially in Norway.

In the North Atlantic the U.S.S.R. is now conducting a "super" hunt into the possibilities of aquaculture from a floating cannery town on the Grand Banks. With far-sighted and well-financed oceanology, the Soviet Union maintains the largest research operations on the world's oceans. (See *Fishing*.)

ARABIA

The Federation of Arabian Emirates came into formal existence at the end of March, 1968. States involved are the Bahrain archipelago, Qatar (the peninsula south-east of Bahrain), and the seven Trucial States—Abu Dhabi, Dubai, Sharjah, Ajman, Umm al Qaiwainn, Ras al Khaimah and Fujairah. All are on the Persian Gulf—or the Arab Gulf as it is firmly known in the Arab world. The total population is about 300,000. Because of the oil wealth of Abu Dhabi, Qatar, Bahrain and Dubai this is the richest federation, in terms of per capita income, the world has known. The "big three" Gulf states—Saudi Arabia, Kuwait and Iraq—support the federation; Saudi Arabia and Kuwait as well as Britain and the U.S.A. will give technical and economic aid during the development stages. Bahrain international airport, formerly directed by the British Board of Trade, has gone to the federation. No doubt many strains and possible breakaways face the federation, which is the direct result of Britain's decision to withdraw all military forces.

Dubai is the commercial heart of the Trucial States and is known as the Beirut of the Gulf; it is the main port for imported goods to the federation and consequently has a big entrepot trade. Imports in 1967 amounted to £33.7m (£23m in 1966).

ARGENTINA

1.1m sq. m. Pop. 23m. During 1968 the Argentine economy entered a phase of recovery, helped by a 40% devaluation—the tenth since April 1964. The cost of living rose 24% in 1967, only 5% less than in 1966. Major investments include the construction of an oil pipeline from Mendoza to Cordoba, a £180m HEP complex at El Chocon-Cerros Colorados and improvements to communications; a large amount of investment money was raised in West Germany. Industrialists from the U.S.A., Italy and Japan are playing a greater part in Argentinian industry. Although 32% of the labour force is engaged in industry Argentina remains highly dependent on agriculture, which accounts for over 90% of the exports. In 1968 the industry faced several major problems. Higher wheat prices discouraged European buyers and apart from a 1m-ton contract with Brazil few overseas sales were made.* Port congestion and delays are blocking deliveries of corn for export. Argentina also suffered heavy losses from the British ban imposed in December 1967 on meat exports from countries where foot and mouth disease is endemic. (The ban was removed in April 1968.) Low world commodity prices, especially for meat and wool, and increasing competition from New Zealand and Uruguay, following the devaluation of their currencies, are also affecting Argentina's agriculture.

ARTIFICIAL FOODS

On present trends mass starvation is virtually inevitable by 1980; measured by protein deficiency it is already with us. Synthetic amino acids are already made on a huge scale in the U.S.A. for supplementing animal feeds. Cereals are deficient in one amino acid (lysine) and legumes in another (methionine) and adding these in small amounts to feeds does dramatically increase meat, milk and egg production. For animal feeds synthetics could and should be vastly extended. In Western Europe half of all agricultural produce goes to animals, in America far more—all to turn out animal protein with a net efficiency averaging 10% (3% on beef). It is uneconomic for animals to be living off land that could be

* In 1966 Argentina's own harvest was so poor it imported 180,000 tons from Rumania and Spain.

producing high-protein bulk foods far more effectively; they eat animal protein at the level of British people—70 to 90 grammes a day or ten times the average for more than half the human population. In the last two years cows have been healthily raised on ground corn cobs, synthetic urea and a little molasses.

By 1980 the population of South-East Asia alone will be about 2,300m. On the Freedom from Hunger target of 20 grammes of animal protein per person by 1980—the present consumption is only 8 grammes—South-East Asia would need 10m metric tons of synthetic protein. This is about five times the free world's output of synthetic rubber, an old-established industry with strong commercial incentives. The basic task is to improve protein production in the farmer's fields, despite the apparent promise of biosynthesis—getting yeasts or algae to synthetize proteins (i.e. themselves) from wastes. Under ideal conditions 1,000 lb of yeast can produce a ton of protein from a ton of petroleum and some fertilizer. In 1969 about 380,000 tons of yeasts will be grown on molasses and wood pulp liquor for animal food; in 1968 it became possible for them to grow on straw, bagasse and other plant wastes that are now burned by the tens of millions of tons each year. It must be remembered that on a factory scale the economics of such synthetics could be formidable. In Britain Supro Laboratories are selling a high-protein powder in East Africa to supplement protein-deficient staple diets. Where rice, maize or wheat is the staple, less than 1 oz a day, costing 1d to 2d, provides adequate protein.

The INCAP programme in Latin America is now making high-protein supplements from locally grown oil seeds at a rate sufficient to feed 100,000 children a day with all their protein needs in the form of three glasses of milk. Such supplements are necessary wherever sago or cassava are staple foods since they have practically zero protein; even rice has only 8% protein. (Wheat has 15%.)

ATOMIC ENERGY

Atomic energy has unlimited potential for economic development and is already changing geography. Since 1958 the IAEA—98 member states in 1968—has achieved much, especially in the last two years.

AGRICULTURE. Improvements of rice yields through collective research to make better use of fertilizers are being studied in twelve countries, and for maize in eight countries. Production of better rice, wheat and barley through radiation-induced mutations; control or eradication of insect pests, preservation of food against contamination; fullest use of water in soil are some of the other ways in which atomic energy is being used to improve agriculture.

DESALTING. This is an increasingly important application of nuclear energy. The IAEA is adding to its basic work the idea of linking the nuclear power/desalting operations with chemical and fertilizer plants to create new agro-industrial centres. The region of Mexico and the U.S.A. around the Gulf of Mexico is the major area under survey but in 1968 missions were also sent to Chile, El Salvador, Finland, Korea, Pakistan, Peru, the Philippines, Thailand, Tunisia and Turkey.

HYDROLOGY. Since 1962 a continuous world survey of the content of tritium (the radioactive isotope of hydrogen) in water as well as some stable isotopes has been carried out jointly with the World Meteorological Organization to determine the water turn-over on earth. More than twenty countries have been helped to estimate their local water development problems; studies of twenty large rivers were carried out jointly with UNESCO as part of the programme of the International Hydrological Decade (to conclude in 1972).

The injection of radio-isotopes which can mix with water, like bromine, iodine and tritium, has helped to trace the movement of subsoil streams and to discover underground reservoirs for pump irrigation. Similarly the directional flow and volume of seepage water from the beds of irrigation canals can help in the study of the problems of water balance in the waterlogged areas. One very successful application of the tracers is the use of labelled sea-sand to determine the movement of silt harbours. Such studies not only help in the dredging of the silt but in dumping it at an appropriate spot so that it is not brought back into the harbours by the undercurrents. The Port of London Authority seems to have cut its dredging budget by half as a result of the studies carried out with the help of labelled sand. (See *Hydrology* in alphabetical section.)

INDUSTRY. Increasing efforts are being made to acquaint industrialists with radio-isotope techniques for improving the quality of production of manufactured goods in processing, wear and tear and flow control, and sterilization of medical products—all ways of saving vast amounts of money as well as leading to more rapid industrial development.

REVOLUTIONARY DESERT CULTIVATION. In Warsaw, late in 1967, Dr. G. T. Seaborg, chairman of the U.S. Atomic Energy Commission, announced new progress in plans for making the desert "bloom" around an atomic city by providing desalted water from the sea and electricity from a nuclear power station. Dr. Seaborg describes the desert atomic city as a "near-term possibility". Its centre would be an atomic power station of 1,000 megawatts, producing 400m gallons of desalted water a day. This could be used to grow 500,000 tons of grain a year—enough to feed 2.5m people. The land needed for this would be 200,000 acres, fertilized by chemicals made with the electricity from the nuclear power station. As this would absorb only a fraction of the available electricity the rest could be used for making more fertilizer with, for example, the nitrogen from the air, and exporting it from the atomic city to other areas where water for agriculture is available. One such city could thus feed 10m people. In addition to fertilizers many other chemicals could be made. Among the many benefits imaginative use of nuclear power could bring, Dr. Seaborg envisages an atom-powered reclaiming and reprocessing plant. This would take in at one end all the waste and "junk" of modern living and produce at the other end raw materials for factories.

AUSTRALIA

2.968m sq. m. Pop. 12m. There has been no slackening in development since the first edition of *New Geography*. The one retarding factor is the recurrence of drought. As this edition went to press estimates indicated that the value of the agricultural output for 1968 would be 600m dollars less than the 3.7m for 1966-67. Agricultural products account for over 60% of total exports and concern already expressed over a fall in world commodity prices was intensified by the devaluation of sterling; over half the country's fruit and dairy exports are marketed in the U.K.

Continued growth in earnings from minerals—output for 1967 was 13% higher than for 1966—is compensation for a decline in the value of agricultural exports. The most important development since 1966 has been the exploitation of oil fields, indigenous oil having been the one major raw material Australia lacked.

The formation of the Australian Resources Development Bank has been a major step in ensuring capital for exploitation of the newer industries. Sales to Japan and the U.S.A. now account for 20% and 12% respectively of total exports, while the U.S.A. has become Australia's largest supplier.

Australia is the first country to enter its main period of development in the age of electronics and automation, thus it does not have the social problems these advances have brought to the older industrial nations.

With about one-third of 1% of the world's population Australia is surpassed as an exporter of raw materials only by the U.S.A., the Soviet Union, Canada and France. Australia exports about 18% of its gross national product and a similiar proportion is spent on imports. (By comparison, the U.S.A. exports about 5%, Eire 37%.)

Among other developments an American-Japanese combine will spend 100m U.S. dollars on a new export coalfield, a railway line and a port in central Queensland. Another American company is to build a large truck assembly plant in Queensland. These are typical of contracts signed each month.

BAUXITE. An important bauxite discovery is reported in Western Australia. More than 100m tons of bauxite with some extremely high grade deposits have been proved in the remote Admiralty Gulf area of the Kimberleys.

BEEF. Pasture experiments in the Northern Territory show that many square miles of country could carry twice as many cattle with improved grasses and proper management. For instance, the coastal plains region from Adelaide River to East Alligator at present carries only one animal a square mile on unimproved native pastures.

"BEEF" ROADS. The Federal Government and the governments of Queensland, Western Australia and South Australia will spend 77m dollars on new roads in Australia's outback cattle country.

IRON ORE. The largest single cargo to leave Australia was 90,000 tons of iron ore sent from Dampier, Western Australia, to Rotterdam, late in 1967. Valued at 1m dollars the ore was loaded in fifteen hours by a bulk carrier. Contracts with Japan cover the next fifteen years and involve at least 500m tons of ore. The Northern Territory is the latest region to begin shipping ore to Japan.

LITHIUM. Western Mining Corporation has found big reserves of lithium, a constituent of some light metal alloys, at Mount Marion, 22 miles south of Kalgoorlie.

MANUFACTURES. Australia's exports of manufactured goods have doubled since 1964, to 464m dollars.

METHANE. A 486-mile pipeline is being built to carry natural gas from the Gidgealpa-Moomba field in the far north of South Australia to Adelaide.

Australia

OIL. Barrow Island oilfield, Western Australia, has achieved targets set when it became a commercial oilfield in 1966. The daily flow is now 30,000 bb. The Victorian offshore fields will produce nearly half of Australia's crude oil needs by 1970—i.e. the fields will yield 240,000 bb a day. With the fields at Barrow and at Moonie-Alton in Queensland total output should be about 300,000 bb of the national requirements of 500,000 bb a day.

PRAWNS. The Northern Territory lists prawning among its new industries. Seven companies are operating between the Joseph Bonaparte Gulf and the Gulf of Carpentaria. Three are joint ventures with Japanese interests; the other four are all-Australian. Surveys show that 20m lb of prawns can be taken from the Territory's waters each year without endangering the vast prawn beds. This could be worth 30m dollars on the Japanese market. Eventually the industry will take 50m lb a year, worth 75m dollars.

RICE. Many rice crops in Australia's 1967 and 1968 harvests yielded more than four tons to the acre, a world record. The 1968 harvest was 200,000 tons.

SHIPBUILDING. Australian shipyards are now engaged in the biggest programme in their history, with orders worth 180m dollars in March 1969. Most of the vessels will be used in the construction and service of offshore oil and gas rigs and for the Australian coastal trade.

SHIPPING. Australian ports are expected to feel the first benefits of containerized ships from overseas in 1969; more than half of Australia's future seaborne trade with Britain and Europe will be containerized. Several ships have been built in Hamburg and a few on the Clyde, in Scotland.

TIMBER. The value of Tasmania's forest products has risen by 21m dollars to 90m dollars since 1966. This follows vigorous attempts to reduce the annual £200m Australia at present spends on imported wood pulp, paper and paper boards.

TIPPERARY CORPORATION PROJECT. Grain, sorghum, peanuts, rice and soya beans are being grown on the huge Tipperary land development project, 100 miles south of Darwin: one of many attempts to open up large areas of the arid north.

WATER. Australia has much greater potential as a food-producing nation than has been developed. The total flow of rivers is 240m acre-feet a year, but little more than 5,000 acre-feet is used on the land. Full development of Australia's water resources is now being accepted as a national responsibility and will result in greater productivity.

A major water storage, irrigation and power complex is under construction in the Ashburton-Pilbara region of the Fortescue River, Western Australia. Most of the water will be pumped from underground.

WOODCHIP INDUSTRY. This new major industry has begun operations on the far south coast of New South Wales as a direct result of Japanese interest. Japan has so far imported most of its woodchips (for pulping) from the west coast of North America.

AUSTRIA

32,376 sq. m. Pop. 7.3m. Industry stagnated in 1967, with the output of capital goods actually declining while most industries were working at a tenth below capacity. This has happened largely because productivity has not kept pace with pay increases. As early as May 1968 forecasts for the 1969 budget indicated a deficit of at least 16m schillings. A major, and interesting, step towards overcoming economic difficulties was, in mid-1968, to group all state-owned companies under a single management in order to co-ordinate investment, facilitate research and foster technical integration. Austria's sales to co-members of EFTA have increased but those to the EEC and especially to Germany have fallen. Disturbingly, net tourist earnings from tourism fell by 6% in 1967-68 because of increased spending overseas by Austrians. However, agricultural production increased by 7% in 1966 and again in 1967, largely owing to increased mechanization made necessary because of a growing shortage of agricultural labour. As in Britain, coal mining is declining in importance as more HEP stations are built; eight were under construction in September 1968.

AVALANCHES

To lessen the danger from avalanches, commissions were set up in the Bavarian, Tyrolean and Swiss Alps in the winter of 1966-67. Co-operating closely, these commissions not only carry out scientific measurements and observations but cordon off dangerous areas and disperse dangerous accumulations of snow with explosives.

AVIATION

Aircraft designers are already talking seriously of an orbital transport capable of carrying passengers from any terminal on earth to any other in less than an hour. This is looking ahead of the supersonic transports—already designated SSTs—which will be in operation, though perhaps not carrying paying passengers, by 1969. Slightly behind the stage reached with the Anglo-French Concorde, two U.S. manufacturers (Boeing and Lockheed) and two engine builders (General Electric and Pratt and Whitney) are working towards prototypes of an SST. It will be bigger and faster than anything developed by the British, French or Russians, with a cruising speed of up to Mach 3 and a capacity of 240 passengers. The SST has been the subject of much controversy with many people questioning the investment of vast sums of money merely to cut a trans-ocean journey from seven hours to three. Leaders of the air transport industry say that passenger preference and economics determine investment. Bigger, faster planes can move more people at a lower cost than smaller, slower ones. Certainly they carry more than 90% of all passenger traffic. Operating costs will rise with tomorrow's jet: it will burn 25,000 gallons of fuel during a trans-Atlantic crossing, or about twice as much as a jet of 1969.

Smaller airline companies are now tending to merge because of economic difficulties. This is best shown in Alaska (571,000 sq. m.) where in March 1968 two pioneer bush airlines, Wien Alaska and Northern Consolidated Airlines, merged their 8,500-mile routes and became public companies. The reason for the merger was to finance the purchase of three Boeing 737s. Most of the company's 81 pilots will continue to fly De Havilland Otters and Harland Skyvans. Air tourism is a major feature of Alaskan airline business; in 1967 Wien Alaska carried more than 5,000 passengers on its packaged Arctic tour. Further mergers are imminent among Alaska's eight other airlines.

ROUTES. The major new air routes are:—

Denmark—Indonesia, SAS. November 1967. Copenhagen, Tashkent, Bangkok, Singapore, Djakarta.

U.K.—Australia—Pacific route, BOAC. April 1967. London, New York, San Francisco, Honolulu, Fiji.

U.K.—Spain. April 1967. BUA. Twice-weekly, Gatwick—Ibiza.

U.K.—Canada. May 1967. Aer Lingus. Belfast—Montreal.

U.K.—Hong Kong. October 1967. BOAC, all-cargo jet service. London, Bahrain, Karachi (sometimes Bangkok), Hong Kong.

U.S.S.R.—Japan. April 1967. Moscow, Novosibirsk, Tokio.

U.S.S.R.—U.S.A. May 1967. Direct weekly service, Moscow—New York,

West Germany—Rumania, September 1967. Lufthansa. Bonn (Stuttgart), Munich, Zagreb, Belgrade, Budapest, Bucharest.

AIRPORTS. The major new airports (excluding minor landing strips or new airport buildings) are:
Italy: Santa Eufemia, north of Reggio di Calabria; an international airport to be completed by 1971.
Pakistan: Islamabad International Airport is under construction and should be serviceable by 1970.
Netherlands: Schipol Airport (Amsterdam) opened April 1967.
Indonesia: Bali now has an international airport at Denpasar.
Israel: Kalanida became Jerusalem's airport in July 1967.
Rhodesia: A new airport at Victoria Falls, mainly for tourism.
Seychelles: A transit airport of great capacity is being built to serve airlines operating between India and Africa.
Zambia: A new international airport, sixteen miles from Lusaka, was opened in July 1967.

B

BEEF

Since 1966 beef producers have been watching the success of beef farming in the three French departments of Haute-Vienne, Corrèze and Creuse, the home of the Limousin (or Limoges) cattle. It is a damp, highland country through which the Vézère and Corrèze rivers flow to join the Dordogne. There is scope for development and redevelopment on the Millevaches shelf, but in the main the region is thriving. The Limousin strain of cattle has spearheaded the new growth of the beef industry. They are only modest milk producers, which means they can be used without adding to the chronic butter over-production crisis. They also grow quickly. Farmers are used to selling $5\frac{1}{2}$ cwt beasts to the St. Etienne market and $7\frac{1}{2}$ cwt ones to Lyons at the age of 8-10 months. They are now finding a more profitable substitute in the half-ton baby-beef sales at a year old, compared with the conventional slaughter-age of about $2\frac{1}{2}$ years. Baby-beef farming is as much an embodiment of "industrial" farming as the British battery hen or Danish battery pigs. To be an economic success it is necessary to make the most of the pasture; the Limousin farmers turn out their animals in all weathers for 365 days a year. They are never milked but the calves go with them and feed wholly from their mothers' milk for the first six months with only slight and brief supplements before they go to the shed for fattening. With a guide price in Europe of 240s 6d per cwt for beef cattle on the hoof the success of the Limousin cattle scheme has brought observers from several countries, notably Britain, Australia, the Republic of South Africa and Canada. New South Wales, for instance, is introducing the cattle to the lush pastures of the coastal plain. With the increasing world demand for beef—consumption in Britain alone increased by 10% in 1967—the French methods will certainly be copied in many places.

BELGIUM

11,870 sq. m. Pop. 9.9m. Since 1966 the government has been more active in promoting industrial development and diversification, particularly in the depressed Walloon regions, notably Hainaut, Limbourg and Liège, but there is still undue reliance on steel, coal, glass and textiles. The newer industries such as those producing chemicals and electrical goods need to be further exploited. Company profits fell by nearly a quarter in 1967, and the coal industry has suffered heavy losses. (Output in 1960 was 30m tons; in 1968, 16m tons, and the estimated figure for 1970 was 12m tons.)

The language problem is still a major cause of political and therefore social and economic discord. French-speaking Walloons in the south fear that a split with the Dutch-speaking Flemings on a linguistic basis would be a serious economic setback to their region, which remains dependent on declining industries. In 1967 Belgium exported goods worth £146m to the U.K. and imported products worth £184m. The Netherlands and West Germany together constitute a market for almost half of total sales and changes in conditions in either of these countries are automatically reflected in the pattern of Belgian trade.

Some Belgian economists believe the country does not take sufficient advantage of its strategic trading position: a circle with a radius of 200 miles centred on Brussels would include a population of 100m. Still, Antwerp's rapid port development should bring about the exploitation these economists suggest. External capital remains vital to Belgian development but in 1968 the U.S. government's restriction on American investment overseas was damaging; since 1961 the U.S.A. has invested 800m dollars in Belgian industry.

Belgium probably has the most modern textile-producing equipment in Europe, but the industry is suffering in part because of lower-priced imports from developing countries such as Pakistan and Egypt.

BIAFRA

In June 1967 a Nigerian province sought to secede from Nigeria and proclaimed itself the independent Republic of Biafra. Most of the 8.5m people in Biafra are members of the Ibo tribe; at least 325,000 of them have died in the war. By June 1968 Biafra had lost about three-quarters of its original territory and late in the year its eventual extinction seemed inevitable. Portugal, and despite the disapproval of the Organization of African Unity, Tanzania, Gabon, Ivory Coast and Zambia, recognized the secessionist regime.

The effect on crops—oil palm, cotton, coffee—has been disastrous in the border regions and in Biafra itself. Mineral oil production has also been drastically reduced, for the major fields are in the Niger delta area, which is Biafran controlled. Economists among the agency workers taking relief to Biafra say that the whole region's economy has already been set back a decade.

BIOLOGY, INDUSTRIAL

Biologists are becoming as vital to industry as chemists in the early nineteenth century and physicists in the 1930s and 1940s. Fields in which they are working include the discovery of new products and processes; devising new, cheaper ways of making things; helping to evolve new materials that will stand up to biological interference with manufacturing processes, and dealing with the many problems that arise from the new legal and public attitudes to the manufacture of food and drugs. The rapid rise in the popularity of processed foods for example has not only led to more public and official interest in food additives and preservatives, it has also led to new work for the biologists leading back to the crop itself. Thus the mechanized harvesting of crops such as peas and beans requires not only a uniform product but also one which ripens at the same time for any given sowing, instead of over a long period, as is desirable with hand-picking. Similarly, to ensure a steady supply of the crop for economic operation of the canning or freezing plant research is needed to determine optimum rates of fertilizer, herbicide and pesticide application, as well as to evolve new cultural methods. Other examples of the increasing demand for biologists are concerned with industrial effluent disposal, testing of new drugs, and whatever biological processes play a direct part in actual manufacture. Opportunities exist for biologists outside their normal sphere; some aspects of central management are considered fields for people with a training in biology.

BOLIVIA

415,000 sq. m. Pop. 3.8m. In spite of constant efforts to diversify the economy, tin still represents about two-thirds of all exports. COMIBOL, the State Mining Corporation, reduced the number of its workers by 4,000 to 23,000 in 1967 but its losses were still so great in 1967-68 that the International Tin Council bought a considerable amount of tin to prevent prices sinking even lower. A dredging operation, the first in Bolivia for twenty years, is currently in progress by an American consortium at a cost of 5.5m dollars. The U.K. government has given £1m for building another dredger. Another major development is a 9m-dollar smelter (West-German built) at Oruro which will start production early in 1969, with an annual capacity of 7,000 tons annually. An American company, exploring mineral deposits, aims eventually to produce up to 100,000 tons of lead and zinc concentrate annually. In 1967

9m bb of oil were exported by pipeline from Santa Cruz through Chile via the port of Arica, to the U.S.A.—Bolivia's first exports of crude oil. The petroleum industry may in future provide the diversification Bolivia so badly needs. The FAO has announced long-term plans for a beef cattle industry. Bolivia exports to the U.K. about 70% of all its tin concentrates for smelting. Development of the recently discovered gold mines has begun. The government plan to resettle farmers from the *altiplano* has been started and 56,000 farmers were transferred in the year ended June 1968.

BOTSWANA

275,000 sq. m. Pop. 580,000. If enough water were available this young republic could support 2.5m cattle. The government is aiming at this figure but its realization depends on the success of scientific waterdrilling methods. An annual export quota of 200,000 is planned and in 1967 the figure reached 178,000. A large, modern slaughter-house at Lobatsi is helping exports. Britain is the main market, with West Germany second. A census in December 1967 showed that the livestock and dairying industries employed part and full time about 90% of the population and contributed roughly 86% of the value of exports. The traditional reluctance of farmers to part with cattle is gradually being broken down as the African farmers learn to concentrate more on quality stock. In 1954 there were only twelve registered African farmers of stock for sale to the abattoirs; the number had risen in March 1968 to 1850. There is serious over-grazing around the boreholes and other sources of water, owing to increasing numbers of cattle and the not-so-rapid opening up of new grasslands and water points. The best prospects are in the more remote northern lands. The immediate solution to the problem is in the control of grazing and use of water and in more rapid turnover of stock. Irrigation is now being successfully used by European farmers in the Tuli Block and the Tati Concession in the east; the main cash crop is citrus fruits. Considerable potential for developing a coalfield now exists following the discovery of two large seams of medium grade, non-coking bituminous steam coal at a shallow depth with easy access to the railway line from South Africa to Rhodesia. A trans-Botswana railway and 4,700 miles of new roads are under construction as part of the overall beef project. There is a practical plan to develop the large wild animal reservations in the north as tourist attractions. However, in 1968 at least 80% of income was from meat, with cotton, gold, silver, manganese and asbestos providing the rest of the foreign money.

BRAZIL

3.3m sq. m. Pop. 84.8m. In 1967 Brazil's gross national product rose by 5% compared with 1966, but of greater significance was a reduction to 25% in the rise of the cost of living compared with increases of 60% and 40% in 1965 and 1966 respectively. Unfortunately government expenditure in the 1968 budget doubled that of 1967 and another huge increase will occur in 1969.

It is now possible to see that efforts to industrialize the underdeveloped Amazon and north-east regions have been largely successful, mainly because of fiscal and other incentives being given to firms establishing themselves in these areas, which are becoming increasingly important for their rich mineral deposits such as oil, copper, iron ore, salt and barium. Petro-chemicals, plastics and concrete are manufactured here. It is significant that major industries are receiving direct investments from overseas: 1,224m dollars from U.S. sources; 668m dollars from France; U.K., 466m and Switzerland, 249m.

In relative terms coffee is gradually diminishing in importance as an export earner. In 1967-68 it accounted for 40% of foreign exchange earnings compared with 60% in 1965. Almost daily low-yielding coffee groves are being uprooted to give way to more profitable crops such as corn, cotton, peanuts, citrus fruits and vegetables.

Brazil is now the third largest producer of beef and the development and reorganization of beef, wool and mutton are being supported by a World Bank loan of 40m dollars.

The first stage of an HEP plant on the Parana River has been completed. Several similiar plants have been completed since 1966 but the output of HEP is still less than 4% of the country's full potential.

BRIDGES

BALTIC. German and Scandinavian engineers are working on plans for a short and stable road link from the European continent across the Baltic to Helsinki. The latest project in this field is a plan drawn up by Finnish experts for a road link across the Gulf of Bothnia. They propose to advance from southern Finland by means of bridges and moles as far as the Aland Islands and from there carry the bridge on to Central Sweden. This would mean that, at a cost of 1.2 thousand million marks, Europe Road No. 4 from Stockholm to Helsinki could be cut from 1,300 to 300 miles. At the same time, efforts are going ahead to provide road links between the Federal Republic of Germany, Denmark and Sweden. The bridges to be built at this end—across the Great Belt and between Copenhagen and Malmö—are estimated at 1.2 thousand million marks each, while the bridge across the Fehmarn Belt, which continues the end-of-flight railway link between continental Europe and Scandinavia is estimated at 800m marks. Altogether the scheme is one of the most complex and ambitious ever. In 1968 work actually started on the longest bridge in Europe—to link the city of Kalmar with the island of Aland. More than 6,060 metres long, the bridge is due for completion in 1972.

FRANCE. A bridge has been completed over the Seine's main

arm at Courbevoie, west of Paris. Part of national road 308, it carries 40,000 vehicles daily. A smaller bridge, Grande Jatte, crosses a secondary arm of the river.

SWEDEN. The country's largest suspension bridge—900 metres and 6 lanes—across the Gota River, west Gothenberg, came into use late in 1966.

SWITZERLAND. Via Mala Gorge is now bridged south of Thusis (Grisons canton).

VENEZUELA. The Angostura, the longest suspension bridge (5,507 feet) in Latin America and the ninth largest in the world now links Ciudad Bolivar, on the Orinoco's south bank, with Soledad on the north bank.

BRITISH HONDURAS

8,900 sq. m. Pop. 110,000. So much attention has been drawn to the quarrel with Guatemala over the future of British Honduras that it is perhaps not widely realized how much the spirit of self-determination has grown among the local population, who are better known for political indifference. Belize, as the country will be renamed after independence, has some interesting new developments but remains economically vulnerable with oranges and grapefruit in glut and its chicle (gum) forests almost exhausted. The most promising new venture is the £8m investment made by Tate and Lyle in a new sugar factory near Corozal. American firms are shipping lobster tails and cucumbers and there is a small trade in coconuts. Hondurans have been emigrating to the U.S.A. and Mexico in relatively large numbers. The country will become independent in 1970.

New Geography 1968-69

BRITISH WEST INDIES

Early in March 1967 Britain granted "associated statehood" to Antigua, Grenada, St. Lucia, Dominica and the group of St. Kitts-Nevis-Anguilla. The new states conduct most of their affairs through elected legislatures but by mutual agreement Britain manages and pays for their foreign affairs and defence. The islands have precarious one-crop economies which have been hurt by increased competition abroad. The St. Kitts-Nevis-Anguilla group (Pop. 60,000) suffers from uncertain prices for its sugar; St. Lucia (100,000), Grenada (88,000) and Dominica (67,000) depend on fluctuating prices for bananas. Only Antigua with its casino and 33 hotels attracts a large tourist influx. The best hope for prosperity

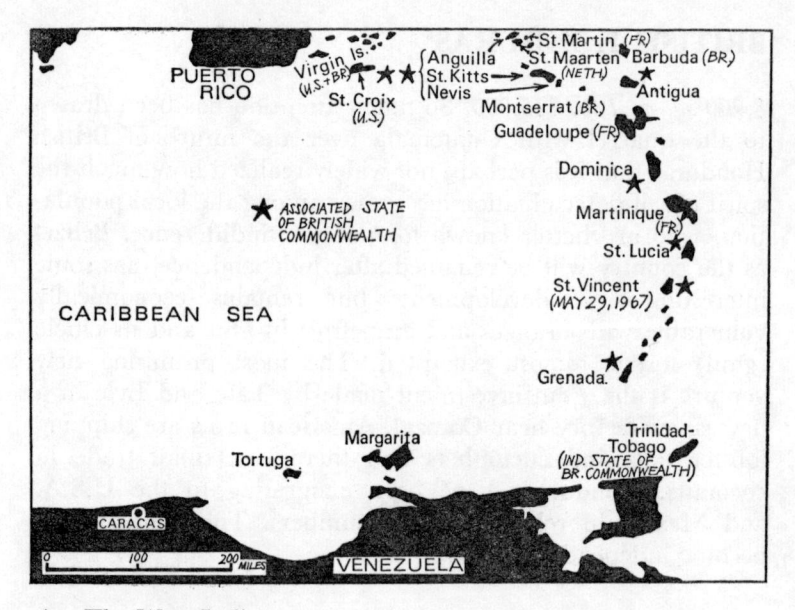

1. The West Indies

seems to be some form of regional grouping that would enable the West Indians to combine their resources. (Past attempts at federation have failed. The most notable collapse was in 1962 when the larger islands of Jamaica and Trinidad-Tobago, fearing that the smaller islands would become an economic burden, opted for full independence instead of a federal arrangement.)

BULGARIA

43,000 sq. m. Pop. 8.3m. Bulgaria is developing at an impressive rate, especially in heavy industry—engineering, iron and metallurgy. The importance of agriculture is lessening steadily, though it provides a third of all exports, as industrialization has advanced, but Bulgarian horticulture is steadily making an impact in European markets. A rapid expansion of orchards, especially apples, is in progress. Sales of horticultural produce have been most profitable in West Germany, despite EEC barriers, and Bulgaria is emerging as a serious competitor to Italy and Holland. Progress towards a realistic price system— i.e. with some profit incentive—is being hampered by Bulgaria's close integration with the U.S.S.R. and its increasing reliance on Russian raw materials. In 1967 receipts from tourism amounted to 60m dollars, from 2m tourists (150,000 in 1960).

C

CAMBODIA

70,000 sq. m. Pop. 5.9m. It should be noted that the desperate land hunger which is typical of much of monsoon Asia is notably absent in Cambodia; nine-tenths of the peasants own their own land. Although the great majority of Cambodians are peasants, only one-ninth of the country is cultivated. This is concentrated in the alluvial lowland of the Mekong River and its tributary, the Tonle Sap. Four-fifths of the cultivated land is devoted to rice—1 ton per acre compared with Japan's 7 tons—but the surplus, about 250,000 tons, makes rice the

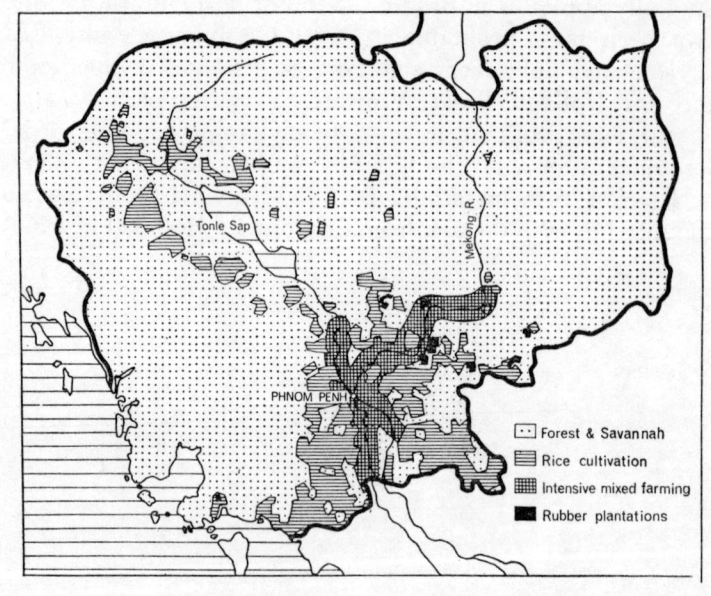

2. Land Use in Cambodia

major export crop. Co-operative purchasing and marketing, a new development in Cambodia, is bringing larger profits all round. Maize, vegetables, sugar cane, oil-seeds, tobacco and many fruits are being much more intensively farmed on the sandy river terraces. Per acre, Cambodian rubber plantations now have the highest yield in the world. The most important new industries are the state ones established with Chinese aid. These include a paper mill at Cholong, plywood at Phnom Penh, cement at Chakrey Ting, a cotton mill at Kompong-Cham. The latest Sino-Cambodian aid programme includes the establishment of a small iron and steel complex at Pnonom Dek. Czechoslovakia has helped to set up a sugar refinery, tyre factory and tractor assembly plant.

The whole country's development is being so carefully planned that it could serve as a model. This care can be seen particularly in the new port of Shikanoukville, just finished after ten years' building. This city, cut out of the rain forest on the south coast, is one of South-East Asia's most impressive achievements. The label given to Cambodia as an "oasis of peace" is not inapt as long as it can avoid becoming embroiled in South-East Asian violence.

CANADA

3.9m sq. m. Pop. 19.9m. In 1967 Canada celebrated the centenary of its Federation with EXPO 67 and more than 2,500 "centennial projects". No fewer than 21m visitors attended EXPO—on two islands in the St. Lawrence River—between April 28 and October 27, 1967.

Canada has completed a natural resources survey. The major findings include these points. In Saskatchewan are potash reserves sufficient to fertilize all the arable land on earth for the next 500 years. There are 20,569 producing oil wells, conventional oil reserves of 8 billion bb and natural gas reserves of 44 trillion cubic feet. In addition there are the Athabasca tar sands, potentially one of the largest oil deposits—

at least 300 billion bb of recoverable oil clinging to the sticky black sand cover over 11,000 sq. m. of northern Alberta. In September 1967 a company began a daily output of 45,000 bb a day (about 38,000 bb a day are exported to the U.S.A.). In the Labrador region one HEP project by 1971 will be the biggest single power source in the world, capable of supporting the annual domestic needs of 85m people. The country has an assured export market—mainly the U.S.S.R., China, East Germany—of 500m bushels of wheat annually from its average annual production of 825m bushels.

Larger sales of motor vehicles and parts (as a result of a motor trade pact with the U.S.A.), non-ferrous metals, wood pulp, petroleum and machinery account for substantial rises in exports. In an average year Canada exports to the U.K. materials worth £450m, about twice the value of goods imported.

Water, not oil or wheat or timber, is the key to Canada's future, in more ways than one. Many American politicians, predicting that the U.S.A. will face a severe water shortage by 1980, have urged Canada into an urgent study of water resources. Nationally, Canada is worried about provincial governments making water deals with the U.S.A., as did British Columbia in the case of the Columbia River Treaty in 1964. The treaty provides for the extension and harnessing of rivers common to both countries on the western seaboard on such a grand scale that it will eventually account for nearly a quarter of the potential HEP in North America. Though primarily a power-sharing project from which the U.S.A. stands to gain the most benefit, it has raised the spectre among many Canadians of what could happen if, in the absence of a national policy on water, provincial governments tried to do similiar piecemeal deals using water instead of electricity. Some American interests have gone so far as to produce the blueprint of an imaginative and costly project that would aim to trap about 20% of Canada's northern waters. Known as the North America Water and Power Alliance, it would reverse, at a cost of 120 billion dollars, the rivers of north-western Canada and Alaska and divert them through canals, tunnels and natural waterways on the pattern of the Snowy River Scheme, Australia. The core of the project is a 500-mile storage trench in British Columbia, from which water would be piped 2,000 miles across the Canadian heartlands to the Great Lakes, feeding 33 American states, three Mexican states and seven Canadian provinces.

It is stressed that this is not a firm project but it does indicate American interest in Canada's resources. Even some Canadian economists think that the answer to Canada's own needs may lie in devising a sort of national grid system similiar to that of electricity, so that water can be channelled, at the touch of a button, to wherever it is needed most. (Canada has 292,000 sq. m. of fresh water, 14,000 miles of navigable rivers and lakes, and a flow of about 70,000 gallons of water per head per day.)

CANALS

A 250-mile canal linking the Caribbean and Pacific is to be built through Colombia at a cost of about £250m. It will run from the Gulf of Uraba to the Bay of Malaga and 200 miles of it will be through two large lakes which engineers plan to create by damming the Rivers Atrato and San Juan with earth dykes. Colombia stresses that the new waterway is not intended to compete with the Panama Canal and, indeed, it cannot do so since it will take ships of only up to 20,000 tons. But it will be a shorter route to or from the west coast of South America. This is not a substitute for the "grand" new Panama Canal, the final route for which has not been decided.

It is possible that the Saar River will be canalized to develop this busy region still further. Plans are speculative but basically the idea is to exploit the earlier canalizing of the Moselle, of which the Saar is a tributary, by extending the Saar to the Rhine. (See *New Geography 1966-67*.)

CENTRAL AMERICA

The Central American Common Market (Costa Rica, El Salvador, Guatemala, Honduras, Nicaragua, Panama) has completed its seventh year. It covers an area about the size of France (212,000 sq. m.) with a population not much bigger than Greater London (approximately 8m) and has achieved one of the fastest growth rates in Latin America—an annual increase of nearly 7%. The initial aim was a free trade area within six years with a common external customs tariff. By the end of 1968, 98% of internal tariffs had been abolished, but the remainder represents in value a fifth of the area's trade and includes such important items as coffee, sugar and fuel. A commission is studying ways of amalgamating the CACM with the Latin American Free Trade Association and in due course this will probably be achieved.

CEYLON

25,332 sq. m. Pop. 11.55m. Following the devaluation of sterling Ceylon devalued the rupee by 20%. The trade deficit has been reduced substantially but pressure on balance of payments remains because the majority of Ceylon's imports are from countries which did not devalue. Ceylon's tea output fell slightly in 1967 to 487m lb, but the country remains the world's principal exporter and the volume of exports (478m lb in 1967) was 8m lb higher than in 1966. Because of the world rice shortage in 1966 much more attention is being given to the cultivation of rice and the improvement of techniques; the 1968 crop was expected to increase by more than a tenth to 60m bushels. Under a loan agreement signed in March 1968 Britain is able to sell to Ceylon more fertilizers, tractors, engineering stores and commercial vehicles. Industrially the Japanese are active, especially in electric power transmission and steel. Ceylon's first oil refinery commenced operations early in 1969. A vigorous tourist campaign is expected to attract 150,000 tourists between 1969-79. (See *Tea, Rubber.*)

CHILE

300,000 sq. m. Pop. 8.81m. Although copper remains of major importance to the economy, progress in agriculture is no less important. At present Chile produces less than a third of its food needs, the remainder being imported. These imports, particularly wheat and beef, account for a quarter of the country's total import bill, using foreign exchange which could otherwise be used to buy capital goods for industrial development. An agrarian reform programme has yet to reverse a long-term trend of food supplies lagging further and further behind the growth in population. Several important industrial developments have occurred. A British firm is completing a pulp mill (£8.6m) and France is building a motor assembly plant. Chile's exports to Britain in 1968 amounted to £50m, 85% of it in copper. The increase in the cost of living was held to 10% in 1967 (see *New Geography 1966-67*) and was expected to be about 8% in 1968.

CHINA

4.3m sq. m. China's population in September 1968 was 796m according to Barclays Bank Economic Intelligence Department, and 800m by U.S. State Department figures. Some disruption followed political upheavals in 1966-67 but in general the economy was remarkably well sheltered from these disturbances. In 1968 exports and imports increased by a sixth. A lack of official statistics makes it difficult to assess China's progress in developing the economy. However, because the country's ability to import capital equipment for industry is dependent on earnings from the sale of agricultural produce, and also because of the need to provide for a vast population, increasing by 2.5% annually, the basic emphasis in the third five-year plan (1966-72) is on improving farm productivity, mainly by extending irrigation and the use of fertilizers. Cotton production is also rising and record harvests have been claimed; the 1.5m tons produced annually is sufficient for China's textile industry. In 1967 the output of steel was about 12m tons (less than two-fifths of the U.K.'s total) of which about half was produced in the Anshan complex and a quarter at Paotow. Steel to the value of £50m was purchased from the West in 1967. China is now claiming to have vast oil supplies, with a production of 9m tons annually. If this is so, the country could only refine about half. Since the breakdown of Sino-Soviet relations, trade with the West has practically doubled and trade with other Communist countries was, in 1968, less than a quarter of the 1959 level. The scope of China's foreign trade is little realized. Figures for 1968 are: with Japan, £222m, Hong Kong, £176m, and large amounts with West Germany, France and Canada. In the same year Britain exported to China goods worth £40m and imported others worth £41m, fertilizers, textile machinery and machine tools being exported.*

CITIES

The distinguished Greek town planner, Constantinos Doxiadis, in 1968 presented an analytical forecast for city-settlements of the future. He cites the megalopolis of the east coast of the U.S.A. where the cities of Boston and Washington are, for

---

* The author has had several queries regarding British imports from China. In the twelve months ended December 31, 1968 they comprised: textile fibres, £5,923,000; crude inedible materials, excluding fuel, £3,795,000; textile yarns, fabrics and made-up articles, £3,610,000; vegetable oils, £3,443,000; chemical products, £2,405,000; oil seed, £1,506,000; animal hairs, £1,372,000; coffee, tea, cocoa and spices, £1,128,000; hides, £1,076,000; miscellaneous manufactured articles, £912,000; other items, £9,830,000. (Supplied by Barclays Bank Economic Intelligence Department, and verified by Board of Trade.)

all practical purposes, part of one sprawling amorphous mass. This illimitable conurbational growth will result, Doxiadis believes, in a world-wide city which, if left to its own devices, will continue to use its existing centres to serve its expanded populations. "The world-wide city (Dynamegalopolis) which is being created will be asphyxiated in its own cradle." If the World City is to come about, as appears inevitable, it is necessary to co-ordinate action for both the expansion and renewal of our existing cities. Doxiadis demands that in the development of this world-wide city we must know how to save the values of the past and create the best values for the future. Its dimensions by the end of the twenty-first century will be the largest that are comparable with man's survival. Since this city (Ecumenopolis) will be incapable of expansion it will, in theory, represent the ideal city state, which once existed, having undergone massive magnification. He sees this new world network comprised of a multitude of human communities which in themselves would be replicas of the whole of the earth's surface pattern on a human scale, society finding its shell within this community. From the village and earliest township we have seen, in historical progression, Dynopolis, Metropolis, and Dynametropolis.

It is interesting to note how the highest points of various cities are becoming progressively higher. Tokio has duplicated the Eiffel Tower for its radio transmissions—only 40 feet higher. London has a tower of 620 feet, Stuttgart 702 feet, Dortmund 715 feet, Hamburg 892 feet, and Munich 951 feet. East Berlin will have a tower 1,185 feet tall in 1969 and West Berlin may counter with one 1,312 feet. Moscow's tower is 1,722 feet, 250 feet more than the Empire State Building. (In 1966 Rotterdam's Euromast of 365 feet was the tallest in Europe.) (See *Urban Development*.)

COAL

Coal is still fighting a losing battle against oil, methane, water and nuclear power. In the EEC alone in 1968 there was a 10m-ton cut on the quantity used in 1967. In Belgium between 1966-68 no fewer than 175,000 miners were re-deployed. The EEC has estimated that out of the 220m tons produced annually in the Six, only 90m tons are mined in conditions which are competitive on the open world market. This is one reason for the sharp cuts. The figure of 190m tons has been given for the Six after 1970. In Britain the drop has been from 223 tons in 1953 to 180m in 1965 and 150m in 1970. However, the Middle East War of 1967 and the action by the Arabs to deprive the West of Middle East oil has reminded the EEC and other countries that their oil requirements are at the mercy of one of the world's least stable areas and that it would be unwise to allow coal to be cut back too much. In any case, the world's known oil reserves amount to 85,000m tons of coal units with the reserves of natural gas about two-thirds this figure. The reserves of coal amount to 7,500,000m tons of units. Even nuclear energy will not yield much more than the equivalent of 400,000m tons by 1980. Various promotion methods are being used to exploit coal. In Britain, for example, the Coal Board arranged a 25-year contract to supply cheap coal for the generating station of the proposed £49m Alcan bauxite smelter at Invergordon.

It is not generally realized how closely transport in Britain has been geared to coal movement and how radically since 1966 this transport pattern has changed. Coal comprises 60% of total rail freight, over 80% of dry cargo for coastal shipping; it is the second largest bulk commodity on the road and the biggest user of inland waterways. Until 1966 the whole transport system was tuned to move about 200m tons of coal annually. With that figure down to 145m tons in June 1968 and falling, road, rail and barge operators, shipowners and ports are all badly affected. The railways ascribed, in mid-1968, £12m of their losses to the fall in coal traffic. If gas replaces coal to any appreciable extent in British power stations the railways will suffer even more.

Coal-concentration depots planned as recently as 1964 find their traffic dwindling below viability level. Ports and coastal shipping are as much affected. Though the National Coal Board is building a modern stocking and loading facility at Immingham, practically all other traditional coal ports are finding it difficult to justify purchases of new specialized coal-handling equipment. When a port loses a million or more tons of coal traffic the reduction in shipping is substantial. Every other port cost rises and hampers remaining trade. Shipowners are also concerned at dwindling prospects for their specialized colliers. Under the British Transport Bill of 1968 coal is one of the commodities which is to be diverted from road to rail as a matter of policy. Since more than 30m tons were moved by road the rigid uncommercial restrictions now applied will stifle efficient movement and deprive coal of an essential transport flexibility.

COCOA

The 1967-68 world cocoa bean crop was 1,321,600 metric tons, only 1% below the harvest for 1966-67. Reserve stocks may have to be used to meet growing world requirements, though there is no risk of a shortage. International control of cocoa growing and marketing is having the desired effect of doing away with over-productivity and glut.

COFFEE

Barclay's Bank Economic Intelligence Unit research shows that coffee, after oil, is the largest commodity entering into world trade. It provides employment for 20m people and fifty producing countries. Understandably, then, repercussions from sharp price fluctuations are widespread and profound. For instance, a price reduction of only one U.S. cent per lb results in an annual loss of 8m dollars to Colombia.

The main objectives of the International Coffee Agreement,

renewed in April 1968 for a further five years, are to stabilize prices at a "fair" level and to bring production more into line with consumption. (When the first Agreement was signed in 1962 coffee prices had been declining for eight consecutive years.) Because of increasing competition from other beverages much money is being spent on publicity and diversification is being actively encouraged in those countries highly dependent on coffee. With member countries accounting for 95% of the world coffee trade the ICO is in a powerful position and to date has succeeded better than any other commodity organization in stabilizing prices. But control of production has been more difficult. Production exceeds consumption by about 10m bags (1968) and present stocks are capable of meeting two years' demand. (A bag contains 60kg.) In Brazil alone stocks are almost sufficient to supply the entire quota of 55m bags for the 1968-69 coffee year. By 1970 the coffee surplus will exceed 100m bags unless more effective control measures can be found. Financing the cultivation and storage of surplus stocks is a serious problem and is a major cause of inflation in some countries, e.g. Brazil, Colombia. Survival of the Agreement depends on how long producers can withhold coffee from world markets in the face of mounting surpluses at home. Despite serious economic and social consequences which would arise if the Agreement were to be abandoned, the present quota system cannot control the surpluses indefinitely. (See *Brazil*.)

COLOMBIA

461,606 sq. m. Pop. 19m. Most intensive efforts are being made to lessen the country's dependence on coffee and on agriculture generally. To this end there has been since 1967, a vigorous "Buy Colombian" campaign, which has given new life to local industries. The textile industry is one of the most highly developed in Latin America but most of the wool is imported. Man-made fibre factories are going into operation. In conjunction with the Andean Development Corporation (an attempt by Colombia, Venezuela, Ecuador, Peru and Chile to achieve more rapid integration), special emphasis is being placed on the expansion of the petro-chemical industry. Colombia hopes to supply the Andean market with nylon and polyester and an expensive aromatic plant is being built at the Ecopetrol refinery at Barrancabermeja. Petroleum ranks second among Colombian exports. Development of a new field near the border with Ecuador with estimated reserves of 1,000m barrels, could mean a doubling of output (70m bb in 1968) and a substantial boost in foreign earnings. Colombia is, enterprisingly, trying to expand two-way trade with East Europe.

COLONIES

With the hand-over of Aden, and the granting of independence to Mauritius and Swaziland in 1968, Britain's shrinking overseas possessions are now nearing the point of an almost irreducible "hard core" of small dependencies. Decolonization may be going into reverse. Anguilla's 6,000 people were persuaded to end their revolt against joining St. Kitts in a Caribbean associated state only after the restoration of a temporary British administrator. A similiar threat by tiny Barbuda, also in the Caribbean, was also narrowly averted. The Seychelles are strictly anti-independent. The indigenous population of Fiji and Gibraltar have demonstrated their desire to retain the British link.

Even if Britain wanted to abandon her remaining, and not inconsiderable empire, the step would be difficult. By the end of 1968 Britain was still responsible for about twenty territories with a population of about 5m. Excluding Hong Kong, which accounts for about 3.75m and is, in any case, self-supporting, the remainder live mainly on islands—about 15,000 altogether —generally in conditions of extreme isolation, overpopulation and vulnerable one-crop economy. Most of them need financial aid and in 1968 Britain paid out about £43m. One factor militates more than others against any easy solution for the smaller territories: island populations tend to double every 25 years without their possessing economic potential for absorbing the increased burden. Attempts to "tidy-up" geographically have proved abortive. Parochial insularity, conflicting ethnic and religious origins conspire to defeat the economic advantages of regional federations.

COPPER

In mid-1967 the world's four largest copper exporters—Zambia, Chile, Peru and the Congo (Kinchasa)—formed the Inter-Governmental Council of Copper-Exporting countries with headquarters in Paris. The founder members see the club as an instrument for freeing them as developing nations from economic subservience to Europe and the U.S.A. They want Lusaka, Santiago, Lima and Kinchasa to dictate copper prices rather than London or Washington. The four countries produce about three-quarters of the world's copper available for export, but some factors make scientific planning of the copper industry difficult. For instance, scrap metal—sale of which is beyond the control of the mining industry—provides 42% of the metal consumed.

In April 1968 Japan formed an investment company to buy into the Congo copper industry; this marks the start of massive Japanese involvement in the mineral-rich Congo.

Mining has started on the Baluba area of the African Copperbelt and the Rio Tinto-Zinc Corporation is operating on Bougainville Island, New Guinea, where there is a big low-grade copper deposit, similiar in some ways to the group's new Palabora mine in South Africa which produced 85,000 short tons of copper in 1968.

In 1967 the world copper output (excluding China and the U.S.S.R.) was 4,410m metric tons. The estimated Soviet production was 750m tons.

COSTA RICA

19,653 sq. m. Pop. 1.5m. Costa Rica now has the highest standard of living and the least illiteracy in Central America, at the cost, however, of a credit squeeze. New ventures include mushroom-canning, textiles, paper, plastics, medical products and banana derivatives. Large new banana plantations have been established on the Pacific Coast. A U.S. firm is to exploit and build a sulphuric acid plant.

COTTON

The world output for 1967 was 11,812m tons. This breaks down to: U.S.A., 3,268m; U.S.S.R., 1,900m (estimated); China, 1,260m; India, 1,000m; Brazil, 668m; Mexico, 580m; Egypt, 530m; Pakistan, 421m; Turkey, 332m. Students should note the development of cotton growing in Australia (Ord River, Atherton Tablelands) and in Papua, New Guinea (Goroka Highlands).

CUBA

44,178 sq. m. Pop. 7.8m. Cuba has ambitious plans to develop its industry and agriculture and Britain is very much involved. Early in 1967 the Stockport firm of Simon-Carves Ltd. signed a contract to build a £14m fertilizer plant, the biggest venture in Anglo-Cuban trade in a decade. The plant, designed for an enormous output of nitrogen fertilizer, is being built in Cienfuegos, an important sugar port in south central Cuba. It will be in production in 1970.

Cuba lives with perhaps the harshest rationing system ever formulated by a modern government—2 oz of butter and 2 oz of cheese a month, one pair of shoes and two pairs of trousers a year, for example. According to estimates by the U.S.

State Department, the Soviet Union is still giving Cuba between £107m and £142m a year in the form of direct grants, as well as buying the bulk of Cuban sugar.

CYPRUS

3,572 sq. m. Pop. 607,000. Substantial progress and development has been achieved in all sections of the Cyprian economy but especially in agriculture and mining, on which Cyprus so largely depends. The 1967-68 citrus production amounted to about 100,000 tons; citrus exports are worth £5m annually and will probably rise to £7m in 1970. The U.K. is the main importer. Planting of new citrus groves is forbidden without government permission, a step taken in 1967 to protect underground water resources, which are being rapidly exhausted. The government is encouraging intensive mineral exploration, since the life of known ore reserves (except asbestos) is believed to be short. Mineral exports increased by 2% in 1967 to bring in £12.2m in export money.

The tourist industry is catering for 100,000 visitors a year, but the Middle East War of 1967 lost Cyprus 25,000 of its anticipated 80,000 tourists. The natural resources of the country are being exploited as never before and products include brandy, sherry, beer, plaster and plastic-boards, detergents, flour, cigarettes, pottery, aluminium, furniture and clothing. About a third of Cyprus's imports come from Britain and a little more than this of its exports go to Britain. West Germany, Spain and Italy are its other main trading partners but new trade agreements have been made between Cyprus and Poland and Rumania.

CZECHOSLOVAKIA

49,000 sq. m. Pop. 14.275m. The dispute with the Soviet Union in the late summer of 1968 will have adverse effects on Czechoslovakian geography—human, economic and social—for a long time, but until this happened the country was in an enviable position among Eastern European countries, with industry and agriculture both developing, and with many more tourists in the summer of 1968 than ever before. Production at the Skoda factory is a success story in point. By August 1968 daily production of cars had reached 450. This is a miniscule figure compared with General Motors, Ford or Volkswagen but it proves that Communism can at least try to compete in highly competitive motor-vehicle markets. Such products as the Soviet Union's Zil and East Germany's Trabant have failed on the Western market but Skoda has become increasingly popular. Nearly half the Skoda output is exported to the West.

The budget for 1968 allowed for considerable development in relatively neglected sections of the economy, such as transport, forestry, agriculture, communications and tourism. Early in 1968 there was criticism that little money had been allowed for Slovakia, the least developed part of the country, and in the 1968 budget Slovakia's share was raised from a quarter to a third.

No Eastern European economy had suffered so painfully under the stagnation of Stalinism as Czechoslovakia's. As the "machine shop" of the Eastern bloc, Czechoslovakia had been forced by Moscow to concentrate its energies—without significant Soviet investment—on building the machine tools (and weapons) that the Soviet Union needed.

D

DAHOMEY

45,000 sq. m. Pop. 2.45m. An agricultural revolution is taking place in Dahomey—draught-oxen are being used for the first time. Until 1968 Dahomey farmers had used nothing more complicated than a hand-hoe and could produce nothing more than the food needed to subsist. Through FAO help some farmers now have oxen, which can increase cultivation four-fold. With the densest population in West Africa and with no industry, minerals or other resources and with the population increasing by 2.8% annually the draught-ox has arrived just in time. To qualify for a grant of oxen farmers must cultivate at least 2.5 acres. Ox-carts are now replacing women as the main form of portage; one cart carrying 1,500 lb is equal to twenty women. By the end of 1968 only 200 farmers were oxen-equipped but the Swiss, French and Belgian volunteers in charge of the system say that use of oxen will now rapidly increase.

DAMS (For irrigation and/or HEP)

AUSTRALIA. In July 1967 the last of the large tunnels for the Snowy Mountains Scheme was finished, so that 24.5 miles of tunnels now permit the river to flow backwards and inland. Several associated systems, over a vast area, are still under construction. South Australia will have its first HEP station—near Hahndorf on the Onkaparinga River, in 1969.

BHUTAN. In February 1967 the country's first HEP project

commenced operations in an attempt to stimulate local industry.

BRAZIL. The Furnas Dam, part of the Jaguara Project, on the Rio Grande will provide power for the burgeoning industries of São Paulo, 200 miles south. Two dams on the Parana are already providing power.

CAMBODIA. The Prek Thnot project west of Phnom Penh will irrigate 150,000 acres.

CANADA. In October 1968 the Portage Mountain Dam at Hudson Hope on the Peace River commenced power production. The dam created a lake of 228 sq. m. The Duncan Lake Dam, August 1967, created a 29 sq. m. lake. The Mactaquac HEP system on the St. John River, New Brunswick, commenced output in February 1968. Of the numerous other projects the main one is the Manicouagan complex, Quebec, which commenced operations in 1969.

ETHIOPIA. A dam and power station is being built across the Fincha River.

FRANCE. A new power station is in operation on the Rhône at Pierre Benite and HEP works are nearly completed on the Durance and Verdon rivers.

INDIA. During 1967 the country gained several new dams. The main ones are the Kotah Barrage and Gandhisagar HEP station, Chambal River; Sabarigiri HEP plant in Kerala; Bhakra, Sutlej River. In mid-1967 a barrage across the Giri River, in Himachal Pradesh, was begun.

MOZAMBIQUE. Of the several dams under construction the chief is that at Cahora Bassa on the Zambesi; it will irrigate at least 1m acres. A dam under construction at Alto Molocue interestingly incorporates the Mutala Falls.

NEPAL. An HEP project at Trisuli, begun early in 1967, was showing results late in 1968.

NEW ZEALAND. In September 1968 the Aviemore HEP station on the Waitaki was completed.

PAKISTAN. A French-Italian consortium is building the Tarbela Dam at a cost of £375m in West Pakistan.

SPAIN. At least thirty dams are under construction on several sites as part of a major programme to bring irrigation and power to undeveloped areas. The major HEP/irrigation works are at Puerto Moral on the Huelva River, Ternadilla on the Tera, Susques on the Ter. The main HEP-only dams are at Alcantara on the Tagus, Almendra on the Tormes, Peal de Becerro on the Guadalquivir, Ribarroja on the Ebro.

SOUTH AFRICA. Late in 1968 the Jozini Dam in the Lebombo Mountains (northern Natal) was completed, forming a lake 22 miles long.

THAILAND. Two new power and storage reservoirs are in operation in Thailand—at Nam Pong and Nam Pung—on tributaries of the Mekong. About 125,000 acres will be irrigated.

TURKEY. A large dam has been completed at Kesikkopru near Ankara.

U.S.A. The major dam of the 26 listed by the U.S. Department of Works is the John Day Lock and Dam multi-purpose complex, which includes thirty dams and associated pipelines in the Columbia River Basin. Power was being produced in October 1968.

U.S.S.R. On the Dnieper River the Kanev Dam will be complete late in 1969 and on the Daugava the Riga Dam will be completed soon after. In Georgia a dam 900 feet high on the Inguri will provide irrigation and power. The Soviet Union claims that the Nurek Dam across the Vakh, near Dushanbe, will irrigate 3.7m acres of arid land, but this figure is suspect.

VENEZUELA. In 1968 part of the Guri Dam system came into use as well as the Macagua HEP plant on the Caroni River.

ZAMBIA. About 30 miles south of Lusaka a dam is being built across Kafue Gorge and another one, at Meshi Teshi, will regulate flow in the Kafue River and thus prevent flooding of the Kafue polders.

DEAD SEA

A recent estimate notes that the Dead Sea contains 45,000m tons of valuable chemicals—sodium, chlorine, sulphur, potassium, calcium, magnesium and bromine. Both Israel and Jordan are exploiting the minerals, but development has decreased as a result of the 1967 war. Between them the two countries are taking about one-fifth of the Jordan's normal yearly flow into the Dead Sea which could mean about a 10-inch yearly drop in the Dead Sea's level. It seems likely that within perhaps as little as ten years the Dead Sea will lose its entire shallow southern portion. In a few centuries the far deeper northern part could dry up, too, leaving a huge expanse of dried white chemical salts in layers hundreds of feet deep. In 1968 it was proposed to bring water from the Mediterranean, 50 miles away, by tunnels and canals, to generate vast amounts of HEP and save the Dead Sea. (The idea was first mooted by geophysicist Walter Lowdermilk, in 1944.) By early 1967 Israel had enclosed by dykes 30 miles long all its half of the southern shallow section to form a complex of evaporating pans so as to secure harvests of potash-fertilizer. It hopes for an annual production of 1m tons.

DENMARK

16,000 sq. m. Pop. 4.77m. For the first time, in 1968, Danish industry employed more people and answered for a greater part of Denmark's total production and exports than agriculture, but 21% of the country's export earnings is still

71

coming from bacon. In 1967 Britain spent £85m on Danish bacon imports and £200m in all on Danish imports. The *degree* of specialization in the Danish bacon industry is not generally appreciated. One breed, the Landrace, has been perfected. Meticulous feeding ensures that pigs entering a Danish bacon factory are as similiar as peas in a pod. Careful breeding and research enable every part of the pig to be used commercially. It is well-known that bristles are used for upholstery and brushes. The pituitary glands and other parts are used for medicines and cosmetics; the blood produces albumen for textiles and plywoods; the skin is used in the leather industry, and the bones make glue and bone-meal. Even the feet, dyed red, are a delicacy in Ghana. Because the pig's head is difficult to market the Danish researchers are reducing its size by selective breeding. It is now 2 lb lighter than in 1965. By transferring the useless 2 lb to the rest of the pig the Danes estimate that they are making an extra £2.5m a year.

The big expansion of Danish exports since 1966 is due mostly to small and medium-size firms new to the export trade and encouraged by the Foreign Service Department. The Trade Fund makes grants to groups of firms operating in the same line of business and engages an export consultant to handle their joint export production and marketing efforts.

It should be noted that the number of Danish farms is declining steadily as the larger, more prosperous farms absorb smaller ones. The average farm in 1965 was forty acres; it is now seventy acres. The loss of valuable markets in the EEC, particularly the West German market for cattle and meat, has led to enthusiastic support for Denmark's application for EEC membership. Estimates suggest that if Denmark joined the Common Market pastoral earnings would increase by about 25%.

DISEASE

Increasing numbers of people are contracting bilharziasis, the most dangerous tropical disease after malaria. According to WHO, about 200m people are suffering from the disease in many areas of Africa, tropical South America and the Middle and Far East. Enormous numbers of the water snail which is host to the bilharziasis virus breed in reservoirs, canals and irrigation ditches. In the Congo, after completion of irrigation ditches, the number of cases of bilharziasis increased tenfold. A probable solution to the problem is *bayluscid*, developed by the Bayer dye works at Leverkusen (Rhine). Even heavily diluted in water it is fatal to water snails, their eggs and the larvae of the bilharziasis worm, yet it has no ill effects on human beings, warm-blooded animals and plants.

Chagas's disease, a mostly fatal intestinal infection, may also decrease now that a substance has been found to spray the bed-bugs which carry it. However, no specific cure has been found for the disease from which 12m South Americans are suffering.

DROUGHT

Drought gripped many parts of South America during 1968. This was due as much to scant snowfall in the Andean watersheds as to lack of rain. In Chile, which suffered its longest drought, 700,000 sheep, 300,000 cattle, half the corn and two-thirds of the potato crop were lost. Peru lost nearly all its cotton in 1968, Ecuador vast areas of coffee and rice. In the Patagonian region of Argentina at least 200,000 sheep died. The Chilean weather bureau warned, in January 1969, that other parts of the country could become as desolate as the Atacama Desert.

E

EARTHQUAKES

CAUSES. In the quest for more definite causes of earthquakes geophysicists are concentrating on two recently postulated rival theories. The newer theory holds that earthquakes originate where the molten core of the earth meets the mantle about 1,800 miles below the earth's surface, a view that is questioned by supporters of the older belief that earthquakes can be best explained by the fact that the earth's sea floor is spreading and its continents are drifting.

The protagonists of the new theory, the Americans Bisque and Rouse, speculate that the core and mantle work against each other like old clutch plates, slipping here and catching there. As a result pockets of turbulence develop that send seismic waves to the surface; these waves create stress and ultimately fracture the granite and basalt crust, causing earthquakes. Bisque and Rouse believe that the waves travel along stress planes that may be created by differences between the speeds at which the plastic-like mantle and the liquid core rotate. The theory does appear to fit with several observations. Rouse has calculated that most earthquake areas, volcanoes and other signs of geological activity lie on sixteen belts or circles. One circle, for instance, lies along the west coast of South America, crosses the Atlantic to southern France and arcs through Italy and the Indian Ocean. At nineteen points three belts intersect—and significantly most of these points mark areas of major seismic or volcanic activity. Even more significantly the belts outline planes which run tangent to the earth's core, cutting the earth's surface at an angle of 60 degrees—the angle at which most major earthquakes strike the earth's crust. The pockets of turbulence are located at these points of tangency.

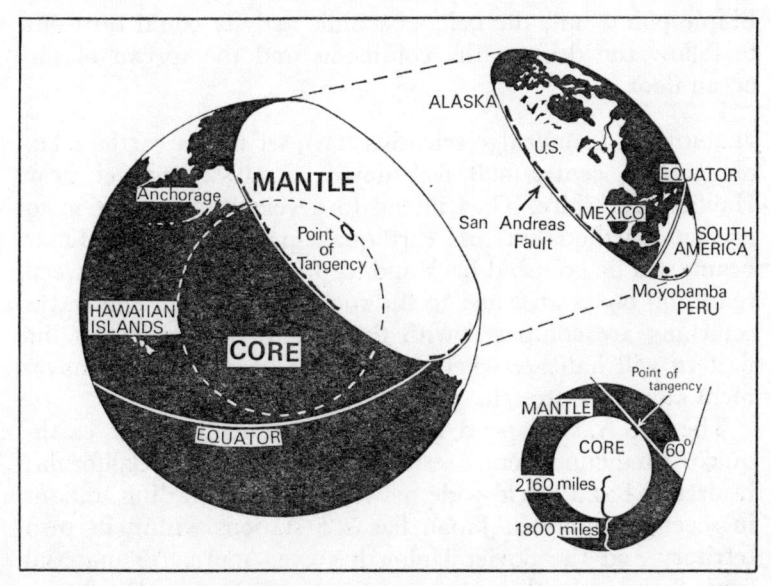

3. The Rouse-Bisque Theory of Earthquakes

Giving the theory additional support, Bisque and Rouse point out that variations in the earth's gravitational field and its magnetic field (called geoid and magnetic anomalies) are found over areas where these stress planes would intersect far below the earth's surface. Core and mantle material, they suggest, mix in these regions causing instability, hence magnetic and geoid variations.

Seismologists who dispute the Bisque-Rouse theory point out that earthquakes measured so far have originated at depths no greater than 400 miles—far shallower than the path Bisque and Rouse postulate. Bisque, however, claims it may be only the initial impulse of energy that comes from the greater depths, not the shattering quake itself.

Perhaps the greatest counter-pressure to the Bisque-Rouse theory comes from the growing popularity of the fifty-year-old concept of continental drift, though in fact Bisque and Rouse say that their belts and planes of seismic activity may yet conform with the continental-drift theory. For instance, Bisque points out, the belts of seismic activity could turn out to follow the drift of the continents and the spread of the ocean floor.

PREDICTION. Cambridge scientists have set up an earthquake-observation centre 400 feet down a railway tunnel near Halifax, Yorkshire. They intend to develop a laser system to predict earthquakes in earthquake-prone regions. Laser beams will be bounced back and forth along a tunnel between reflecting boxes attached to the rock at each end. The waves returning are compared with those emitted. Changes in the pattern will indicate whether there has been any rock movement along this stretch.

The U.S.A. will spend 150m dollars annually on an earthquake prediction centre established in 1968 in California; it already has a world-wide network of 130 recording stations in seventy countries. Japan has 285 stations within its own territory and the Soviet Union has even more. All material from these and other sources is now collected at the International Bureau of Seismology in Strasbourg.

Near the notorious San Andreas Fault, south of San Francisco, the U.S.A. completed an underground laboratory in 1968—three 100-feet tunnels in a Y formation, 200 feet below the surface. Many seismologists expect, within a decade, another major earthquake in San Francisco.

The major earthquakes since 1966 include:

ALBANIA-YUGOSLAVIA. An earthquake which hit the border region near Debar left 7,000 people homeless in November 1967.

COLOMBIA. On February 9, 1967, Gaucamaya, in the Andes, was destroyed in the worst earthquake ever to strike Colombia.

FRANCE. The village of Arette, Pyrenees, was practically destroyed in August 1967; 1,200 people were left homeless.

GREECE. Within the triangle formed by the cities of Arta, Ioannina and Trikkala, Pindus Mountains, an earthquake caused widespread damage in May 1967; twelve villages were affected and eight people were killed.

INDIA. Koyna Nagar, 125 miles south of Bombay, December 1967, was the epicentre of a series of tremors which affected an area within a radius of 300 miles. The region is outside the accepted earthquake belt which runs through northern India along the rim of the Himalayas. A hundred people were killed, 1,300 injured.

INDONESIA. The Malang region, eastern Java, was severely shaken in February 1967; 51 people died and 400 were injured. About forty died in a quake at Madjene, southern Sulawesi. On February 23, 1969, about 600 people died in earthquakes in the Celebes.

IRAN. Two major earthquakes devastated parts of north-east Iran on August 31 and September 1, 1968. Kakhk was the worst hit region. At least 20,000 people died and 100,000 were left homeless in the quakes, the nation's worst.

TURKEY. In an earthquake at Adapazari, 80 miles east of Istanbul, in January 1967, 68 were killed.

VENEZUELA. An earthquake on July 29, 1967, hit Caracas, Macaray and La Guaira; 100 people were killed and 10,000 left homeless.

EAST AFRICAN COMMUNITY

Established in December 1967, the Community—Kenya, Uganda and Tanzania—has been acclaimed as a major step to promote free trade. In mid-1968 the Community reached a draft agreement with the EEC, offering trade concessions on a number of products in return for the abolition of import tariffs on all East African produce with the exception of coffee, cloves and pineapples. Ratification is likely to take some time.

EAST GERMANY (German Democratic Republic)

41,479 sq. m. Pop. 17.4m. As in other COMECON countries economic reforms have been introduced since 1966, with individual managers being given much more control and greater reliance being placed on the control of credit through the banking system. The chemical industry is making the maximum use of the country's limited natural resources, while petro-chemicals are also growing in importance, based on crude oil pumped direct from the U.S.S.R. Oil, methane and nuclear power are noticeably replacing coal and lignite as sources of power. The majority of trade is with other East European countries but exchanges with the West are expanding rapidly, notably with West Germany. U.K. sales have undoubtedly benefited since 1966 from the Leipzig Fairs held in the spring and autumn, directed respectively at the promotion of capital and consumer goods. Leipzig is regarded as a shop window between East and West. East Germany is particularly interested in the participation of British industry in capital projects and there are opportunities for increased sales of British chemicals, dyes, insecticides and synthetic fibres. (See *Shipping*.)

ECUADOR

226,000 sq. m. Pop. 5.387m. Ecuador's basic problem still lies in excessive dependence on agriculture, with expansion averaging about 4% annually. Banana exports were worth £28m in 1967 compared with £25m in 1966. The country is seeking new outlets, notably in East Europe. Better packaging methods and techniques in fighting plant disease are being improved. The small amount of arable land available and poor communications make agricultural diversity difficult. To support ambitious industrial plans several HEP plants are being built and a recent discovery of oil in east Ecuador will provide further incentive. Ecuador's imports from the U.K. amount to about £3m, her exports to the U.K. to only £250,000.

4. The Industries of East Germany

EDUCATION

After twenty years of striving many nations are still endeavouring to attain the goal of education for all, but the goal is constantly receding; UNESCO does not believe that education can outpace the demographic population. As the world's population increases its average age decreases.

In Pakistan only 25% of children are being educated, in Bolivia 40%, in Brazil 50%, 80% in India, 14% in Afghanistan. The comparison between 1965 and 1970 shows the position starkly. In that five-year period places have to be found for a further 40m children in primary schools, 12m more in secondary schools and 1m more in universities. More than 1,154,000 more primary school teachers and 250,000 more secondary teachers will be needed. In the Arab countries great progress has been made, largely owing to the money available from oil. Between 1960 and 1966 the population rose from 92m to 105m while school and university population increased from 8m to 12m. Against an annual rate of population growth of 2.5% that of school enrolments is nearing 10%. Even so, 8m children (1968) are not yet in school. Added to all this is the fact that nearly half the pupils in the primary schools of the developing countries drop out in the first or second years; less than a quarter of those who start school complete the course. (In the U.S.A. only a quarter of university students complete their courses; in French universities only one student in five obtains a degree.)

EIRE (Republic of Ireland)

26,600 sq. m. Pop. 2.9m. Much of Eire's current progress stems from the government's industrial development plans, though the future of the initially most promising of these, the Shannon Estuary Scheme, which is largely dependent on international air traffic developments, is uncertain. An agreement in May 1968 with U.K. car manufacturers regarding imports should

Eire

result in growth of the Irish car assembly industry. Mining, particularly of lead, zinc and silver, is an area of potential expansion worth £12m a year. Peat was worth £6m in 1968. Stimulus for the new mining comes from Canada; about 8,000 sq. m. are under prospecting licences. For any new mine starting operations before 1986 there is twenty years' total exemption from tax.

A drop in emigration together with an end to the centuries-

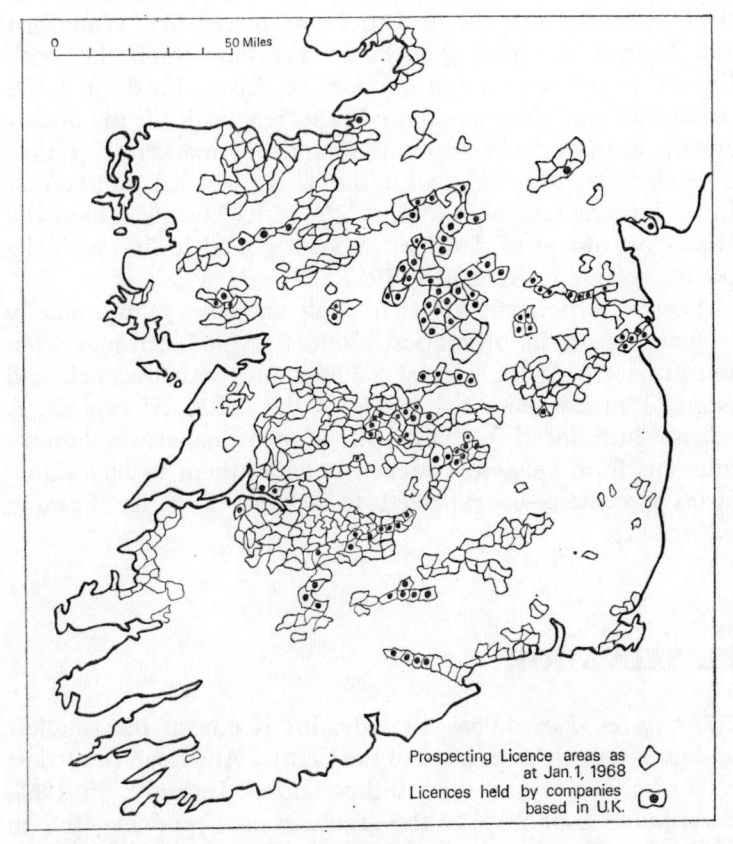

5. Prospecting Licence Areas in Eire

old decline in population, has added to the pool of unemployed, already enlarged by a continuing outflow of labour from agriculture. However, in 1967-68 agricultural production rose by 2%, or £13m in value, on 1966 figures. Farmers cut down on the breeding of cattle in 1967 and again in 1968 and the numbers of cattle and sheep on farms dropped in 1968.

The largest rises in exports in 1968 were of electrical machinery, petroleum products, textile yarns, clothing, professional and scientific goods and chemicals. The effort to set up rival industrial centres to Dublin at places like Waterford and Galway is working well. In February 1968 the Irish Export Board announced an export drive aimed at 1,300 companies regarded as potential exporters, which is to encourage the formation of co-operative exporting marketing groups. The close trading links with the U.K. which supplies half Eire's imports and buys about 72% of its exports caused the Irish government to devalue the Irish pound in line with the pound sterling in November 1967.

There is a powerful effort to push tourism—£2m annually is being spent in promotion alone. In 1967 earnings from tourism were £83m, almost £30m more than livestock and only £22m less than the whole of the industrial exports. A scheme introduced in 1967—provision of loans to voluntary migrants from congested areas to enable them to buy viable farms elsewhere—is expected to achieve a better farming pattern.

EL SALVADOR

7,722 sq. m. Pop. 3.06m. El Salvador is one of the smallest and most densely populated of the Central American countries; it is also one of the most industrialized. Industry, in 1968, contributed over 20% to the gross national product (10% in 1958). In 1967-68 more than forty new factories were established including a container factory, a sugar refinery and a food-processing plant. A Japanese-owned synthetic fibre factory and an American-owned paper bag factory began operations in 1968. The economy's vulnerability to fluctuations in the world prices of coffee and cotton has, apart from the industrial drive, led to agricultural diversity. Apples, mangoes and citrus fruits are being newly cultivated on marginal land. By 1969 El Salvador will be self sufficient in corn.

ETHIOPIA

395,000 sq. m. Pop. 22m. Industry, largely inspired and financed by West Germany, is growing up around Addis Ababa— (pop. 455,000). Nearly all industry is concerned with consumer products, thus reducing the country's expenditure on imports. With foreign help, Ethiopia's public health service is developing, although the number of notifiable cases of illness is still high, 129,381 of malaria, 97,398 of syphilis and 85,588 of dysentery being registered in 1967.

EUROPEAN ECONOMIC COMMUNITY
(Common Market)

Pop. 180m. The Common Market has, in the last two years, mastered many of its problems and is now consolidating itself. The most prominent symbol of its solidarity is the new EEC headquarters in Brussels, a vast thirteen-storey building which Belgians, at least, believe will one day be needed for a European Foreign Office and Economic, Finance and Defence Ministries. Late in 1968 common rules were applied and as the industrial and farm union leads on to full economic union Eurocrats will begin to set up at least the framework of a Ministry of Economics. Common economic policies must, they say, call for common trade policies towards the outside world, particularly towards the Communist countries, and therefore to the beginnings of a common foreign policy.

Ordinary workers in all six member states have been able to move freely across national frontiers and take permanent jobs in any part of the EEC, but each of the six governments was able to exercise a safeguard clause under which its own nationals had first call on any vacancies. The countries are now waiving this clause. By 1969 nearly all self-employed people will also be able to establish themselves by right in any country of the Six.*

July 1, 1968 is one of the milestones in the history of the Common Market. On this date, with the removal of the tenth and final instalment of duties on goods traded between the members and with the establishment of a common external tariff on imports from other countries, the EEC achieved their initial objective, a fully-fledged customs union. But the French authorities, who introduced in August 1968 a range of economic measures without consulting their colleagues, have underlined the fact that they do not feel that the final removal of duties has placed them under any obligation to maintain closer co-operation on economic policy.

The next goal of the Common Market is economic union; only when this has been achieved will political union, the ultimate aim, become feasible. Progress towards the former will be helped by the merger of the EEC with the other two Communities, the European Coal and Steel Community and Euratom in July 1967. Solutions to many of the problems now facing the Common Market countries—agriculture, transport and foreign trade competition—depend on their being prepared to yield a greater measure of national sovereignty to the EEC Commission than has been apparent hitherto. On the way this challenge is met will depend whether the Common Market can make the transition to a genuine European economic community.

---

* The French Ministry of Education informs me that in spite of development of the EEC there has been no increased interest in the languages of its members and that in all existing organizations, public or private, the English language had a distinct priority and that while during 1964-66 German made some progress it has now yielded to English.

EUROPEAN FREE TRADE ASSOCIATION (EFTA)

(Britain, Norway, Sweden, Denmark, Austria, Switzerland, Portugal.) On January 1, 1967 almost all EFTA tariffs were abolished, making EFTA a free industrial trade zone almost eighteen months before the EEC. The influence of tariff reductions is probably best seen in the timber and pulp trade, with vast increases in exports from Finland and Sweden and corresponding increases in imports by Britain and Denmark.

The question preoccupying EFTA is how to crack the Common Market, which has about twice the population (180m), production and trade of the EFTA nations. Exports to the Common Market are all important, particularly for Austria which trades much more with the Common Market than with its fellow members.

Yet trade among EFTA countries grew by 9.7% in 1967 (9.4% in 1966). It brought to 129% the total increase inside EFTA since 1959. EFTA imports from EEC rose by only 4% in 1967 (6% in 1966), and exports to EEC fell by 2.4% following a 4.4% rise in 1966.

Within EFTA the Nordic countries are becoming stronger because the trade between themselves is growing much faster than their trade with Britain and the other EFTA states. On the other hand, Britain is the best customer of every one of them.

($ million)

IMPORTER / EXPORTER	Austria	Denmark	Finland	Norway	Portugal	Sweden	Switzer-land	United Kingdom	EETA
Austria		35.0	16.1	22.2	11.5	64.8	156.4	100.5	406.5
Denmark	31.2		50.6	182.6	11.9	344.3	58.6	573.4	1,252.6
Finland*	7.5	59.3		38.6	3.4	138.6	14.6	318.4	580.4
Norway	8.5	136.9	35.9		9.5	271.5	18.0	335.7	816.0
Portugal*	10.2	18.9	7.5	8.4		32.8	12.8	152.7	243.3
Sweden	53.9	427.5	232.1	539.0	24.2		100.0	604.1	1,980.8
Switzerland	179.9	76.6	38.6	44.4	40.0	117.8		261.8	759.1
United Kingdom	111.9	405.4	201.3	358.6	134.4	620.9	324.4		2,156.9
EFTA*	403.1	1,159.6	582.1	1,193.8	234.9	1,590.7	684.8	2,346.6	8,195.6

6. Intra-EFTA Trade

F

FALKLAND ISLANDS

4,600 sq. m. Pop. 2,200. Ever since British occupation in 1848 these islands have been claimed by Argentina and talks have taken place spasmodically since 1966. Falkland islanders see their situation as parallel with that of Gibraltar and resent any suggestion of the islands being given to Argentina. A Scottish Company plans to harvest seaweed to make alginates; the industry could yield £100m annually.

FAMINE

Famine is endemic and there can be little "new geography" about it but it should be noted that in northern India during 1967-68, especially in Bihar, it reached even worse proportions than usual. Of the 50m people in Bihar at least 30m were suffering from famine, a famine aggravated by the religious reluctance of the inhabitants to exploit the sacred Ganges for irrigation. The shortage of grain has encouraged hoarding and in 1968 it was estimated that up to 3m relatively rich farmers eat the better grain themselves, hoard some of the rest and sell the poorer grain at high prices. Government rationing has been completely ineffective. In spite of food brought in by the government, Oxfam and CARE (Co-operative for American Relief Everywhere) hundreds of thousands of people have died.

One of the world-wide problems which the United Nations is tackling is how to avert an impending protein crisis. Most people in the wealthy Western nations are not aware of the existence of the crucial problem of the protein gap between their own part of the world and the under-developed countries. They are inclined to assume that where there is enough food to go round it will be adequately nourishing. But one-third of the world's population is suffering from protein deficiency. In vast stretches of Asia, Africa and Latin America even where sufficient quantities of food are available hundreds of millions of children are condemned to ill-health and to be swept away by epidemics because of insufficient protein intake. The U.N. Advisory Committee on the Application of Science and Technology to Development has set out proposals for international action. They note that, unless their proposals are vigorously implemented the physical, economic, social and political development of many of the poorer nations may be completely arrested. In 1968 they prepared a ten-year "action" programme, costing more than £100m, to be carried out by several organizations including WHO, FAO and UNCF.

The world's oil industry is one of the main hopes of filling the protein gap; good progress is being made in the U.S.A., U.S.S.R., Britain and France in producing protein-rich food from petroleum fermentations.

An experimental farm was set up in Nigeria (1967) to study the use of protein concentrates derived from petroleum for stock raising in tropical regions. The world potential of the oil refining industry is a production of nearly 20m tons of proteins a year; this is greater than the amount of protein contained in the world's annual catch of 50m tons of fish.

Scientists emphasize the need to develop sources of protein such as oil seed cake and food from sunflower seeds and soya. A successful example is vitasay, a soft drink especially rich in proteins, in strong demand in Hong Kong. Another successful mixture is incaparina, a mixture including maize meal and cotton-seed flour with a high protein content. This flour has been developed in Guatemala by the Institute of Nutrition for Central America and Panama (hence *incaparina*). But much else needs to be done to control famine. (See *Artificial Foods, Hunger.*)

FAROE ISLANDS

540 sq. m. Pop. 37,000. In December 1967 the Faroes formally became part of EFTA, on Danish application. Faroese agriculture, supplemented by inshore fishing, has proved wholly inadequate to support the growing population (increasing by nearly 1,000 annually). The old agricultural settlements are becoming depopulated as their inhabitants move to larger centres offering better prospects of work on sea-going vessels; a third of the population get their living direct from the sea. No longer a matter of inshore fishing from open boats, it is now chiefly deep-sea fishing from ocean-going vessels ranging as far as Iceland, Greenland, Newfoundland and the Barents Sea. Italy is now the principal market for salted fish, displacing Spain. Brazil is an important new market, taking 75% of all exports of dried cod. A very new branch of Faroese production is quick-frozen fish fillets; the U.S. bought 20m kroner-worth in 1968. Two large factories were built—at Thorshavn and Klaksvig in 1967-68. At Thorshavn, too, steel ships of up to 1,000 tons are being built.

FINLAND

130,165 sq. m. Pop. 4.7m. Almost two-thirds of Finland's foreign exchange earnings come from sales of timber and timber products and this overdependence has made Finland peculiarly sensitive to conditions in the major West European markets. Weak demand for timber and paper because of competitive trading from the Soviet Union, Sweden and Canada has caused much uncertainty since 1966. Rationalization programmes in forestry and agriculture have reduced the number of jobs available. However, the basic metal-using and electrical industries are expanding. Indeed, Finland is among the world's top fifteen industrial nations. Finland's recovery depends largely on conditions in the major markets. As a supplier Britain, once in first place, now ranks behind the

U.S.S.R., West Germany and Sweden. Sweden has 60,000 Finnish workers, but the contribution of women to the economy is higher than in most countries; 40% are employed. In the country they retain responsibility for many dairy herds and most poultry.

The intensified forest renewal and cultivation programmes initiated in 1966 will clearly make room for further expansion of the industry. A new board mill, opened in January 1969, is one of the biggest of its kind in Europe. In the meantime there is interesting growth in exports of textiles, furniture, ceramics, glassware, toys, cutlery and domestic utensils.

FISHING

Initially, it should be noted that the fishing industry has further developed along the lines explained in the 1966-67 edition of *New Geography*, with larger trawlers travelling further afield and with the use of more scientific equipment. Because of competition—even Thailand is now a leading fishing nation—fishing companies complain that fishing from conventional sources has become less profitable. The catch for 1967 was 51m tons, in 1968 53.5m tons. That for 1970 is anticipated as 61.5m tons.

CRABS. Since 1956 the American king-crab catch has grown from 9m lb to 175m lb in 1968; the expected annual rate of increase is 20%. Supply cannot meet demand, although several companies are now involved. A large packing plant has been opened at Seldovia, on Kenai Peninsula, Alaska.

DRIED FISH. The Norwegians in 1967-68 successfully commercialized surplus production of dried fish to Africa and South America and are now starting up in the starvation-stricken Kerala province of India.

FISH ALBUMEN. The scientists of a Swedish medicinal drug firm have succeeded in reducing fish albumen to an odourless and tasteless concentrate which can be added to low-calory human food. This concentrate is obtained in the form of a powder which consists of 83% albumen and 13% mineral salts and which can be used like powdered milk. The first large-scale delivery of this nutritive additive was sent (April 1968) to Ethiopia where it has been used, under scientific control, to enrich local food. This easily digestible fish albumen concentrate is expected to come into world use.

FISH FARMING. As fishing from conventional sources has become less profitable—an inevitable result of the intense competition between the fishing fleets of the world—attention is being focused on the possibilities of rearing fish under artificial conditions. There are precedents: oysters, mussels and shrimps have been cultivated in various parts of the world for many years, though, admittedly, for the purpose of supplying a minority market rather than for the production of large quantities of a basic foodstuff.

The main factors to be considered in the rearing of fish are temperature, salinity, light, water exchange and food. If the expense of creating a totally artificial environment is to be avoided, each country must concentrate on rearing its native fish, in the case of the British Isles plaice, sole, brill, halibut and turbot. Research is being carried out at Port Erin in the Isle of Man and at Lowestoft to discover the most suitable combination of factors for the rearing of a particular type of fish.

The problem of feeding the fish is considerably eased by the existence of the brine shrimp, artemia. The eggs of this shrimp can be stored for years and, after immersion in sea water for only two days, the life cycle continues, the shrimp reaching maturity in three to four weeks. Thus artemia provides an ideal fish food, ranging in size from 0.35 mm to 12 mm. The capture and culture of artemia can now be carried out mechanically; similarly the shrimp, at selected stages of growth, can be fed to the fish.

There are two practical areas for the culture of fish: in enclosed inlets relying on semi-natural conditions, reinforced where necessary by artificial means, or in the regions around coastal power stations where the cooling water would supply plentiful quantities of warmed sea water at a very low cost.

Sole is perhaps the most suitable fish for cultivation. It is a fish popular with consumers and it will live and spawn in captivity in a water temperature just above the average found around the coasts of Britain, which makes it suitable for power station sites. Experiments in raising sole to a salable size have shown that it will, throughout its growth, feed on the various states of artemia and fully grown will eat chopped mussel, although more dependence would probably, in a commercial project, be placed on a pelleted food. Plaice is also suitable for rearing under artificial conditions; large quantities of fertilized eggs can be obtained from the North Sea in January and February, and again the fish can be fed on artemia. Turbot and brill are more difficult to "farm"; feeding as they do on live fish, they do not feed readily in captivity, although, by cross breeding, it may be possible to produce a strain suitable for cultivation in these conditions. Indeed, perhaps in the future, food from the sea will not be from fish as we should now recognize them, but from much larger creatures, artificially bred and artificially raised.

FISH FLOUR. If the potential American fish catch were turned into fish flour the diet of 1,000m people could be balanced for 300 days at the cost of half a cent a head a day.

PRAWNS. The Persian Gulf is one of the biggest natural breeding grounds for prawns and the trawler operators, the Ross Group, have set up four companies to exploit it in Saudi Arabia, Bahrain, Qatar and Iran. Nearly forty boats and four factory ships are providing markets in the U.S.A., Europe and the Far East with 100 tons of prawns daily. (See *Mosquito Control.*)

FOOD

The world food situation is now (1969) more precarious than at any time since 1945-46, according to Dr. R. B. Sen, Director-General of FAO. World food production failed to rise in 1967-68 but population increased by about 100m. The FAO estimates indicate that food-per-person output has dropped back to the 1957-58 level in many developing regions. The danger is that where many millions of people are already undernourished there is little margin against the effects of a poor season and drought-affected harvests.

WORLD FOOD PROGRAMME. This is an organization, the offshoot of the U.N. and the FAO, which began operations in 1963. Its purpose is to collect and distribute food and in 1968, for the first time, it became clear that the WFP is being successful. At the end of 1967 no fewer than forty countries had pledged food and WFP was operating in another forty. Among the most difficult problems are those of earmarking and allocating the variety of foodstuffs from the large number of countries which have pledged them to the many projects or emergency operations needing them, and in the quantities and units in which they are needed. At the end of 1968 the resources available to WFP were worth less than 60m dollars: the target was 275m dollars. (See *Atomic Energy*, also *Hunger* for information on food related to population statistics.)

FRANCE

212,700 sq. m. Pop. 50m. Political reasons apart, much of President de Gaulle's obstructiveness over British entry to the Common Market represents a rearguard action to protect France's relatively weak industry from still keener competition for as long as possible. The overdeveloped Paris region has distorted the economic balance of the whole country. At least a third of France, the vast region west of a line from le Havre to Marseilles, is underpopulated and underdeveloped. Rural living standards rise more slowly than urban standards and there is a flight from the land of 110,000 workers a year. As in Britain, coal mining is declining, making depressed areas out of Lorraine, St. Etienne and other fields. Alarmed by unemployment the government has been establishing labour exchanges. Fully a third of French industry is government-controlled and its 160 state-owned companies have massive deficits. Yet it is true that French industry is "underpopulated". Only 16% of the people hold industrial jobs, compared with 22% in Britain and 23% in West Germany. (Of the thirty biggest industrial companies outside the U.S.A., twelve are German, ten British but only two French—Renault and Rhone-Poulenc.)* The government has granted 600m dollars in low-interest loans to steel firms on condition that they merge and modernize.

The French tourist industry was severely hit in 1968 by the students' riots, industrial strikes and violence. By some estimates about a quarter of all tourist enterprises were irreparably damaged.

---

* *The Times Review of Industry & Technology*, July 1966, listing the 100 leading European companies (excluding the U.K.) ranked by capital, put Rhone-Poulenc as the highest French firm but eight German, five Italian and three Dutch firms ranked higher.

G

GEOLOGY

The major centre for geological research is now the Federal Geological Research Institute of Hanover, where 250 scientists and 450 technical assistants provide the basis for geological work in which West Germany is engaged in many countries. The Institute is now so well established that in 1967 no fewer than 800 foreign geologists were given advice at the Institute. One of the most important homeland tasks of the Institute involved work carried out in preparation for the cultivation of Emsland, the large moorland area of north-west Germany. In this once poverty-stricken province considerable fallow areas were made agriculturally and industrially useful after systematic and exhaustive geological, hydrological and soil analysis studies.

Investigating the disappearance of the sophisticated Minoan civilization on Crete, geologists and archaeologists found during 1967-68 that a violent volcanic eruption on the island of Thera (now Santorin), 75 miles to the north of Crete, in about 1470 B.C. caused the central and western parts to sink and generated *tsunamis* between 100 and 165 feet high. These waves hit the Cretan coast with devastating force and were accompanied by a rain of volcanic ash that buried nearly everything left standing and by fumes that poisoned the population. (It is thought that Thera's eruption affected the Exodus and caused the ten plagues of Egypt 450 miles to the south.)

GEOPHYSICS

Ever since physicist James Van Allen discovered the earth-circling belts of radiation that bear his name scientists have been trying to answer a simple but perplexing question: how do the electrons and protons get there in the first place? Having summarized data that he and other scientists had collated from many satellites, Van Allen himself reported (December 1967) that the charged particles are drawn into the belt by a high voltage generated across the earth's magnetic field. For years scientists have been reasonably certain that the electrons and protons in the outer belt come from the solar wind, a stream of charged particles emitted continuously from the sun at velocities up to 1.6m mph. But at these speeds, relatively low in the world of high energy physics, the electrons and protons are travelling too slowly to penetrate through the earth's magnetic field and into the outer belt. They should bounce off the magnetic lines of force and be deflected back into space. Van Allen states that an electrical potential of 50,000 volts is generated across the earth's comet-shaped magnetic field by two complex effects. As the solar wind blows by the earth, compressing the magnetic field into a rounded shell on the daylight side and sweeping it into a long tail on the night side, it produces friction on the outer boundary of the magnetic field. This friction generates a positive electrical charge on the morning side of the boundary and a negative charge on the opposite, or evening, side. The charge is supplemented by a dynamo effect caused by the rotation of the earth and its magnetic field. As a result protons striking the morning side of the boundary are attracted into the field by the negative charge on the evening side. Similarly electrons hitting the evening side of the boundary are pulled into the field by the positive charge on the morning side. This new theory may also explain why the auroral displays consist entirely of electrons or entirely of protons streaming down through the atmosphere. The solar particles have apparently been segregated by the high voltage in the sky.

GHANA

91,753 sq. m. 8.2m. In July 1967 Ghana devalued its currency, a step which boosted gold exports, diamonds, manganese and timber. The marketing board price paid to cocoa farmers was increased by 30% to give incentives for improved cultivation. Over half the country's revenue still comes from cocoa, but the 1966-67 crop was only 375,000 tons—the smallest since 1959. The 1967-68 crop of 400,000 tons was still below average. Timber provides (1968) 11% of the export income. British-Ghanaian trade is roughly at par, a different situation from that of 1966-67 when Britain had a £15m credit balance.

GIBRALTAR

2.25 sq. m. Pop. 25,000. Gibraltarians voted (September 1967) to retain links with Britain; Spain claims possession of the rock and the U.N. has voted that it be "decolonized". In 1968 Gibraltar began to style itself the "shopping centre of the Mediterranean", but it has an artificially maintained economy, strengthened temporarily by the Middle East War of 1967 which forced many more ships to use it as a transit port. By applying a tightening grip at La Linea, which links Gibraltar to Spain, the Spanish government has forced the Gibraltarians into making the Rock as impregnable economically as it used to be militarily. Fresh fruit and vegetables (£1m annually) are no longer bought from Spain but Morocco. By concentrating on tourism Gibraltar's efforts, as the gateway to Africa, are now geared to Morocco as they were at one time to Spain.

GLACIERS

Late in 1966 Steele Glacier in Yukon, Canada, suddenly began to move at the spectacular rate of 2 feet an hour; even the most rapid glacier in Europe moves no faster than a few feet a day. The glacier, 22 miles long and a mile wide, attracted American and Canadian glaciologists to observe the effects of glacial movement. The glacier slowed down in 1967-68 but late in 1968 was still moving relatively rapidly. The movement is believed to have followed subterranean disturbance.

The Allalin Glacier, south-west Switzerland, has been moving intermittently since November 1966. In 1965 a 60m cubic feet section broke off and killed 100 workers on the Mattmark HEP site and caused £5m damage. The glacier is under observation. (After receding 2300 feet in 36 years the glacier had been practically stationary since 1956.) (See *Ice Ages*.)

GOLD

The South African gold mining industry has reached one of the most critical points in its history. Rising production costs have forced managements to initiate a searching reappraisal of operations. The government is being urged to plan for a gradual but relentless decline in output and economists are calculating the effects on the Republic's economy should the gold mines cease production within fifty years. The Chamber of Mines has stated (January 1968) that without any further inflation the industry could survive until 2015; but with an increase of 2% annually it could last only until 1996. (For 1967 and 1968 the inflationary increase has been 4% annually.) Searches for new deposits are not encouraging.

GREECE

41,328 sq. m. Pop. 8.6m. The rate of expansion in the Greek economy during 1967-68 was only one third that of previous years; business conditions remain depressed because of political uncertainty following the military takeover in April 1967.

Under an agreement made when Greece became an associate member of the EEC, 125m dollars were to have been made available by the EEC over the five-year period ended October 1967. But at the end of 1968 more than two-thirds had not been paid, a measure of the Common Market's lack of confidence. Again, a major project to develop Crete and the western Peloponnese over twelve years at a cost of 840m dollars has found little support. Agriculture remains a major weakness in the economy, accounting for only a quarter of the national product but still employing half the labour force. Output of wheat, constantly in surplus, is to be reduced and cotton, citrus, raisins, figs and wines expanded. In June 1968 the government cancelled all debts by farmers incurred before April 1967; the total figure is probably £65m. Plans for tourism, which until 1967 had been expanding rapidly, are based on a calculation that numbers will have trebled by 1972 and that the tourist income will have reached 400m dollars annually. But this aim is now far from being fulfilled.

GUATEMALA

42,042 sq. m. Pop. 4.65m. In contrast to other CACM countries the government is relying heavily upon industries which make use of Guatemala's vast agricultural and mineral resources rather than those which rely heavily on imported raw materials. Recently factories to make antibiotics and vitamins, electric stoves, water heaters and kitchen utensils have commenced operations. Agriculture is being diversified under a national agricultural plan announced in 1967. The first two stages, concerned primarily with the cultivation of citrus fruit, avocado pears and sesame, have been completed. The third stage entails planting of bananas and plantains and flower growing, mainly for export. Guatemala expects foreign exchange earnings of 5m dollars annually by 1970 from exports of flowers to the U.S.A.

GUYANA

83,000 sq. m. Pop. 0.71m. After the first year of independence (May 26, 1966) the country had an unfavourable trade balance of £15.6m, but bauxite and alumina, sugar, rice and shrimps all brought in more money. During 1967-68 the Guyana Development Corporation granted concessions to sixty new industries. The Development Programme 1966-72 requires about £300m for its implementation and most of this is coming from overseas loans and grants. With a rapidly growing population, high unemployment and a shortage of skilled manpower the need to accelerate the pace of development is urgent. It places much emphasis on the harnessing of the numerous rivers and waterfalls for HEP schemes. A survey is in progress to see how the forests can be exploited. (About 90% of the country is forested but only about 14,000 sq. m. are accessible.) The main supplier is the U.K.; in 1967 £16.2m, but the U.S.A. now has a larger share, £9m.

H

HAWAII

6,420 sq. m. Pop. 740,000. Tourism is now Hawaii's largest source of income—500m dollars in 1968—larger than the pineapple and sugar businesses together. In 1960 this U.S. state had 296,517 visitors; in 1966, 700,000; 1968, 900,000. By 1972, 2m are anticipated. Tourism's latest surge is now to outer Oahu and what the Hawaiians call the Neighbor Islands—Maui and Kauai, Lanai, Molokai—all of which have spectacular scenery. Much of Kauai is accessible only by helicopter, including the rim of the crater of the extinct Mount Waileale, which with 400 to 800 inches of rain a year is the wettest place on earth. (See *Hydrology*.)

HEATING

Britain has the biggest air pollution problem of all countries. The annual death rate from bronchitis is about 72 per 100,000 in England and Wales but only 2.5 in the U.S.A., 8.4 in Japan and 14 in West Germany. About 87% of all smoke pollution in the U.K. is caused by open coal fires. The U.K. is far behind other industrialized nations in district and group heating; the most up-to-date scheme is that at Billingham, where an entire town centre of 34 acres is heated from a single coal-fired boiler house. West Germany has about 650 separate schemes, most of which operate from waste heat from electricity production. Denmark has more than 200 such schemes. In the U.S.A. most of the large cities have complex networks which use steam and not hot water. The Communist countries have developed district heating further than even the most "district heated" Western countries. Moscow has more than 300 miles of pipelines. A new development is the production of heat as a by-product of electricity generation in new Russian super power stations, with hot water delivered in insulated pipes for distances of up to 140 miles. Russian engineers say this is economical if the station has a capacity of at least 500 MW. The method would be useful in Britain as some of the new British power stations are capable of producing between 2000 and 4000 MW and it would seldom be necessary to transport water over distances as great as 140 miles.

HONDURAS

43,227 sq. m. Pop. 2.37m. Economically, Honduras has made relatively little progress except in the San Pedro Sulas region where the establishment of small local industries is growing rapidly. Since mid-1967 the country has gained a sugar mill, rice mill, poultry processing plant, seed processing plant, starch (from maize) factory, two rubber and plastics factories and a distillery. By 1971 a great pulp and paper mill in the north will be in operation. Sales of timber to the U.S.A. are providing a larger source of income.

HONG KONG

398 sq. m. Pop. 4m. (80% of the population lives in 12 sq. m.) The banking system, the bulwark of Hong Kong's prosperity, withstood the riots and political discord of 1967; local Communist banks suffered the worst. Hong Kong offers the best facilities to investors to be found in Asia, though a shortage of finance for small manufacturers, who make up 90% of all Hong Kong's industry, has led to a loan institution being set up. The electronics industry is expanding rapidly while another export earner which has developed quickly is the wig industry. Textiles remain the biggest industry, employing 40% of all workers. Several ambitious projects were at the planning stage at the end of 1968, one of the largest being a cargo handling complex at Kai Tak airport. A reservoir is being built at Plover Point.

HUNGARY

36,000 sq. m. Pop. 10.2m. A reliance on coal has been steadily superseded since 1966 by the use of more economical fuels. The discovery of immense quantities of methane in the south will help to reduce the country's power problems and should meet all increases in demand for energy. The chemical industry will benefit in particular. Many factories now have more incentive to export by being allowed to engage in trade directly and being entitled to receive the actual amount earned by their sales (under the old system manufacturers were paid only the Hungarian internal value of their goods).

However, Hungary has been unable to take full advantage of the trade treaty signed with West Germany in 1967 because many of the goods it would most like to sell—bicycles, sewing machines, textiles—proved so inferior that the Germans would not buy them. With a glut of such things as shirts and shoes, Hungarian manufacturers have been forced to unload them on home consumers at cut-rate prices. Foreign trade—exports account for two-fifths of national income—is vital to development, so that the 1967 increase in imports by 13% (over 1966) compared with a mere 7% increase in exports is disturbing. An Anglo-Hungarian trade agreement 1968-72 should lead to an expansion of interests; there is scope for a wide range of goods. In particular, British companies are making and installing electrical transformers to raise Hungary's electric power production substantially by 1970. Britain is importing dairy products, textiles, meat, fruit and vegetables from Hungary.

HUNGER

The population of the world is growing faster than the supply of food available to it. The result is a deficient diet for many millions of people, malnutrition for millions, and for hundreds of thousands death by starvation or by some disease which makes short work of their weakened bodies which no longer have any power to resist its inroads. A man who weighs 165 lb needs 2,500 calories a day, a woman who weighs 125 lb needs 2,100 calories. If performing heavy manual labour, the man will need 4,000 calories, the woman 3,000 calories. Only 38% of the world population have a daily intake of 2,300 calories, 42% have to make do with 2,000 to 2,300, while 20% have to content themselves with less than 2,000.

Two out of three human beings are undernourished, and every second person is particularly susceptible to disease because of a lack of vitamins, minerals and, particularly, proteins. Every diet should contain 25 grammes of animal albumen every day. The daily average intake of albumen is fourteen grammes in Peru, eleven grammes in Egypt and Pakistan, six grammes in India and China, and five grammes in the Congo (according to J. L. Lebret).

The world's total population is estimated at around 3.4 thousand million, 2.5 thousand million of whom live in the developing nations. United Nations demographers estimate that, by 1980, the world population will have risen to 4.5 thousand million, including 3.5 thousand million in the developing nations, and that by 2000 it will amount to 6.6 thousand million people, of whom 5.4 thousand million will be living in the developing nations.

By 2000, the population in Latin America will probably have increased by 194%, in Africa by 181%, in Asia by 99%, in the U.S.A. by 78% and in Europe by 24%. It is a terrifying prospect, for several thousand people are already dying every day of starvation when the total world population is only 3.4 thousand million; estimates vary between 10,000 and 70,000. There are 900 million children under the age of fifteen in the world today; it is likely that every second one of these children will die as a consequence of undernourishment long before he or she reaches adulthood. In India 40% of all children in India die before they reach the age of five. Out of a thousand children, 974 live beyond their first year in Germany, 800 in India, 770 in Bolivia, 650 in West Africa, and, in some towns in Brazil, only 550. (See *Famine, Food, U.S.A.*)

HURRICANES

BRAZIL. In January 1967, storm rains flooded the Paraiba River; in Rio de Janiero State at least 700 people died. The Camburi River floods in March 1967 killed 400 people east of São Paulo.

INDIA. Monsoonal storms and associated floods destroyed hundreds of thousands of acres of sugar, banana, rice and other crops in north and central India in September 1967. Hundreds died in these storms. In October 1967 a cyclone killed about 1,000 people at Cuttack, Orissa State.

JAPAN. A typhoon devastated the west coast in July 1967, damaging towns and ports and killing 350 people.

MALAYA. Storm-caused floods in January 1967 were serious enough to force 0.5m people from their homes, mainly in Trengganu and Kelantan states.

PAKISTAN. A cyclone wrecked much of the Madaripur area, East Pakistan, in April 1967, and in July monsoonal storms and floods left 100,000 people homeless in Karachi.

PORTUGAL. Portugal experienced its worst storm in a century at the end of November 1967. More than 300 people died in the Lisbon area. Badly damaged were Alenquer, Alverca, Odivelas, Kueluz and Ulmeria.

U.S.A. Hurricane Beulah, September 1967, was the third most powerful blow ever to strike Texas, but the low death toll is attributable to technology. Several aircraft and the weather satellite Essa (Environmental Science Services Administration) gave the Texas Gulf Coast twelve days warning of her course. Damage amounted to 1 billion dollars, including 70% of the Rio Grande's citrus and pepper orchards. At least 100 tornadoes spun off the hurricane, which degenerated into a mammoth rain storm causing the worst floods in the Rio Grande basin for 34 years.

HYDROLOGY

Of the 13 billion gallons of rain that fall every day on the island of Hawaii only 3% is retained by the land. Much of the rest soaks rapidly through permeable rock and soil and seeps into the sea. The continuous loss leaves three-quarters of the island with no streams or lakes to supply fresh water. In 1967, as a result of volcano research, scientists found new freshwater sources that could enable Hawaiians to move into previously uninhabitable areas and could help meet the needs of the island's growing population for generations. The techniques involved could be used anywhere in the world with similiar results.

While charting temperature variations in the vicinity of Kilauea, the island's largest volcano crater, the scientists, using infra-red scanning equipment, enlarged their thermal survey by following two great rifts that led from crater to sea. Under the shore and in nearby coastal waters their infra-red detector revealed the opposite of what they were searching for—large areas that were not hotter but as much as twelve degrees cooler than their surroundings. The infra-red scanner had located streams of cool, fresh water flowing into the ocean. After a survey of the island's entire coastline, 219 areas that could have underground freshwater springs were mapped. In one five sq. m. area in Hilo Bay the discharge of fresh water is probably 100m gallons a day. The U.S. Geological Survey has published an atlas showing locations; government

Hydrology

and other developers will now be able to establish communities close to water supplies. By the end of 1969 it is hoped to use more sophisticated techniques to find water under deserts, chart the best locations for wells and discover new hot springs for health and tourist sites.

I

ICE AGES

In January 1967 Dr. A. T. Wilson, Victoria University of Wellington, New Zealand, offered a solution for recurrent ice ages. During relatively non-glaciated eras, such as the present, the ice builds up on Antarctica and the southern ice-cap becomes higher and higher. The top of the ice remains very cold but the bottom is warmed slightly by heat escaping from the interior of the earth. Finally the combined effect of pressure from the thickening cap and geothermal warming melts the ice at the bottom; this frees the polar ice-cap from friction with underlying rock and it begins to spread out over the surrounding ocean as a floating ice shelf. At its maximum, Dr. Wilson estimates, the ice shelf covers 10m sq. m. of ocean and its white surface reflects so much sunlight that the earth's heat input is reduced by 4%. The earth's general temperature falls a few critical degrees and ice sheets begin to grow larger in the northern hemisphere. The more they spread the more solar energy is reflected back into space and the colder the earth becomes. The glaciers retreat when colder ice comes once more into contact with the rock below it, stops moving and is eroded by the ocean. Part of Dr. Wilson's theory has been born out by research made by U.S. Army geologists who have drilled through Greenland ice to a depth of 4,450 feet. They have found the temperature at the bottom of the ice sheet was 9° F. while on the surface it was —13° F.

ICELAND

40,500 sq. m. Pop. 195,000. Reduced incomes from fish and a serious falling off in the size of the catch in 1967-68 has affected Iceland. The white fish catch, of which cod is the most important, has been declining for some time, but only in 1967 did herring register a fall. Herring shoals have not come as close as usual to Iceland and a failure to move back would have a serious effect on the economy. The number of people employed in agriculture has been decreasing for many years and in 1968 only 16% of the population was so employed. However, improved methods and increased mechanization have resulted in increased output. Horticulture is the big new industry, using glasshouses heated by geothermal power. One of Iceland's most important projects is an HEP scheme on the Thjorsa River, associated with an aluminium plant near Reykjavik using power from the project. A new harbour at Straumsvik, open in 1969, handles ships up to 60,000 tons.

ILLITERACY

In 1968 UNESCO adopted a new strategy in the campaign against illiteracy. Departing from the procedures of attempting to solve the problem on a world-wide scale countries have adopted a more selective approach with crash-training courses aimed at groups where incentive for literacy is high and the promise of results considerable. At least fifty countries asked for UNESCO aid and by the end of 1968 preparatory missions had visited 38 of them. In some countries, e.g. India, the project is linked with increased food production, in Venezuela to the oil industry. All countries concerned contribute to the costs of the programme, the largest sum coming from Algeria with 3m dollars. Functional literacy programmes are linked with a large number of selected pilot schemes, for example, with textile workers at Chbin-el-Kom (Egypt), fishermen in Qatar, rubber workers at Cap Vert (Senegal), miners at

Tuncbilek (Turkey). Iran's fourth five-year plan (1967-72) envisages a 30% reduction in the illiteracy rate. Some countries are making it compulsory for certain sections of the population to participate in literacy programmes. In Libya and Iraq illiterate adults are compelled to attend classes; in Cambodia and Ecuador 1968 laws require literate adults to help teach illiterate fellow citizens.

In 1968 national "literacy services" were established in Argentina, Congo Republic, Dahomey, Ethiopia, Korea and Mauritania. Since fully trained teachers tend to follow the conventional approach to education and traditional teaching methods, volunteer teachers are being recruited, in several countries, from other callings—agricultural instructors and nurses in Nigeria, rural development leaders in Laos, factory foremen in Tunisia. According to UNESCO reports results are extremely good, but the population growth outstrips inroads into illiteracy. In the years 1961-66 UNESCO estimates that the number of illiterates in the world increased by something like 200m. Of the 373m schoolage children in 1966 only 30% were in school; the majority of these will not complete the primary course and will relapse into illiteracy. (September 8 is now celebrated each year as International Literacy Day, to mark the date, in 1965, of the meeting of The World Congress of Ministers of Education on the Eradication of Illiteracy.)

INDIA

1.2m sq. m. Pop. 513m—517m. Hopes that a record grain harvest in 1967, following two years of drought, would lead to a marked recovery did not materialize. In December 1967 the fourth five-year plan (1966-71) was discarded since the targets could not possibly be met. From April 1969 a new plan will attempt an average agricultural growth of 5% and less dependence on overseas support. The jute and tea industries have had difficulties. A fibre shortage has necessitated the reduction of output in the Indian jute mills and high grade fibre is being imported from Pakistan. Exports of tea amounted to 460m lb in 1967 but declined by 30m lb in 1968, coupled with a fall in prices. Because of Russian investment in heavy industry Indian sales to the U.S.S.R. are rising steadily. U.K. sales to India have declined disappointingly, falling from £97m in 1966 to £72m in 1968. The 1965 aim to increase fertilizer capacity to about 2.5m tons by 1970 was seen, at the end of 1968, to be certain; sixteen plants were then in operation. Far greater quantities are required and a target of about 5m tons by 1975 is contemplated.

The government's family planning policy aims at bringing down the birthrate from 41 to 25 per 1,000 of population by 1975. Free consultation and services are provided through a network of 1,634 urban and 21,000 rural family welfare centres, but the success of the scheme is doubtful, because illiteracy hinders the propaganda campaign.

INDIAN OCEAN

In April 1967 Britain paid £1m for three sparsely inhabited islands in the Indian Ocean—Desroches and Farquhar to the north of Malagasy and a third in the Chagos Archipelago. They are to become defence communications centres. (The islands of Gan, Mesira and Cocos also form part of the communications network.)

INDONESIA

887,000 sq. m. Pop. 112m. Prices rose by 100% in 1967 (600% in 1966) and the rise for 1968 was estimated to be about 60%. Emphasis up till 1971 will certainly be on mining and agriculture. Several foreign oil companies are drilling offshore; about 220m bb were produced in 1968 (189m bb in 1967).

A U.S. company is spending large amounts on copper exploration, and a Canadian company is seeking nickel. A major source of finance comes from several Japanese consortiums exploiting minerals and agriculture (rice). The population is increasing at 3.2%—one of the world's highest rates—thus crippling the country's planning. Smuggling, costing £30m in foreign exchange annually, is rampant.

Many of the 2.5m Chinese residents of the country want to leave the country now that political feeling is running against China. The best sign is that several big U.S. companies, forced to leave the country with the loss of immense investment, are returning to rebuild. This applies also to the Dutch; Philips is investing 6m dollars in a joint venture with the government. British, Belgian and West German industrial groups are also setting up industries.

IRAN (Persia)

628,000 sq. m. Pop. 26m. Much of Iran's progress depends on oil. The oil companies have agreed to return a quarter of their 100,000 sq. m. concession area to make available 20m tons of crude oil for the government to sell to Eastern Europe. The U.S.S.R. is building a steel complex at Isfahan, taking payment in methane. Rumania is building a tractor plant in exchange for oil and Czechoslovakia has arranged a similiar deal for a turbine factory. British and American firms are involved in petro-chemical complexes, fertilizers and paper. A further Russian scheme provides for the building of a dam and HEP scheme which will irrigate 23,000 acres of border land. The maintenance of water supplies is a national problem, but the Shah believes that with intensive irrigation he could triple Iran's present arable land—now only 10% of the total area—and produce enough food to sustain 75m people. He has been negotiating with the U.S.A. for a series of desalting plants along the Persian Gulf.

A notable development is the construction of the Kharg

Island terminal to handle all Iranian Consortium crude exports; a jetty can accommodate ten tankers simultaneously. Completed in 1968, the loading terminal is the world's largest; Iran's oil output exceeds 2.6m bb a day. The closing of the U.S. AID mission in December 1967, on the grounds that Iran could now support itself, is a promising sign. The U.K. provides about 13% of Iran's imports, ranking behind the EEC countries and the U.S.A.

IRAQ

172,000 sq. m. Pop. 8.3m. There is considerable potential for an expansion of oil production in Iraq but it is difficult to assess how much of this can be realized because of uncertainty regarding official policy towards foreign companies already operating and towards the awarding of contracts for new fields. The Iraqis have decided, after protracted negotiations with Spanish, Italian, French and Japanese companies, to develop certain fields, notably North Rumaila, themselves. The Iraq and Kuwait governments are developing rich sulphur resources in Mishraq. Following the Arab-Israeli War Iraq is giving greater preference to its trade relations in the Eastern bloc and to countries which they regard as neutral, e.g. France, Japan and Spain. Because of a ban on the import of consumer goods from the U.K. and U.S.A. there are opportunities for industries to develop, but it is more likely that the void will be filled by the neutrals.

IRRIGATION

Considerable space was given to irrigation projects in *New Geography 1966-67*. See *Irrigation* in the general index for several references under national entries. See also *Dams*.

EGYPT. Work on the Aswan Dam was due to be completed at the end of 1968, thus providing irrigation for 2m more acres; Lake Nasser, formed by the dam, will be well stocked with fish.

GHANA. A dam at Vea in northern Ghana irrigates 3,500 acres.

INDIA. An 116-mile canal will open arid areas in Mysore and Andhra Pradesh; Nagarjunasagar Dam impounding the waters of the Krishna River and forming a very large artificial lake, is irrigating 0.5m acres; the Ghandi Sagar Dam, Kotah Barrage and Ranapratap Sagar Dam are irrigating 550,000 acres.

INDONESIA. On the Tjitarum River, south-east of Djakarta, about 5,000 acres of rice are newly irrigated.

LIBYA. An interesting scheme is under way to irrigate many parts of a 600 sq. m. region with water from a subterranean lake south of the Tarhuna Mountains.

PAKISTAN. The irrigation schemes completed since September 1966 are: 19,000 acres at Dacca-Narayanganj; 300,000 acres in Kushtia-Jessore; Tanda Dam, West Pakistan, irrigating 11,000 acres and Dungi Dam across the Hochiari River irrigates 1,500 acres. (See *Pakistan* for information on the Mangla Dam.)

PORTUGAL. The Rio Cavado has been dammed in three places but the principal new scheme is at Povia on the Rio de Nisa, east central Portugal.

RHODESIA. Several schemes have been completed: Chikwarakware on the Limpopo; the Makwe Dam at Gwanda; Silalbuhwa Dam, near Filabusi; and the Ngwesi Scheme.

SOUTH AFRICA. The major Lubisi Dam on the Indwe River at Qamarapoort in Transkei is beginning to irrigate 10,000 acres. The Orange, Fish and Sunday Rivers are being canal-linked to provide grid irrigation water.

SPAIN. Various dams are under construction as part of a vigorous and complex irrigation scheme. The Rivers Magro, Calcon, Asmat, Cinca, Arlanza, Rambla Salada, Mao, Barranca Laja, and Barranca Liria have all been dammed, but a few years must elapse before the schemes are in operation and crops growing.

U.K. At Little Leighs, Essex, water is being stored for irrigation from the Ter River.

U.S.A./MEXICO. Amistad Dam, affecting both the Rio Grande and Devil's River, will irrigate new areas.

U.S.S.R. The Kara-Kum Canal, linking the Rivers Murgab, Tejen and Amy Darya, has progressed sufficiently to irrigate a further 200,000 acres.

ISRAEL

7,992 sq. m. (without captured Arab territory which amounts to 18,000 sq. m.). Pop. 2.66m. In May 1968 Israel celebrated the twenty years of its existence. The Israeli achievement, by any standard, is remarkable. Since 1948 the population has nearly quadrupled, the agricultural output has increased sixfold, and industrial production sevenfold. About 500 new cities, towns, villages and kibbutzim (the 246 kibbutzim account for 16% of agricultural output) have come into existence and the desert—which once began just south of Tel Aviv—has been pushed back past Beersheba. Israel is one of the very few countries capable of doubling the value of its domestic product in the next decade. British exports to Israel in 1967 amounted to £50m but of this, rough diamonds—of which the U.K. is Israel's main supplier—totalled £28.3m. (Israel mines no diamonds.) The U.S.A. is the main supplier (27%) but the U.K. gives Israel her largest market for citrus and agricultural produce. Much money is being invested in ports, such as Ashdod, which is now the country's main outlet for chemicals and minerals. Between Haifa and Eilat, on the Gulf of Aqaba, a pipeline will (1969) carry 55m tons of oil annually, much of it for export. Israel plans to transport an immense amount of container freight traffic by road between Eilat and its Mediterranean ports; this route is the quickest link between the Mediterranean and the Red Sea and it will obviate the danger to shippers of having their ships trapped in the Suez Canal in the event of further wars. Long-range, the Israelis plan a deepwater canal.

The estimated number of tourists for 1968 was 400,000 and it is forecast that Eilat will, by 1972, become one of the world's major winter resorts. Tourism is already the second largest foreign currency earner. The only serious problem is the water shortage Israel will face by 1970; it is relying on some basic forms of conservation such as reclamation of sewage, reduction of evaporation, the harnessing of winter flash flooding, but major desalting will soon be necessary.

Apart from giving Israel additional territory—most of it desert and economically useless—the Arab-Israeli War of 1967 has had the effect of making Israel more conscious than ever of the need for self-sufficiency, hence intensified efforts to develop the oil industry, petro-chemicals and small arms.

ITALY

131,000 sq. m. (116,000 sq. m. excluding Sicily and Sardinia). Pop. 52.7m. Italy was the only country in Europe in 1967 which increased its production of motor vehicles—1.5m. As a result demand for steel has been great and in 1967 16m tons were produced—2m more than in 1966. Capacity will rise to 18.5m in 1970. Agriculture was not so severely affected by floods in 1967 as was expected and output increased by 2%, but unless modernization and rationalization of farms are accelerated agriculture is likely to continue an undue decline in importance. Italy's most pressing long-term problem is a widening gap in living standards between the industrial north and the under-

Italy

developed south. Much investment has been made in communications but progress has been disappointing despite a steelworks at Taranto, a petro-chemical plant at Brindisi, a motor vehicle factory near Naples and petro-chemicals at Gela, Sicily. The tourist industry was hard hit in 1968 following the British devaluation and introduction of travel restrictions by the U.S. government. Even so, an estimated 24m people visited Italy in 1968.

Certain Italian firms continue to show much enterprise. The state-owned petroleum combine, ENI, has been buying huge shipments of Soviet oil and offering cut-rate competition to Western oil companies for drilling and refining rights in Africa. Its subsidiary, Snam Progetti, is busy with construction projects in many countries, including a 51m dollar, 500-mile Syrian pipeline and other pipelines in France and Spain, as well as refineries in Madras and West Germany. Another example of enterprise is the new "port" of Rivalta Scrivia, which began operations early in 1967. Designed to relieve the pressure on hopelessly congested and inefficient Genoa, Rivalta Scrivia, forty miles inland, is linked to the sea by its own railway and highways. Incoming cargo is unloaded in Genoa directly on to freight cars or trucks, then expressed to Rivalta Scrivia for customs clearance, sorting and warehousing. Cargo costs are reduced by 50%.

J

JAMAICA

4,411 sq. m. Pop. 1.9m. Jamaica's difficulty in promoting social and economic development on the scale required is a great one, aggravated by the rapidly rising population, composed of many different races and religions, which is only partly alleviated by emigration. There is a drift of population to the towns where employment opportunities are not rising fast enough. Rising costs, labour troubles connected with increasing mechanization and low prices are causing concern in the sugar industry. The Banana Board accelerated its boxing programme during 1966-68 since this method of shipment has proved more successful than the loading of wadding-wrapped fruit. A brighter picture is presented by the increasingly important bauxite and alumina industry. Jamaica is now not only the largest producer of bauxite but the leading exporter of alumina. At St. Elizabeth a consortium of American companies is building what will be the largest alumina plant in the world outside the U.S.A., doubling Jamaica's alumina capacity. Among new products being manufactured since 1966 are printed fabrics, transistor radios, nylon stockings, fertilizers, motor tyres, chocolate confectionery, flour and animal feeds. The principal destinations of Jamaica's exports are the U.S.A. (37%), the U.K. (28%) and Canada (17%). These countries are in the same order of importance as Jamaica's suppliers.

JAPAN

182,700 sq. m. Pop. 99.9m. In 1967 Japan overtook Britain as the third largest motor manufacturer, but labour shortages are serious. Several measures were introduced in 1967-68 in an attempt to attract and retain more employees, including changes in age and educational qualifications. Higher productivity and further rationalization offer the only real scope for further expansion. Large companies are tending to merge, especially in steel, motor manufacturing, paper, sugar-refining and chemicals. The idea is to provide greater capital and better competition in world markets. The shipbuilding industry, despite its advanced stage, has its worries. The value of shipbuilding export orders won by Japan in 1967 fell by a third (to 960m dollars), reflecting the very long order books which the industry has built up and which prevent shipyards from offering early delivery dates. However, Japan launched 7.5m tons of new ships in 1967, half the total world production. In 1967 U.K. exports to Japan amounted to £87m, imports from Japan to £91m. It is worth noting that Japan is already laying the economic foundations for an Asian or South-East Asian Common Market; there is even talk in Japan of a "Pacific Common Market", which presumably would include Australia, New Zealand and the Philippines.

Japan's Mitsui & Co. Ltd., through its various trading companies, handles 80% of the nation's exports and imports and is the biggest of the nation's 6,400 trading companies. By acquiring the necessary patents, winning the interest of Japanese industrialists and arranging financing, Mitsui is almost entirely responsible for Japan's vigorous petro-chemical industry. It is responsible for the delivery of the vast quantities of iron ore Japan is importing from Australia. Japan is spending less on defence than any other major industrial nation—1% of the gross national product.

1968 was the centennial of the Meiji Restoration, the year that Japan broke out of its feudalism.

JORDAN

34,750 sq. m. Pop. 2m. The Israeli occupation of the west

bank lands of the River Jordan—2,165 sq. m.—has seriously disrupted Jordanian civil, commercial and agricultural life. The Jordanians claim that 47% of their people come from the west bank. Certainly about 200,000 Arabs fled to the east bank after the war of June 1967. More than a third of Jordan's population are refugees from Palestine and even before the war 224,138 refugees were living in United Nation camps. Late in 1966 the Jordan Cabinet approved a seven-year 209m-dinar plan to develop trade, reduce the trade deficit and increase the level of employment by 5% a year. Projects include a new HEP station at Zarqa, but because of the 1967 war many projects have been delayed and some cancelled.

K

KENYA

224,960 sq. m. Pop. 9.98m (approx. 42,000 Europeans). Tourism is now such big business that it can be described as Kenya's second largest export (the chief one is coffee); the annual growth of up to 30% is expected to be maintained. The number of visitors—125,000 in 1967—should treble by 1973. New technological advances have produced record grain crops and sugar is expanding well. Tea had an astonishing uplift in 1966 but eased in 1967. Sisal, after a decline in 1967, in 1968 had returned to normal, while much is being achieved with pyrethrum production and horticultural ventures. The production and variety of local manufactured products have increased rapidly. They include nylon, fertilizers, pharmaceuticals, plastics and electrical accessories. A Guinness brewing plant has been built at Mombasa. The first phase of the Seven Forks HEP complex on the Tana River has been completed. All-weather roads to connect Kenya to Ethiopia, Zambia and the Congo are under construction. Since 1966 trade agreements have been signed with the U.K., Denmark, Rumania, Yugoslavia, Pakistan and New Zealand. The U.K. remains Kenya's largest supplier and largest buyer. Much of the country's success is due to its political stability.

KOREA (South)

37,436 sq. m. Pop. 29.3m. The government announced in mid-1968 that the country would be self-supporting by 1981 and that self-sufficiency in food production would be achieved by 1971. A consortium of U.S., German and Japanese companies has built an iron and steel complex near Pusan. Korea has no petroleum resources and as demand is rising several refineries have been built. The U.S.A. remains Korea's chief supplier, with over 40% of the market, but this figure includes a very high percentage (90%) of AID financed imports supplied by the U.S.A. Under the first development plan, which ended in 1966, industrial growth averaged 14% annually. The second five-year plan is aimed at making South Korea self-sufficient in food; this target should be realized. Since the re-establishment of relations between Japan and Korea in 1965 there has been a rapid increase in trade exchanges; in 1968 much more than a third of all Korean imports came from Japan. The petro-chemical industry is a principal growth project. A completely new idea is a series of "reconstruction hamlets" planned for the farmland along the demilitarized zone between South and North Korea. These villages, containing about 100 families each, are to be a mixture of intensive farming and highly trained military outposts. By the end of 1968 about 2,000 families were installed, and by 1971 the farms should be highly productive. Korea remains dependent on foreign aid but this is steadily decreasing.

In April 1967 one of the world's largest fertilizer plants with an annual capacity of 330,000 tons was opened at Ulsan. It was built by the Samsung Group which has been largely responsible for making South Korea an economically viable nation. Its woollen mills have halved the price of worsted goods for Koreans.

KUWAIT

6,000 sq. m. Pop. 470,000. The main development in the past two years has been the Shoeiba, an industrial city with its own water and electricity supply and private port. Tourist development includes an artificial island with hotels, rest houses and sailing. A pharmaceutical factory is planned. Hydroponics and desert afforestation are both growing rapidly; the former is already providing much of Kuwait's vegetable needs.

L

LABOUR

In Europe the demand for migrant labour has slowed down. In 1967 the governments of the Common Market countries permitted about 800,000 workers to come into their countries to fill vacant jobs, but these migrant workers formed little more than 1% of the total EEC work force. About two-thirds of them came from non-EEC countries and most of the rest were Italians. Even the movement of Irish to Britain has declined as has that of Indians, Pakistanis, Africans and West Indians, following immigration restrictions.

LAND RESOURCES AND DEVELOPMENT

Exhortations on the need to "produce more" in the developing countries are many but positive contributions to the technical problems involved are comparatively few. The work of the Land Resources Division is a British contribution to land development in the tropics. The scientific concept of "land resource assessment" is new; a team of scientists—geologist, botanist, soil scientist, agriculturalist, irrigation engineer and forester—can report on the broad potential of a country as large as Malawi in less than four years. The best areas of a previously undeveloped region can be brought into production within a decade, a transformation that once took centuries. Full reconnaissance projects have been completed in Lesotho, Malawi, east Botswana, Tanzania and part of north Nigeria and at the end of 1968 current projects included the British Solomon Islands, north-east Nigeria, east Nigeria and Fiji.

There are four phases to planned development:
1. Topographic mapping (ground survey, aerial photography, mapping).
2. Reconnaissance land resource assessment. Typical size: 10,000 to 300,000 sq. m. Mapping scales: 1:500,000 and 1:250,000. Land resources, including existing land use, are described by a team of scientists who interpret aerial photographs and make ground surveys. Potential land use is assessed in broad terms such as "suitable for cultivation", "suitable for grazing". Promising areas are selected for further study.
3. Intensive land resource assessment. Typical size of areas studied: 1,000 to 5,000 sq. m. Mapping scales: 1:50,000 and 1:25,000.

This is a more detailed study of promising areas. A detailed land capability classification is made of potential land use and areas suitable for particular kinds of development are indicated.
4. Development study. Typical size of area studied is usually small, i.e. less than 500 sq. m. Mapping scales: 1:10,000 and 1:5,000.

After consideration of social and economic factors the areas indicated as "suitable for development" are studied to determine the feasibility of growing specific crops. For each area a plan of development is made, including the crops to be grown and the layout of the farms.

LATIN AMERICA (See also individual nations)

In April 1968 a conference of Latin American countries made several decisions regarding the future of the area. They are:
1. Latin American economic integration and industrial development. This mostly involves the creation of the Latin American Common Market between 1970 and 1985 and the progress of the much smaller and modestly successful Central American Common Market.
2. Joint action to build and improve roads (land communication between countries is often non-existent), tele-

communications, electric power systems and development of river basins.

3. International trade. Latin American exports are not as competitive as they might be. The U.S.A. here faces pressure to grant trade preferences and protection where sharp fluctuations in prices exist.

4. Modernization of rural life and halting of the drift to the cities.

The Council for Latin America, formed in 1965, is now recognized by the U.S. government and the Inter-American Committee for the Alliance for Progress as the chief spokesman of U.S. business on Latin American issues. The major national business associations of the hemisphere, including the Council for Latin America, are united in the Inter-American Council of Commerce and Production.

LEBANON

4,300 sq. m. Pop. 2.36m. The failure of the Intra Bank (October 1966) and the Arab-Israeli War (June 1967) damaged the Lebanon's progress but in 1968 the tourist trade slowly revived and the closure of the Suez Canal enhanced the importance of Lebanon as an entrepot. Two major problems are that the oil-producing countries, an important source of funds, are tending to invest their reserves directly in international capital markets by by-passing Beirut. No way has been found to channel those largely speculative funds still flowing into the Lebanon from the Arab world towards long-term investment that would benefit the economy. Industrial activity occupies only a tenth of the labour force and contributes less than 15% to the national income but its importance is growing fast. A U.S. firm completed a fruit-processing factory in 1968. In 1968 the value of industrial exports—e.g. textiles, plywood, metal products—was twice that of 1967. From July 1968 the EEC made available "most favoured nation" treatment for the Lebanon; increased trade will result.

LEEWARD ISLANDS

The Leeward Islands consist of Antigua, Barbuda, Redonda, St. Kitts, Nevis, Anguilla, Montserrat, British Virgin Islands (11). The major development has been in tourism, especially in the Frigate Bay area of St. Kitts where a company of international financiers has invested £20m. Basseterre, St. Kitts, has become a distributing centre for the Dutch islands of St. Eustatius and Saba, the French island of St. Bartholomew and the Dutch-French island of St. Martin. Montserrat is being actively developed as a resort for retired North Americans.

LESOTHO

11,716 sq. m. Pop. 920,000. The giant Oxbow project, designed to harness the waters of the Maluti Mountains, has become by far the brightest prospect in Lesotho's weak economy. A complicated system of dams, channels and tunnels will feed up to 300m gallons of water a day to the Witwatersrand industrial complex, of which Johannesburg forms the centre. Lesotho will benefit not only from the sale of the water but will also use the HEP. It seems to be not generally realized that Lesotho has tremendous quantities of water, from melting snows, available for exploitation. The Mont Aux sources alone have a flow of 1,600m gallons daily. (The Orange and Tugela rivers rise here, as well as tributaries of the Caledon.)

Several livestock improvement centres have been established to remedy the primitive methods of husbandry. There is now steady movement of livestock, on the hoof, in and out of the country. There is a net import of horses, mules and donkeys and a net export of sheep and goats. Some selected sheep farmers are being induced to start ram breeding on a small scale. The general quality of hides and skins has so improved in the last two years that Lesotho hides and skins are now established in the world market, France being the best customer.

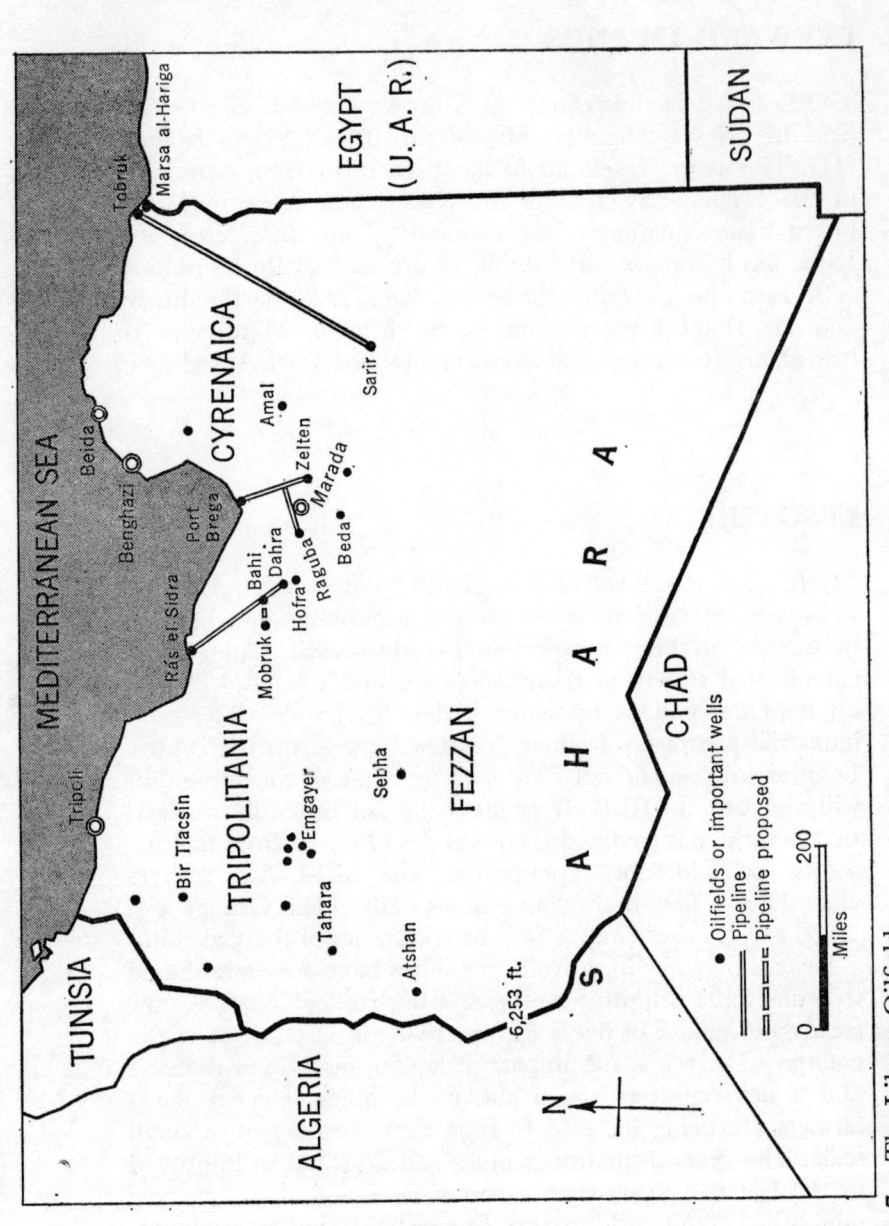

7. The Libyan Oilfield

Prospecting for diamonds is showing encouraging results, especially at Letsand-la-Draai.

LIBYA

680,000 sq. m. Pop. 1.65m. In 1958 Libya had the lowest per capita income in the world; in 1968 it was remarkably high. The 1968 budget was £345m (1967, £226m; 1966, £187m). All this is the direct result of oil and methane; Libya is seventh among the oil-producing nations (after the U.S.A., U.S.S.R., Venezuela, Saudi Arabia, Kuwait and Iran). No fewer than 39 companies have drilling operations in the Libyan desert. The most recent development was the opening in April 1968 of an oil port at Marsa Harigs, close to Tobruk. Gas exports commenced at the end of 1968 to Italy and Spain. There is a drift of population to the towns and oilfields, a decline in agricultural output and a greater dependence on imported food. Libyans have been spending lavishly (note that great wealth differentials exist) so that the U.K., Italy, the U.S.A. and West Germany, in that order, are finding it a better export market, though the U.K. in 1968 had a debit balance of £45m.

M

MALAWI

45,745 sq. m. 4.05m. (inc. 7,000 Europeans). The economy of Malawi, a poor country with few natural resources, depends largely on agriculture and it is to the improvement of agrarian activities that the major effort must be directed. It is probably fortunate that between 200,000 and 300,000 Malawis are out of the country at any one time working on the Zambian copperbelt, Rhodesian farms or in South Africa. The volume of trade with the U.K., both ways, has increased while a new trade agreement with South Africa means larger exports of tea, tung oil, tobacco, groundnuts and coffee. In 1968 Malawi became self-sufficient in sugar, following the development of the Sucoma Sugar Estate at Nchalo. With the inauguration of the Nkula HEP Station in July 1966 the consumption of electricity has increased substantially and, as a consequence, so has industry—cigarettes, radios, footwear and soap.

MALAYSIA

128,703 sq. m. Pop. 9.7m. (Comprising Malaya, 51,000 sq. m. and 8.297m; Sabah, 29,000 sq. m. and 551,000; Sarawak, 48,000 sq. m. and 852,000). Economic prospects are rather overshadowed by the withdrawal of British forces in 1971, leading to a substantial loss in income and heavy defence costs. The rubber market, depressed in 1967, was encouraged in 1968 by new orders from the U.S.S.R., China and Japan. In the long term production is likely to outpace demand. The output of tin is continuing to rise despite a steady fall in prices; this has resulted in many small producers—about 300 between June 1966 and December 1968—being forced to close. Timber and palm oil exports rose markedly in 1967-68. Competition in the Malaysia market is intense and the U.K.'s share has been declining while sales from Japan are rising rapidly. Stronger trade links are being created with the Soviet Union and Eastern Europe. A future source of difficulty will be the Philippine claim to Sabah territory.

MALTA

122 sq. m. Pop. 332,000. Malta has overcome the problems of 1966, which followed the departure of the British. Apart from more intensive manufacturing the island now sees itself as a mid-Mediterranean entrepot; to this end a deep water port at Marsaxlokk, south-east Malta, would be a great asset. The cost of the port would be £35m.

MAPS

Computers have entered the cartographic field. An American company, Bunker-Ramo Corporation, is producing two computers that perform the most tedious and time-consuming steps in map-making. By scanning pairs of serial photographs the computers can measure heights, prepare charts showing contours and automatically correct for parallax displacements and other distortions.

MAURITIUS

720 sq. m. Pop. 825,000. Having gained independence in March 1968, after 150 years of British rule, Mauritius faces serious problems economically and socially with its mixture of Hindus, Moslems, French and Creoles. Many islanders did not want independence, believing that Mauritius can never become economically viable. Sugar accounts for 94% of its exports and in 1970, when the Commonwealth Sugar Agreement ends, Mauritius could easily lose the £25-a-ton subsidy on which it now depends.

METEOROLOGY

After any October in which there is moderate rain Israel's nomadic Bedouins move out of the Negev area into more hospitable land, true to ancient folklore that "early rain means a dry year". The Israeli meteorologist Leo Krown, following a study of October troughs and ridges, has detected a climatic pattern, and announced his findings in April 1968. Whenever a trough hovered over the eastern Mediterranean in the vicinity of Cyprus during most of October while another hung over the Atlantic off Spain, Israel's rainfall was from 20% to 55% below normal for the next three months. When the Mediterranean trough existed near Italy and the corresponding Atlantic trough was located off the U.S. coast, Israeli winter rainfall was from 20% to 60% above normal. The position and movement of the troughs are significant (Krown says) because they are associated with the streams of cold air that suddenly spill down from the Arctic every October, bringing clouds and rain to herald the change of seasons. He claims there should be similiar findings at similiar latitudes—between 30° and 50° N.

METHANE

Pipelines are being built to pump gas to Italy, Poland, Hungary, Czechoslovakia and East Germany. The whole of Italy, the

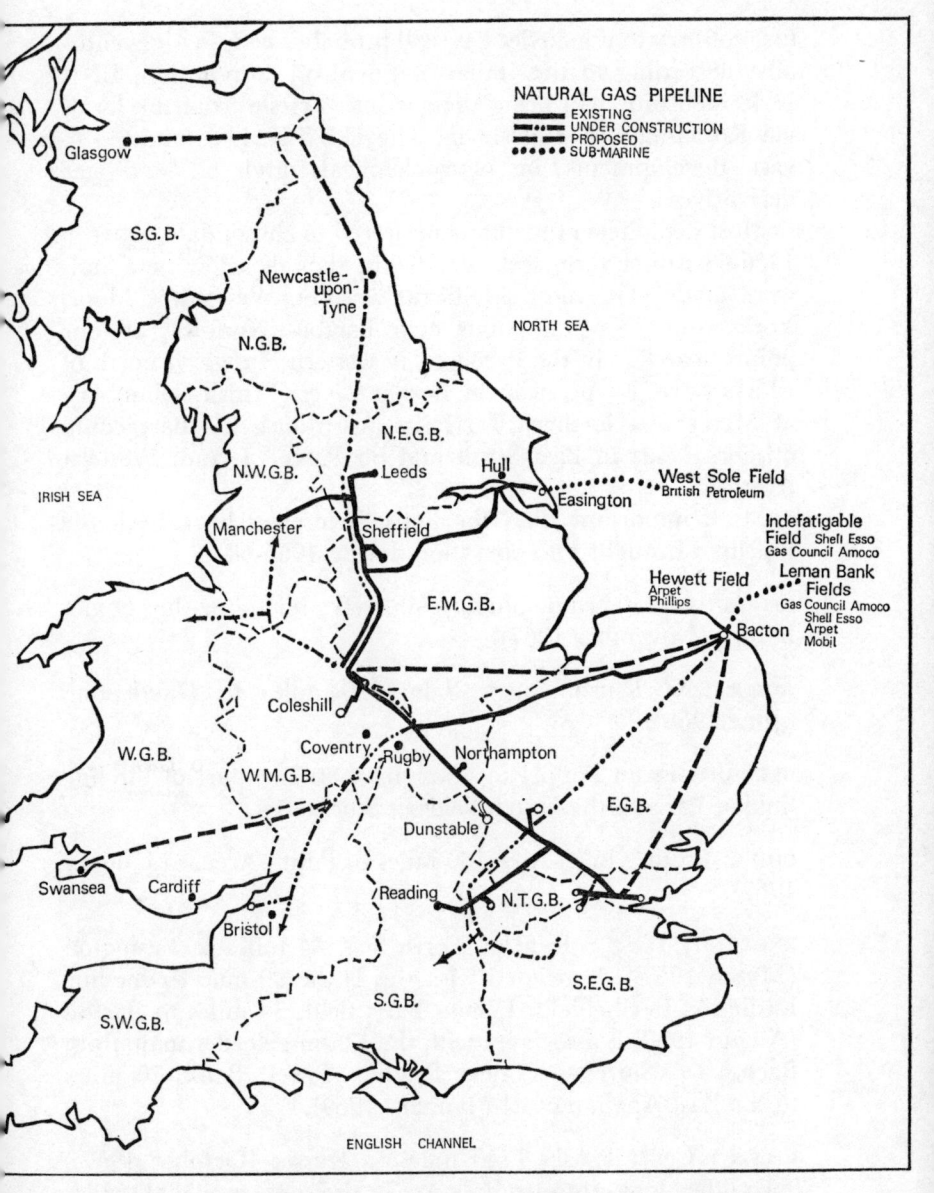

8. The Gas Council Natural Gas Transmission System for Britain

first country to use Soviet gas, will probably be using it eventually, according to the Italian national oil corporation, ENI. A 48-inch pipe will bring the gas into Trieste from the Urals via Rumania and Yugoslavia. The U.S.S.R. is committed to vast developments in petro-chemicals and oil and gas derivatives.

Most exploiters of methane preferred to consolidate between 1966-68 rather than seek new fields, though a few new finds were made. The most significant were on Westerdale Moor, Yorkshire, at several points near Bacton (Norfolk), at four points near Pau in the Pyrenees, in western Hungary, north of El Mansura, Egypt, near the Beaver River (British Columbia), at Mereenie (Northern Territory, Australia), the Barracouta offshore fields in Bass Strait and on Pascoe Island, Western Australia.

More important than the finds themselves have been the pipelines brought into operation during 1966-68.

AFGHANISTAN: From Shibarghan, 60 miles to the Soviet border (November 1967).

AUSTRALIA: Dutson, near Sale, 110 miles to Dandenong (June 1968).

BELGIUM: From Poppel to Blaregnies, 80 km, part of the line linking Paris to the Dutch fields at Slochteren.

CHILE: From Kimiri-Aike 150 miles to Punta Arenas (January 1967).

ENGLAND: West Sole field, North Sea, 44 miles to Easington (March 1967). Associated with this is the 90-mile feeder line Easington to Sheffield. Leman Bank field, 34 miles to Bacton (August 1967) is associated with the 125-mile feeder main from Bacton to Churchover, near Rugby. Hewett Bank, 20 miles to the East Anglian coast (January 1969).

U.S.S.R.: Central Asia 1740 miles to Russia (October 1967). Two other long-distance lines are in progress, one 3,000 miles from western Siberia to near Moscow.

VENEZUELA: Moron, near Puerto Cabello on the Caribbean coast 90 miles to Yaracuy, with three subsidiary lines (January 1968). Anaco 132 miles to Puerto Ordaz, part of a large new industrial area.

WEST GERMANY: From Emmerich 120 miles to Cologne.

MEXICO

758,000 sq.m. Pop. 45.7m. Agricultural output rose by 7.5% in 1967-68 despite damage to crops from hurricanes. Progress under the five-year plan ending 1970 shows that many targets will be exceeded. The use of Mexican raw materials, production of minerals and basic materials has also advanced strongly in 500 industries (Mexican government figure). By 1970, for example, steel capacity is expected to reach 5m tons per annum (3m in April 1968). The importance of increased agricultural efficiency is also reflected in the strong emphasis being placed on expanding the nation's irrigation system. About a third of Mexico's crops are now produced on irrigated land, yet this accounts for less than a seventh of the total cultivable area. Tourism is providing an expanding source of foreign exchange—400m dollars in 1967. Largely as a result of British trade promotion U.K. exports to Mexico rose to £27m in 1967, an increase of 30% over the 1966 figure. The outlook for the country is extremely bright if inflation can be avoided. Major projects indicate improvements in social and human geography: telecommunications and electric power developments (320m dollars); 5,000 miles of roads, and the provision of drinking water for more than 6m people in small towns. Trade relations are broadening with Europe, Japan and Latin American neighbours. (See *Aid*.)

MICRONESIA

2,141 islands spread over 3m sq. m. of the Pacific, Micronesia has only 100,000 inhabitants. A Trust Territory of the U.S.A., Micronesia is a poorer place than in the heyday of the Japanese, who colonized the islands between 1918-39, and in 1968 the U.S.A. budgeted only 14m dollars for the territory—less than a fifth the money allotted for a single Navajo reservation in the U.S.A. However, education is much better, largely through the efforts of missions and Peace Corps workers. In some places development has been notable. For instance, on Tinian a ranch of 7,500 acres carries 12,000 cattle and an equal number of pigs and chickens. There is a slow but steady growth of political consciousness and Micronesians will probably have a vote on their future by 1972.

MINING

CANADA. Following a report published in June 1966 stressing the mutual advantages to be gained by the U.S.A. and Canada in the development and distribution of energy on a north-south basis, ignoring the border, a scheme was put forward by Trans-Canada Pipelines and American Natural Gas Company applying this principle to natural gas. The scheme was a joint proposal by the two companies who formed a subsidiary, Great Lakes Gas Transmission, to construct and operate almost 1,000 miles of natural gas pipeline from Emerson through Austin, Michigan, finishing close to Sarnia, Ontario. This is being done in two stages, starting with the construction of the short pipeline from Austin to a point near Sarnia. The second stage was completed in 1967 with the construction of the Emerson-Austin pipeline together with a branch to Sault Ste. Marie.

A rival scheme was proposed by an American firm, the Northern Natural Gas Company. This scheme proposed to add about 900 miles of pipeline to existing lines, including a pipeline from Emerson to Duluth, another from Ogden, Iowa, to St. Clair and another, extending an existing pipeline, from Marquette to Sault Ste. Marie.

Interesting points of difference exist. In the first, Canadian natural gas will go through the U.S.A. to eastern Canada and sales of gas are being made by Trans-Canada Pipelines to the U.S.A. whereas the Northern Natural Gas Company's scheme provides for gas to be distributed on a "swap" basis between the two countries. Thus Canadian gas will be fed to the American states of Minnesota, Wisconsin and Michigan via an existing network of pipeline and the proposed Emerson-Duluth line, while similiar quantities of U.S. gas will be supplied to Ontario via the new line from Ogden to St. Clair. The second scheme is slightly cheaper than Great Lakes Gas Transmission's project. It uses existing pipelines and storage facilities, and thus hopes to lower future investment costs and to achieve savings to such an extent that customers of the Northern Natural Gas Company will benefit from lower prices in the future. Nevertheless, the Great Lakes Gas Transmission's scheme has the advantage of an earlier completion date.

CONTROLLING STRIP MINING. Many U.S. states are enacting strict laws to control strip mining for coal. Strip mining is a simple, productive and inexpensive method of mining coal, both hard and soft. It accounts for one third of the nation's 500m-ton output. Big power shovels rip off the topsoil, then bite into the underlying seams to depths of more than 100 feet and load the coal onto trucks. But far too often irresponsible strip miners, operating under permissive miner-rights leases, have mined the land and simply moved on, leaving ravaged earth behind them. In West Virginia alone strip miners have been tearing up land at the rate of 6,000 acres a year, annually creating 240 miles of "high wall"—vertical cliffs of overburden—that resist vegetation and frequently slide onto adjacent homes and property. Only eight of the 23 states in which strip miners operate have laws requiring miners to reclaim their land but these eight—Illinois, Indiana, Kentucky, Maryland, Ohio, Pennsylvania, West Virginia and Virginia—produce 80%

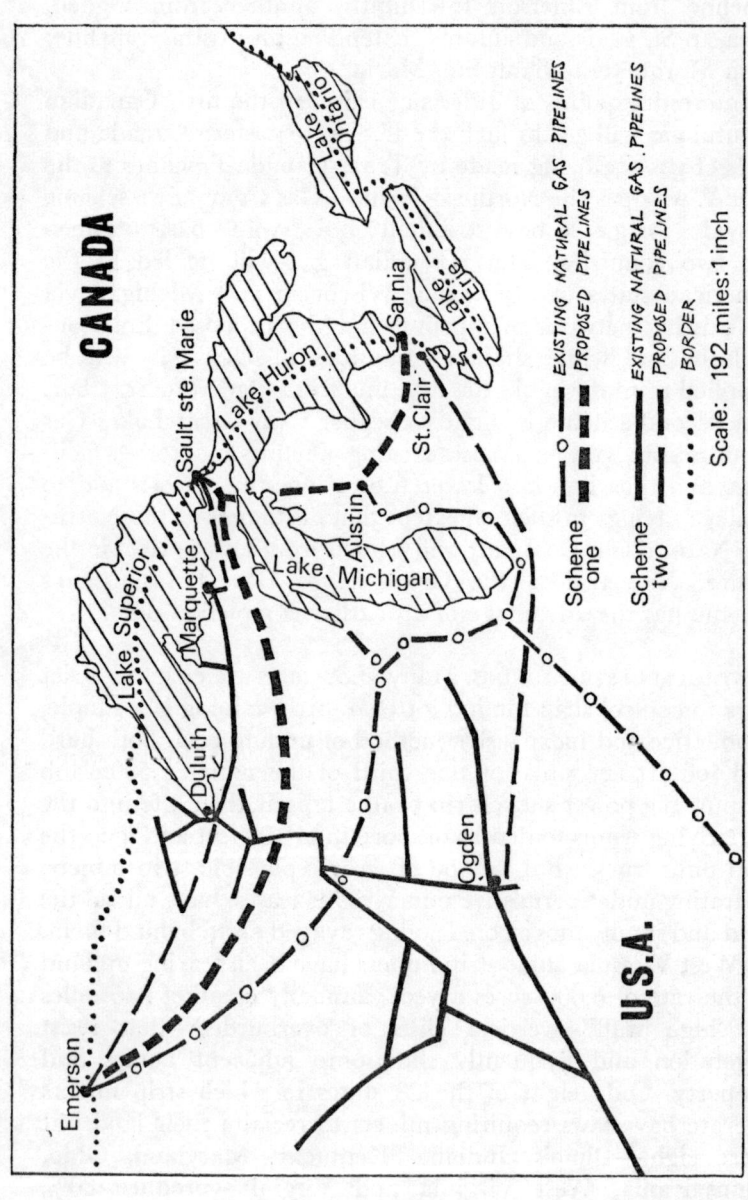

9. Rival Schemes for the Distribution of Energy in Canada and the U.S.A.

of all strip-mined coal. As the realization spreads of how badly strip mining destroys the landscape the laws are becoming more strict, especially in West Virginia, Kentucky and Pennsylvania. The U.S. Department of the Interior estimates that in the twelve-state Appalachian region alone at least 800,000 acres of land have been badly damaged and that reclamation will cost 250m dollars.

DEEP SEA MINING. The encouraging results in the search for oil and methane in off-shore areas are a dramatic indication of the potentialities of the sea bed as a source of mineral supplies. Some metals and minerals are already being won from the seashore environment, including diamonds off South-West Africa, tin off Malaya and Indonesia, iron ore off the Japanese coast and gold off Alaska. Specially equipped Japanese and Russian vessels are known to be investigating manganese nodules covering extensive areas of the sea bed at depths between 5,000 and 18,000 feet. The manganese content ranges between 20—30%, and in addition the nodules contain up to 2% cobalt, 2% nickel and 3% copper. A wide variety of geophysical methods are also available for use in marine prospecting. Clues to the location of placer deposits of gold, platinum, diamond, chromite and cassiterite (the tin mineral) may be found from analysis of local land sources, climatic zones and the shape of the continental shelves and the deep sea floor.

NUCLEAR MINING. The use of nuclear explosives to blast out harbours and canals, to create underground storage cavities and to release methane and oil locked beneath the earth's surface has been under development for a decade. Late in 1967 scientists evolved a nuclear plan to mine billions of tons of copper-bearing ore too poor to be mined by traditional methods. This is a direct result of alarm about the growing shortages of copper in the U.S.A. The plan is shown in the accompanying diagram. "Project Gasbuggy" went into effect in New Mexico on December 10, 1967. A nuclear bomb (TNT equivalent of 26,000 tons) was exploded at a depth of more than 4,000 feet to melt large areas of rock and produce a

New Geography 1968-69

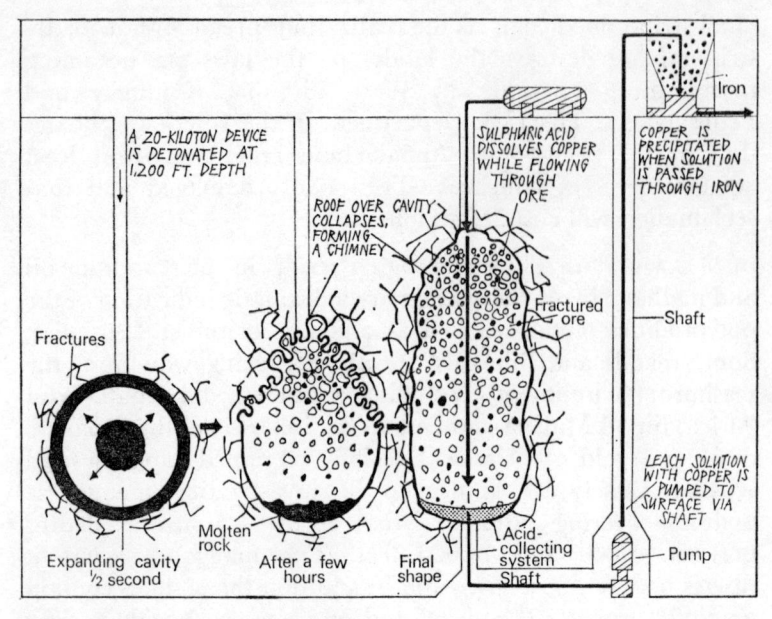

10. Atomic Mining for Copper

hole 350 feet deep and about 160 feet across in which methane would collect. Results will not be known until 1970. The costs of Project Gasbuggy were 5m dollars, but in future a similiar operation would cost only half a million. The explosion in New Mexico could mark the beginning of a new dimension in mining. Technicians using nuclear devices as powerful as 100 kilotons may one day be able to process tens of millions of tons of copper-bearing ore at present beyond man's grasp.

MOROCCO

180,000 sq. m. Pop. 14.1m. Two consecutive years of drought, 1966 to 1968, seriously slowed the pace of Morocco's development, a situation made doubly critical by the 3% population increase. The 1968-72 development programme is to raise production by over 4% annually; with farming providing a livelihood for nearly three-quarters of Morocco's population, one of the principal aims in the new programme is to lessen Morocco's vulnerability to drought and to improve farm productivity. Six new dams will be started in 1969. The River Sebou is the centre of a major scheme involving the construction of dams and irrigation channels, afforestation and terracing of slopes to counter erosion. The output of phosphates between 1966-68 tended to stagnate (though the country remains the largest exporter) in spite of steadily rising world demand and Morocco's share of the market has fallen from two-fifths in 1958 to one quarter. As part of the new programme, production at the two main centres, Youssoufia and Khouribga, is expected to increase by about a half by 1972. A new centre at Benguerir was opened in July 1968. A new plant at Mechra Benabbou is to produce 335,000 tons of chemicals annually; a thermal power station is being built by the U.S.S.R. at Djerada. About 0.5m tourists visited Morocco in 1967 but the government confidently expects to double this figure by 1972; four zones have "tourist developmental priority"—Agadir, Tangier, Smir and Al Hoceima. France still remains Morocco's most important trading partner in spite of a steady decline since the political rift of 1965.

MOSQUITO CONTROL

The rice fields of California's Sacramento Valley are flooded for five months annually between spring and autumn and are ideal breeding grounds for vast swarms of mosquitoes that have become resistant to chemical insecticides. Entomologists are using a voracious and prolific South American fish—*Cynolebias bellottii* or Argentine pearlfish—to control the breeding. The fish keep large areas of Argentina and Brazil relatively free of mosquitoes. Immediately after hatching in the waters of low-lying flood plains the tiny fish, which are three inches at most, begin eating mosquito larvae. A total of 40,000 fish per acre is commonplace. After floodwaters recede the eggs are preserved in the baked mud; the next year, when the plains are inundated again, the eggs hatch in half an hour after moistening. The fish, used in malarial regions, could significantly reduce the disease.

MUSCAT AND OMAN

82,000 sq. m. Pop. 750,000 (approximately). The sultanate's economy, formerly almost entirely dependent on dates, dried fish, limes, pomegranates and firewood, has been given new life by the start of commercial oil operations in 1967. Annual production is expected to be about 7m tons annually. A British company has been commissioned to prepare and carry out a development plan for the Muscat-Matrah region, a scheme likely to take several years. Trade is mainly with India, Pakistan, the Gulf States and Australia (wheat, flour and sugar).

N

NAGALAND

The 400,000 proud, and fiercely determined people of Nagaland have been struggling, in one way and another, for what they call their sovereign rights ever since India won hers 21 years ago. The remote, underdeveloped region has little chance of becoming economically viable but the Nagalanders are set on severance from India. The area has a revenue of only £550,000 annually; India contributes £11m. China's influence is great and to counter it the Indian Army is re-settling villagers in protected hamlets.

NAURU

0.82 sq. m. Pop. 3,000. On January 31, 1968 Nauru became an independent republic. (Since 1947 it had been administered by Australia as a U.N. Trust territory.) Nauruans have a per capita income of about 4,000 dollars, compared with 3,648 in the U.S.A. Fully two-thirds of Nauru contains deep deposits of fertilizer-phosphates, being mined and exported at the rate of 1.5m tons a year. Under an agreement announced in June 1967 Nauruans were given part control of the mining industry. After they finish paying for it, in about 1970, they will get complete control. Phosphate reserves should last at least another thirty years.

New Geography 1968-69

NEPAL

54,000 sq. m. Pop. 10.3m. Various countries have been "investing" in Nepal by building factories. The Chinese have given a shoe factory, a warehouse complex and a highway that runs from Tibet to Katmandu. India is building a road south from Katmandu to Calcutta. The Russians have given a cigarette plant and a sugar refinery. The U.S.A. is working on malarial eradication, family planning and education. A third highway, to open up the fertile rice lands to improverished Nepalese mountain tribes, is planned. In 1967 the country had 15,000 tourists, a large number for this inaccessible country.

THE NETHERLANDS

13,500 sq. m. Pop. 12.6m. A feature common to most branches of Dutch industry is the tendency to promote greater co-operation or mergers among companies. These moves are aimed at strengthening the competitive position of Dutch industry within the EEC. Overseas investment is actively encouraged and is being attracted by big programmes in the chemical and pharmaceutical industries, oil refining, electrical engineering and shipbuilding. Projects in 1968 included exploratory drillings for oil and natural gas off the Dutch coast, and on land, the construction of a 1m-ton dock and the building of four 260,000-ton tankers. A basic weakness, however, is the disparity between the prosperous western regions and the remainder of the country where unemployment tends to be high. This is because of a surplus of agricultural workers, a continuing decline of traditional industries such as coal mining, and a decline in textiles, clothing and leather working between 1967 and 1968. There is to be a great new port at Eemshaven (20m dollars). In 1968 Britain spent £400m on Dutch products, whereas the Netherlands spent £240m on British goods.

NEW GUINEA

93,000 sq. m. Pop. 1.585m. About £140m a year is being spent on developing this large tropical island, where there is a rapid move towards self-government. The World Bank has recommended a five-year £250m development programme. Aims include doubling of earnings from agriculture and forestry by 1970, and a tenfold increase in cattle by 1978. The country has remarkable potential, for tourism as well as for mining, timber and plantation products. A new scheme in operation is the economic production of cheap vegetable protein from grass. New Guinea is the only developing country to play a key role in the production of cheap protein.

NEW ZEALAND

104,000 sq. m. Pop. 2.7m. A major contribution to New Zealand's adverse balance of payments position has been the heavy dependence on wool, world prices for which have fallen very steeply in the past few years. Receipts in 1967 totalled only 140m N.Z. dollars (2.14 dollars to £ sterling) compared with 233m dollars in 1966 and a peak 264m dollars in 1964. The outlook for meat and dairy produce is more favourable. Meat is now the largest single source of foreign exchange and production rose by more than 7% to 890,000 tons in 1967. A rapid boosting of trade with Japan brought mutton up from 149,000 tons in 1966 to 185,000 tons in 1967.

New prospecting techniques together with intensive scientific and industrial research may well lead to the discovery and use of a variety of minerals which will give the nation a broader, safer economy. A consortium of American, British, Australian and Japanese companies is to build an aluminium smelter with a capacity of 105m tons a year and costing 130m N.Z. dollars. Power will come from the HEP plant at Manapouri, which will be in production in 1970. New Zealand is still in a precarious position, with a small home market and

New Geography 1968-69

relative dependence on primary products in a competitive market. More than 11,000 sq. m. of continental shelf, territorial waters and mainland are being oil-surveyed in New Zealand, the first major project of its kind in this country.

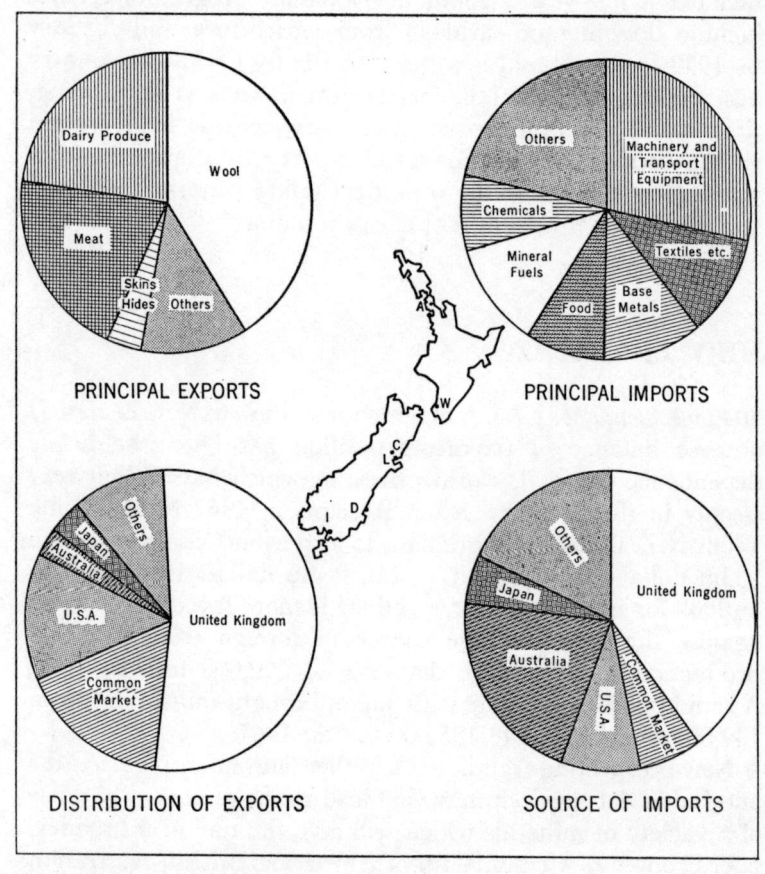

11. New Zealand's External Trade

NICARAGUA

57,000 sq. m. Pop. 1.75m. The remarkable rate of growth (reported in the previous edition of *New Geography*) made possible by much foreign investment has slowed somewhat owing to low world coffee prices and a poor cotton crop through drought. Work is in hand on the irrigation of 36,000 hectares of land in central Nicaragua, the development of new agricultural land in the east, and the intensification of coffee growing through a gradual reduction of the cultivated area by 50%—an interesting move. The land thus made available is being used for maize, sorghum, beans and rice. Factories are being built for the production of communications equipment, pharmaceuticals, chemicals and wood products.

NIGERIA

356,669 sq. m. Pop. 58m. Nigeria's economy and stability have been damaged by political unrest and the war with the breakaway state of Biafra (q.v.). However, a second oil terminal and loading facilities are being built at a cost of £17m. The new terminal will be in mid-western Nigeria with a large pipeline system from the oil centre of Ughelli running more than 50 miles to the coast. But Ughelli is more than 100 miles from the Bonny oil terminal in Biafra. The mid-west terminal should be completed by mid-1969; the area accounts for more than a third of Nigeria's crude oil. Plans to rationalize crops—for instance, more cocoa, less coffee—and to produce more leather rather than raw hides have come to little because of government preoccupation with the Biafra problem. Nigeria has been importing large quantities of munitions from the U.K., West Germany and France at the expense of reduced consumer imports and the growth of a large foreign debt. This debt, nevertheless, is likely to bring about an increase in export figures for 1968-69.

NORWAY

125,183 sq. m. Pop. 3.8m. Norway's outlook is a little uncertain, but economic growth should continue at a slower rate. Costs are cutting into profit margins and to meet this challenge companies are rationalizing and integrating to increase industrial efficiency. Well placed in this movement is the Norwegian shipping industry which earns over two-fifths of the country's annual foreign income. Norway has 372 shipping lines and accounts for 10% of all merchant ships. In June 1967, 20% of all the new merchant vessels under construction throughout the world were for Norwegian owners. Norway is now the third largest producer of aluminium in the West (after the U.S.A. and Canada). In 1968 its production was 0.5m tons.

Late in 1968 Norwegian whaling companies announced their intention of abandoning operations because of high costs and fewer whales—a shortage caused by Japanese and Russian contravention of international quota-whaling. The Norwegian decision will have a profound effect on the regional economy of the southern fiords, the bases of the whaling fleets.

O

OCEANOGRAPHY

CURRENTS. A simple device now makes it possible for divers to test currents near the sea bed. A polythene jar containing a chemical jelly which sets at 32° C. and also containing a magnet is lowered to the sea bed. The current tilts the jar to one side—the greater the current the more it tilts. The slope on the jelly gives the strength of the current while the magnet, set in the jelly, gives the direction.

OCEANAUTS. The first International Conference on the History of Oceanography was held in Monaco in January 1967. With UNESCO help a school for oceanauts has been established in Monaco. The first atom-powered deep-diver has been built in Connecticut, U.S.A. It will carry two scientists and a five-man crew close to the sea bottom for several weeks at a time.

SEAWEED. Forests of giant artificial seaweed anchored to the sea bed might be used to still the currents which relentlessly scour away the sand from around the legs of drilling platforms. The idea is being tried out off the coast of Victoria, Australia, where currents are very strong. It could be useful in the North Sea, where currents menace drilling operations; off eastern Luzon, Philippines, and off Groningen, north Netherlands.

OIL

The most significant new aspect of oil is that the West is no longer as vulnerable to a boycott of Arab supplies. This was shown at the time of the Arab-Israeli War of 1967. At that time, when the Arab suppliers placed an embargo on oil shipments to parts of Europe, the European buyers simply bought more oil from the U.S.A. and Venezuela, though certainly at greater cost. The Arabs found they were losing too much income to sustain the embargo and first Saudi Arabia, then Kuwait, Libya and Iraq—the four major Arab oil states—agreed to resume shipments. The Lebanon agreed to allow oil companies to resume shipments from its Mediterranean ports.

Since 1965 there has been a remarkable transformation in the whole fuel position and many of the suppliers are now anxious sellers in a buyers' market. The only real advantage possessed by the Middle East producers is that of price.

Since the June 1967 war Israel and Egypt have increased oil production at a remarkable rate in the Gulf of Suez. The average production from the offshore El Morgan fields by March 1968 was 15,500 tons a day (7,000 tons in early 1967). The Israelis, mining at El Bilaiyim, sail their tankers through the Egyptians' El Morgan fields, heading for Eilat. It is believed that Israel now has sufficient oil to meet its domestic needs.

Late in 1968 the Oruto oil field in Colombia's Putumayo's field—193 miles from the Pacific port of Tumaco—came into production. All transport has been by helicopter: 150,000 tons of cargo and 200,000 passengers. About 25 wells are pumping an average of 2,000 bb a day, but it is estimated that its peak capacity of 100,000 bb a day will not be sufficient and that another line will need to be built.

OIL PIPELINES

The most interesting and geographically important new line is the great Transalpine Pipeline, which carries oil from the Italian port of Trieste to Ingolstadt on the Danube in southern Germany. TAL is the largest capacity pipeline in Western Europe and early in 1967 it began to carry about 300,000 bb a day, from sea level to an altitude of almost a mile at its highest point. The line itself holds 2.2m bb within its 285-mile length. A remarkable engineering achievement, TAL's planning, financing and construction reflect growing energy needs and changing industrial patterns. (Between 1950 and 1960 oil's share of total energy consumption in Europe rose from 13% to 30%; it is now 53%.)

Ingolstadt (pop. 50,000), is surrounded by expanding refining and petro-chemical complexes which have been supplied with crude oil through the Rhine-Danube Pipeline from Karlsruhe (opened in 1962) and the 475-mile Southern European Pipeline (opened in 1963), originating at Lavera, southern France. TAL is connected with the Rhine-Danube Pipelines.

The explanation of TAL's being built across formidable mountain ranges lies in geography and economics. The shortest distance between Middle East and North African oil fields and the south-central industrial region of Europe lies over the Alps. From the producing countries tankers dock on the Bay of Muggia where two concrete piers can accommodate four tankers of up to 160,000 deadweight tons; 70m cubic feet of the bay's bottom was dredged for deepwater channels. Five pumping stations force the oil towards the slopes of the Carnic Alps to its maximum elevation of 5,084 feet; gravity carries the oil to Ingolstadt. Three tunnels had to be created: Plocken, 4.3 miles at 3,116 feet; Felbertauern, 4.5 miles at 5,084 feet; and Hahkenkamm, 4.2 miles at 3,610 feet. Engineers made 154 crossings beneath roads and 26 beneath railroads; the pipe crosses major rivers 36 times and smaller rivers 136 times.

All three countries through which the pipeline passes, Italy, Austria and Germany, can expect major economic benefits. Austria, with a growing crude oil deficiency, will receive oil supplies from a spur line from TAL, from the point where the line emerges from the Plocken Tunnel and stretches 250 miles to Schwechat, a refining centre close to Vienna. Construction of this line, which began in 1967, should hasten industrial development in the eastern part of Austria. For the city of Trieste itself TAL may be the most important happening in generations, if only because 500 tankers a year are calling to discharge oil, though this will probably double by 1970. From Ingolstadt other spur lines will carry oil to the "chemical triangle" around Burghausen and to refineries near Forcheim.

OLIVES

The best of Spain's eating-olive crop has been damaged by the Dacus fly, which has attacked Queen and Manzanilla olives. Seville and the surrounding territory in western Andalusia produce 98% of the world's green eating-olives and the U.S.A. buys 75%. However, olive oil will be in greater rather than shorter supply, since trees producing olives for oil have not been affected.

P

PAKISTAN

West, 310,403 sq. m.; East, 55,126 sq. m. Pop. 105.1m. In a programme to achieve self-sufficiency in food by 1971 an increase in the wheat crop of more than 50% to 7m tons annually is predicted. Hopes of success rest largely on the cultivation of a high yielding variety of Mexican wheat, which has been planted over about half the wheat belt. Such self-sufficiency would reduce the import bill by £75m. The 1967-68 cotton crop, about 3m bales, was the best for ten years.

The principal irrigation scheme, the Indus Waters development project, entered an important phase in 1967 with the completion of the Mangla Dam, a year ahead of schedule, at a cost of £350m. Water from the dam and a series of link canals will irrigate 3m acres, a quarter of the total area currently under irrigation in West Pakistan. In mid-1968 arrangements were completed for the construction of the Tarbela Dam, the second stage of the Indus Waters project and probably the world's largest dam; the cost will be about 850m dollars. To build Tarbela's 9,000-feet long, 470-feet high main embankment as much earth will have to be shifted as was excavated for the Panama Canal. Four half-mile tunnels, each 45 feet in diameter, must be dug through the rock of surrounding mountains; eventually a fifty-mile reservoir will form behind the dam. However, the Indus carries so much silt—twice that of the Nile at flood season—that the reservoir will be nearly silt-filled in fifty years. To overcome this problem a link will be dug at the Haro River, near the Indus, and a second reservoir created.

Vast sums of money are being invested in the new capital,

Islamabad, which should have 150,000 inhabitants by 1970. The target is 400,000 by 1980.

At Daharki, a small town 400 miles north-east of Karachi, a fertilizer plant costing £11m is being built. With a capacity of 173,000 tons a year, it will considerably boost the nation's economy. The owners, Esso Pakistan Fertilizer Company, claim the urea produced could raise Pakistan's wheat production by nearly 250,000 tons annually, as well as providing substantial increases in the cotton, sugar and rice crops.

During 1968 Pakistan increasingly sought aid from China, while trying to consolidate agreements with the U.S.S.R. and U.S.A. However, the U.S.A. remains Pakistan's chief trading partner, followed by the U.K., West Germany and Japan.

PALEONTOLOGY

In May 1968, a new theory advanced by Paul Martin, a University of Arizona geochronologist, stated that the large mammals which once inhabited North America did not die out through climatic changes of the past 50,000 years. Martin believes that the extinction of such animals as the antlered giraffe (40,000 years ago), the giant kangaroo (14,000 years ago), the European woolly rhinoceros and woolly mammoth (11,000—13,000 years ago) followed the migration of man, the hunter. The pattern and timing of large-scale extinction does appear to correspond with the arrival of prehistoric hunters.

PANAMA

39,890 sq. m. Pop. 1.29m. Two plans, named after the president —the Rural Plan Robles and the Urban Plan Robles—were introduced in 1968 under the "Alliance for Progress". The aim of the first is to check a definite migration from the land to the cities and initially six rural areas have been selected where the emphasis is on increasing production for consumption and on diversification of agriculture. The urban plan is intended to overcome social problems and ease unemployment. Agriculture has been growing since 1966 at an annual rate of 6% and employs half the population, but, interestingly, it is becoming less important relatively. Bananas are clearly the main export commodity but corn and bean production is increasing. Fishing is becoming very important. The catch in 1967 was 170m lb (worth nearly 24m dollars) compared to a catch of only 24m lb in 1960. The textile industry now plays a major role in Panama's economy and a new cotton textile mill will produce at least a third of the country's cotton textile needs. There is also a new petro-chemical plant. In July 1967 the final stretch of the Inter-American Highway between Panama City and the border with Costa Rica was completed ahead of schedule.

One of the most vital factors behind the present buoyant conditions is the completion of negotiations with the U.S.A. on new treaties governing the administration of the Panama Canal and the construction of a new sea-level canal. Panama relies heavily on earnings from the Canal Zone (more than 100m dollars annually) to offset its trade deficit and although details of the new treaties were not revealed it is understood that Panama will have a greater share in the financial benefits from the Canal and that construction of a new waterway will take place on Panamanian soil.

PARAGUAY

157,000 sq. m. Pop. 2.095m. A record 230,000 cattle were slaughtered in 1967 for export but because of lower prices earnings were down. Coffee is becoming of increasing importance as a foreign exchange earner; in 1967 the country had a quota of 70,000 bags. A major project in progress is the expansion of the port of Asunción, due for completion in 1970. The International Finance Corporation has recommended that Paraguay, Brazil and the U.S.A. should participate in the establishment of a 2m-dollar company to provide an all-season freight barge service which could handle 10% of Paraguay's exports and 7% of imports. Major projects completed in 1966-68 include the enlargement of the international airport at Asuncion, building of a bridge over the Parana linking Paraguay with Brazil, a road across the Chaco to the Bolivian border and a bridge over the Tebicuary to replace a ferry. The building of roads accounts for two-fifths of public expenditure, an indication of the importance better communications have in the country's development. Three-fifths of the imports now come from Argentina, the U.S.A. and West Germany.

PERU

514,059 sq. m. Pop. 12.1m. Efforts are being made to develop areas away from the Lima region, which produces two-thirds of the manufacturing output. One such centre is Piura in the north, which has gas petroleum industries on which chemical industries could be based, and Arequipa, where industrial estates are planned. The recent completion of a dam on the River Chancay now makes possible the irrigation and use of a further 220,000 acres. High overhead costs and low returns are causing much trouble in the basically profitable fishmeal industry and the Fisheries Promotion Law of October 1967 encourages mergers and gives tax relief.

PHILIPPINES

114,834 sq. m. (7,107 islands). Pop. 33.5m. The Republic of the Philippines is vigorously applying itself to the task of achieving faster economic growth. Agriculture has traditionally been the mainstay of the economy but a promising start has been made towards building a vital industrial economy. With a population of 33m expanding at an annual rate of 3% the size and urgency of the task cannot be overestimated. Measures taken include the formation of a Private Development Corporation to supply medium and long-term finance. The recent pattern of both imports and investment indicates that the emphasis is changing from the packaging and assembly operations of earlier years to utilization of local resources—timber, copper, nickel, iron ore, lead and zinc. Several new refining and smelting plants are in operation for increasing the production of chemicals and fertilizers, aluminium, steel and tinplate.

PHOSPHATES

One of the world's biggest and richest phosphate deposits, a 1.3 billion ton reserve in the Spanish Sahara at Bu-craa, south-east of the capital El Aiun, is now being exploited. The deposits were discovered in 1963 but the Spanish government refused officially to acknowledge them. American capital is mostly involved. A new port will be built from which to ship the phosphate.

PLASTICS

Few industries can match the recent growth record of plastics. World output of plastic materials has more than quadrupled between 1956 (3.6m tons) and 1968 (18m tons). This explosive growth has been necessary to meet the surging demand for plastics for incorporation in products of all kinds, as manufacturers find new uses for materials that are frequently cheaper, lighter, more easily fabricated and better suited to mass production than traditional materials, and which can offer qualities such as transparency and unbreakability not usually found in combination. In 1968 the U.S.A. was responsible for one-third of all production, Japan and the EEC 15% each, EFTA 1% (of which Britain's share is 7% of the world total). In trade the EEC leads, followed by EFTA.

POLAND

121,000 sq. m. Pop. 31.9m. Profound attempts are being made to decentralize the economy but progress is slow and reforms are hampered by low productivity and growing absenteeism. With incomes rising faster than expected—in 1968 they were up 70% on 1960—more money has been spent on food, notably meat. A chronic shortage of meat in 1968 brought about large price increases. Despite an increase of 14% in agricultural output since 1965 development is insufficient to meet the needs of a growing population. In 1967 Poland had to import 1.9m tons of grain. In contrast to other socialist countries the state owns only 14% of the land—collectivization was abandoned in 1956—but there is neither the capital nor the skilled labour to ensure rapid expansion. Many farms are too small and scattered to be economically viable, and farming is relatively backward. The growth of co-operatives and a high level of investment in fertilizers are hopeful signs. In October 1967 Poland became a full member of GATT, which means that other members will remove as quickly as possible any discriminatory tariffs or quotas against Polish sales. Britain is Poland's largest trading partner in the West; the current boom of U.K. sales to Poland—scientific equipment, rubber goods, dyes, electrical machinery, chemicals, iron and steel, textiles—has led to Polish requests for larger quotas for a variety of consumer goods, food and clothing.

Despite the doubling of British exports to Poland since 1965 there is no doubt that sales could be much bigger. Some British prices are as much as 60% higher than equivalent items from the U.S.A., but Poland dislikes trading with the

U.S.A. because of political upsets, and despite imports of £41m annually from West Germany does not wish to become dependent on what is still generally feared as a potential enemy. Poland would like to sell Britain more manufactures. Big British contracts in 1968 included large electro-plating plant, earthenware pipe-making machinery and fibreglass equipment.

POLLUTION

The entire industrialized world is becoming polluted and emerging nations are not likely to slow their own development in the interest of clearer air and cleaner water. Effluence is overwhelming natural decay, the vital process that balances life in the natural world. Man has tended to ignore his utter dependence on the biosphere—a vast web of interacting processes and organisms that form the rhythmic cycles and food chains in which one part of the living environment feeds on another. The most closely studied example of pollutants is the effect of pesticides, which have sharply improved farm crops but have also caused great destruction of fish and wildlife. In New Brunswick, for example, the application of only 0.5 lb of DDT per acre of forest to control the spruce budworm has twice wiped out almost an entire year's production of young salmon in the Maramichi River. Rain has washed the DDT off the ground and into the plankton of lakes and streams. As another example, every day New York City dumps 200m gallons of raw sewage into the Hudson River. Arctic glaciers now contain wind-wafted lead from tetraethyl in vehicle exhausts. Cities need a systems approach to pollution, as has Los Angeles. Since local governments may be reluctant to levy effluence charges, fearing loss of industry, the obvious need is for regional co-operation, such as inter-state river-basin authorities to enforce scientific water use. The Ruhr is governed this way. An excellent U.S. example is the eight-state Ohio River Valley Water Sanitation Commission which

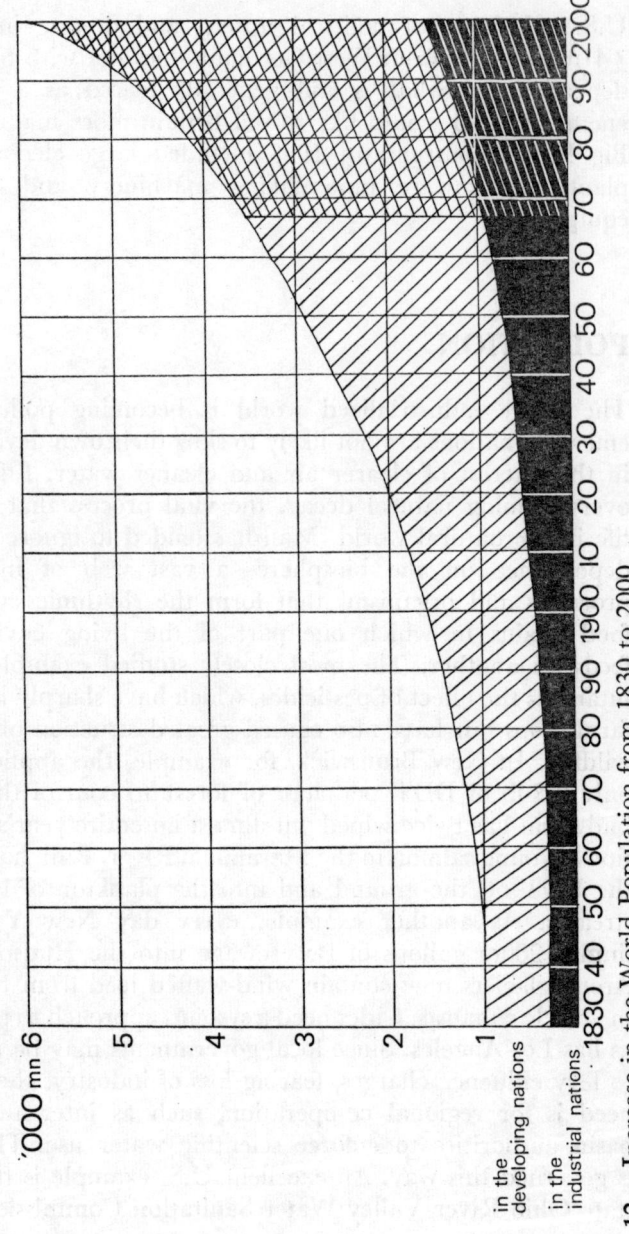

12. Increase in the World Population from 1830 to 2000

persuaded 3,000 cities and industries to spend one billion dollars diverting 99% of their effluent to sewage plants.

The continental shelf, the best fish-populated and most accessible fishing area is being poisoned at a quickening rate. Dr. David Bellamy of Durham University has shown the catastrophic effect of pollution on seaweeds, the base of the marine-life pyramid, on the coast between Blyth and Middlesbrough. A century ago 97 species of ocean vegetation flourished on this littoral. In this century of industry, filthy effluents from mines, furnaces, chemical plants and cities have killed off 56 types. Of those that survive only eleven are useful species.

The Harvard Business Review believes that the U.S.A. will need to spend 105 billion dollars before the year 2000 to abate and control air pollution.

POPULATION

This aspect of geography was discussed at length in the previous edition of this book and in *The Hunger to Come*, and in general terms it can only be stated that the demographic revolution is more acute than ever; several estimates put the world population at the end of the century at 6,000 million. However, in a small number of countries—South Korea, Taiwan, Hong Kong, Singapore and Puerto Rico—there are already signs of a decline in fertility, and an increasing number of developing countries are promoting family planning programmes. In late 1968 there were over twenty government-supported family planning programmes in Asia, Latin America and Africa. The British Ministry of Overseas Development in March 1968 increased its yearly grant to the International Planned Parenthood Federation and has set up a Population Bureau. In the U.K. itself it was evident early in 1968 that the population increase was slowing; up to June 30, 1967 the year's increase in England and Wales was 315,500 (to 48,400,000) but this was fewer than the average annual increase of 389,000 between mid-1961 and mid-1966.

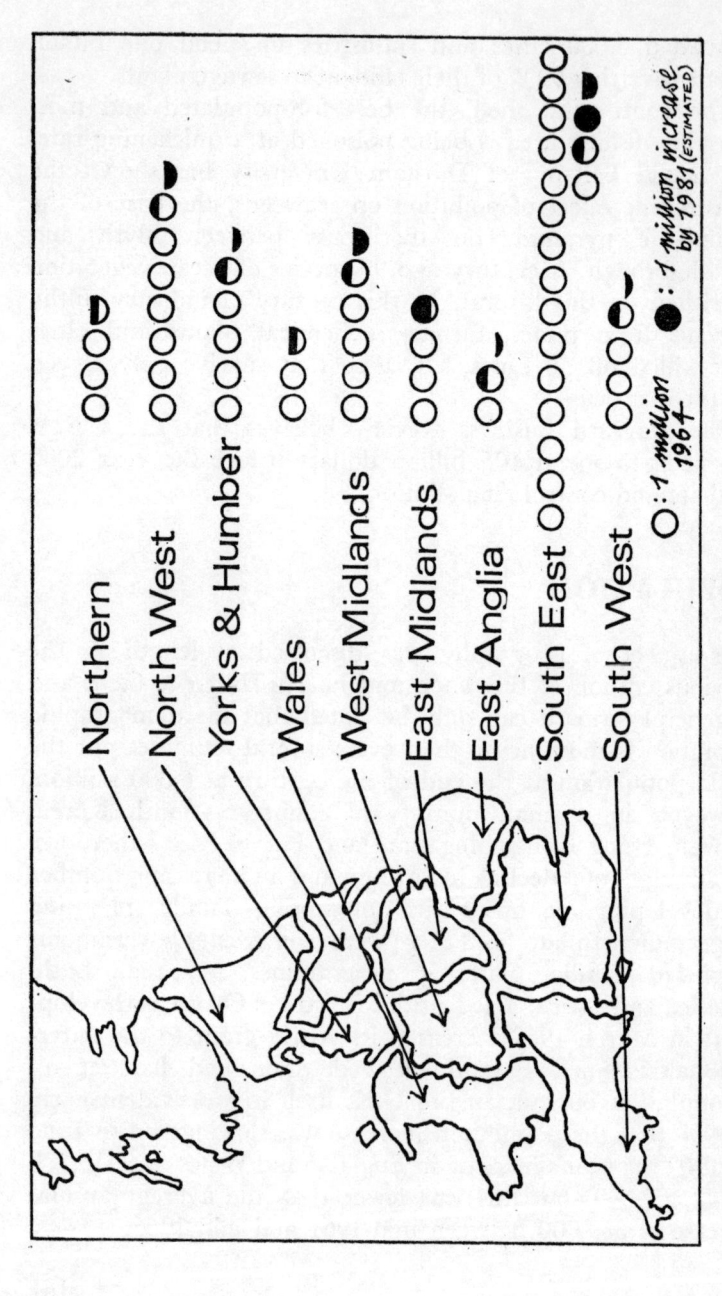

13. Estimated Population Increases in Britain between 1964-1981

PORTUGAL

34,500 sq. m. Pop. 9.2m. The Portuguese government has been trying to reform the country's textile industry, especially in cotton. Between 1964-68 £22.5m was spent on new equipment, and in 1968 about £22m of cotton goods were produced. However, production was affected by a "voluntary agreement" that limited the textiles sold in the U.K., Portugal's main market. Many small firms closed because of this agreement. For the six-year plan 1968-73 Portugal will spend much money on engineering, chemicals, paper and pulp, transport and tourism.

The Portuguese textile industry has seen further spectacular growth in its exports to EFTA countries since the final elimination of duties on industrial products within EFTA—an increase of 60% on 1967 quantities and values. A new steel and tinplate plant has been built at Seixal near Lisbon. Three of Portugal's four sugar refineries are being expanded and modernized by Britain's Tate & Lyle Enterprises. Also, a sulphate factory with a yearly capacity of 80,000 tons of artificial fibre cellulose, mainly for textiles, has started production in Leirosa. The enterprise is using wood of the rapid-growth eucalyptus tree which can be cut after eight to ten years. Under the latest plan for agriculture it is hoped that output will expand by 3% annually. The government is encouraging the integration of small uneconomic units and is paying 20% towards the cost of any farmer's new machinery. Tourism is the most import single earner of foreign exchange: there were 2.7m visitors in 1968. It should be noted that between 1959-68 Portuguese exports to EFTA increased more than threefold, although total exports only doubled. Portugal's position within EFTA has attracted considerable foreign investment from West Germany, Japan and the U.S.A., which can utilize the low-cost labour to manufacture exports to the EEC. In 1967 Portugal spent £47m on British goods and sold the U.K. £56m.

R

RAINMAKING

Until August 1968 nobody had tried, on a monetary basis, to evaluate rainmaking by cloud-seeding. Now the Victorian Department of Agriculture estimates that extra rain resulting from cloud seeding has been worth 2m (A) dollars to Victorian farmers. Also, the Cloud and Rain Physics Section of the Australian CSIRO believes that the 1m dollars spent on research since 1947 has been returned many times over. Research into rainmaking is more developed in Australia than anywhere else.

REFUGEES

The refugees of South Vietnam are changing the familiar picture of families uprooted by war and revolution. They are quite unlike the 50m people displaced by the two world wars or the 5m of the Korean conflict. For the 1.8m refugees in South Vietnam the front line is constantly on their doorstep; only 60,000 have fled to Thailand.

Churches have given much money for help in Africa, Latin America and the Caribbean. During 1967-68 40,000 refugees from the southern Sudan crossed into the Congo, Kenya, Uganda and Ethiopia. Families which fled from the Congo itself, together with refugees from Angola, Mozambique and Rwanda have also to be resettled. Some refugees are of longstanding. In 1967 Christian Aid gave £5,000 towards housing a group of White Russians who fled to Greece in the early

1920s; for forty years they have been living in barracks built by the Greeks for the French Army in the 1914-18 War.

RHODESIA

150,333 sq. m. Pop. 4.3m. Since Rhodesia declared itself independent in 1966 the country has undergone an industrial revolution as a result of being deprived of traditional sources of manufactured goods. Clothing manufacturers lost heavily when sanctions were first imposed because of the loss of the Zambian market, but domestic consumption and exports to South Africa have re-established them. Engineering firms are making goods not previously made such as piping and wire netting. The food industry more than any other has come into its own; canning is prospering and chocolate is being made for the first time. Tobacco markets, however, have been adversely affected, despite greatly increased imports by South Africa. Farms do not appear to be producing less (the government will not release production figures) but great quantities of leaf are being stored.

RUBBER

The low level of rubber prices in 1966-68 has been disturbing the industry. Rubber production has, in general, increased—in Ceylon, for instance, by 9% to 316m lb between 1965-67—but exports have been reduced. Competition from synthetic rubber is steadily being intensified and the level of exports has also been affected by a slowing-down in industrial activity in certain countries, notably in Western Europe. Several Eastern European countries (e.g. Bulgaria, Rumania and Turkey) are now growing rubber, thus tending to eliminate them as markets for the traditional suppliers. World rubber consumption in 1967 was estimated at 2.7m long tons of natural rubber and 3.6m tons of synthetic rubber. By 1971 consumption is expected to rise to 2.9m and 4.3m tons respectively.

In July 1968 an Association of Natural Rubber Producing Countries was proposed. These countries, knowing that production is likely to outpace demand and apprehensive of growing competition from synthetic rubber, want to examine the marketing system and freight rates and to promote the use of natural rubber. The Association may urge an international rubber agreement. By fostering higher-yielding trees Malaysia, for one, is aggravating the situation it most wants to prevent—surplus.

RUMANIA

91,600 sq. m. Pop. 19.1m. The aims of the 1967 plan were exceeded in most industries but returns from agriculture were less successful apart from wheat—13.5m tons. Agriculture in 1968 accounted for a third of the national income and a fifth of the exports and employed more than half the working population but progress is hampered by a lack of fertilizers and of irrigation facilities.

Industry is to be completely reorganized; individual enterprises have been grouped into autonomous trusts—"industrial centrals" is the Rumanian term—which form a basis of forty new regional units and will be directly responsible to an appropriate ministry. Trading ties with the West are gaining in strength at the expense of those with the other COMECON countries; West Germany is the second largest trading partner after the U.S.S.R. Britain, in 1967 and 1968, had a notable deficit in trade with Rumania but an agreement was signed in February 1968 for the purchase of six British aircraft worth £11m, the first order of its kind to be won in East Europe.

S

SCANDINAVIA

Denmark, Sweden, Norway and Finland, collectively the world's fourth largest trading unit (after the U.S.A., West Germany and Britain), plan to form an economic union and by the end of 1968 had evolved a blueprint for the scheme. The four countries economically united will be able to counterbalance Britain's influence in EFTA which, they sometimes complain, is too strong. They will also be in a strong bargaining position *vis-à-vis* the Common Market. The union will in its ideal form apply a common tariff to all countries outside the Nordic area, except Britain and the other EFTA countries (with which tariffs on industrial goods are already abolished). The union's common tariff will be supplemented by a common agricultural market. In this—again ideally—agricultural products will be freely interchanged among the four countries and the four will charge a common price for the produce they export to other countries. While the union will probably not achieve all its objectives it will increase the integration of its members, stiffen their attitude towards Britain and increase their chances of entry into the Common Market. Britain will welcome the union as a rich market for her exports, for average consumption per head in the Nordic area is already 30% above that of the EEC. (See also individual Scandinavian countries.)

SELENOLOGY

Close-up photographs of the moon from spacecraft now suggest that both volcanic and meteoric processes were involved in moulding the lunar surface. (For years astronomers have debated the origin of lunar craters; one school favoured the view that most were formed by the impact of meteorites, while others believed that volcanic processes must be responsible.) There is now evidence of a volcanic origin for a relatively rare type of lunar crater, surrounded by a halo of dark material. The processes responsible for the dark-haloed craters may still be at work. Evidence in favour of this is that changes in the colour of the lunar surface, which many astronomers believe are caused by internal activity, seem to take place in the regions in which the dark-haloed craters are localized.

There is also some evidence that water exists on the moon, though it would be chemically locked in hydrous rocks. Some geologists speculate that in the water released from hydrous rock by volcanic heat a primitive form of life might have evolved, especially near the crater Aristarchus, from which astronomers have reported seeing a red glow—a possible sign of volcanic activity.

The space research craft Orbiter 4, in June 1967, photographed the Cordillers Mountains, 20,000 feet, which ring the Orientale Basin. Within them are six additional rings of smaller mountains separated by relatively flat plains. Giant cracks radiate from the centre of the basin and the lunar surface for another 600 miles is littered by coarse debris obviously hurled from the basin by tremendous force. It is suggested by the U.S. Geological Survey that Orientale is the youngest of the large lunar basins—about 500m years old.

Unlike most scientists, the American Nobel Laureate Harold Urey believes that the moon may have had an atmosphere, rainfall, lakes and even oceans. In a theory put foward in 1967 he states that water, not lava formed the smooth lunar plains and filled-in depressions revealed in space research photographs, and that the dark plains look "precisely like the bottoms of dried-up primitive" areas of water. Material in craters and crevices may once have been flowing mud. Lunar water, Urey suggests, had a terrestrial origin. If the moon was torn from earth it would have carried off substantial amounts of water. Or if, as he believes, the moon was a planetary interloper captured by earth, its gravity would have attracted terrestrial water as well as solid matter during the cataclysmic events caused by its close approach to the earth. Within a few thousand years the lunar waters dried up, before they could carve out major features such as valleys and stream beds similiar to those formed by water flowing on the earth. If any water remains on the moon today, Urey says, it is probably in the form of ice buried beneath the surface and insulated from solar heat. The gradual melting and vaporizing of this ice, which would leave voids beneath the surface, may account for the cave-ins visible in moon-probe photographs. Urey believes that most of the earth's stony meteorites come from the moon, knocked off by other meteorites and occasional comets that have bombarded the lunar surface. Embedded in many of those moon-sent meteorites are smooth fragments that appear to have been shaped by frictional effects like those that would be caused by flowing water; they also contain minerals such as clay-type silicates and calcium carbonates that, Urey says, can hardly be accounted for except by the action of liquid water over some length of time. Observations made during the remarkable Apollo 8 flight in December 1968 will help to clarify some of the problems of selenology.

SHIPBUILDING

Ships are becoming larger and more specialized. Shipowners have two main aims: to reduce labour costs at sea and in port and to obtain more intensive use of expensive capital equipment. Bigger ships cost less per ton to build and require fewer men per thousand tons of cargo carried. Deck cranes (instead of derricks) have speeded up conventional cargo-handling and containers and roll-on, roll-off methods largely solve bottlenecks in ports.

The increase in the size of oil tankers (which in all amounted to only 11.5m gross tons in 1937 and to 66.5m tons at the end

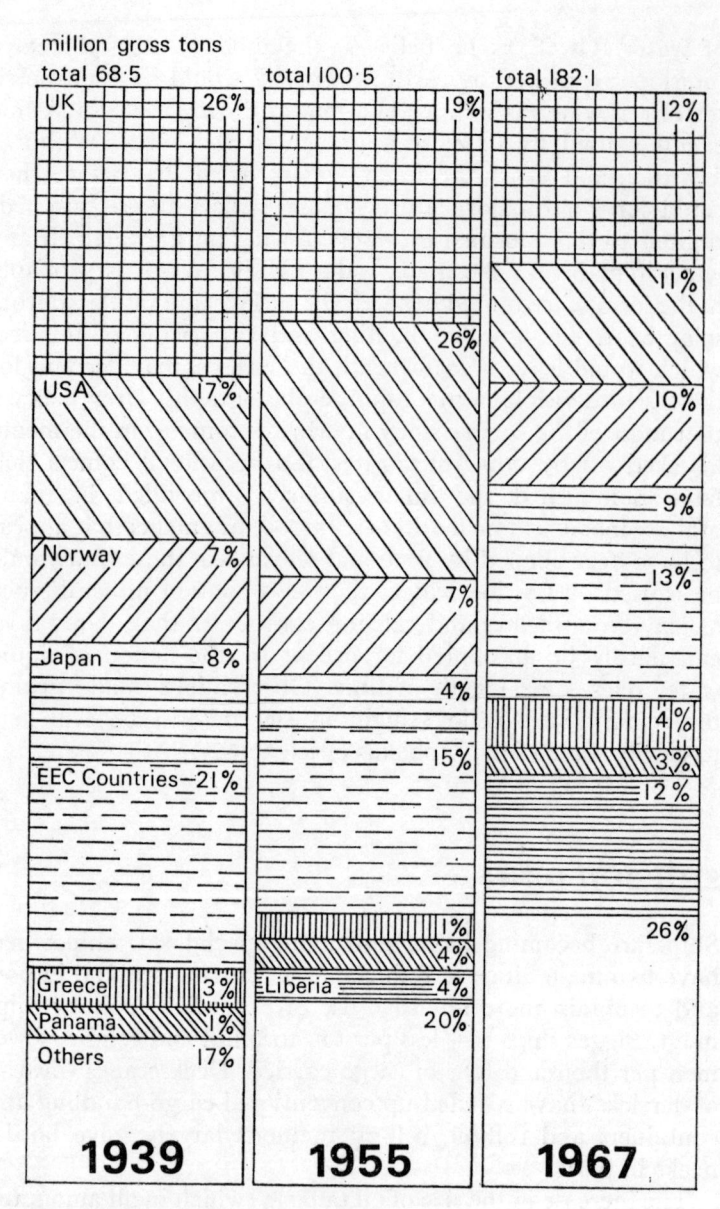

14. World Shipping Tonnage by Flag

Shipbuilding

of 1967) has been remarkable. In 1938 a large tanker was of 12,000 tons deadweight; in 1952, 28,000 tons, and in 1968, 200,000 tons. Even this is now being exceeded. In 1968 the Japanese delivered the first in a series of 312,000-tonners. Such size has its disadvantages: there is a shortage of harbours and drydocks and even difficulties with sea routes. Malacca Strait, for example, is too shallow and the English Channel too narrow.

Japan dominates the shipbuilding trade more than ever. In 1967 figures were: Japan 48%, U.K. 8%, West Germany 8%, Sweden 6%, others 30%. A total of 15.8m gross tons of shipping was built (1962, 8m tons).

Specialization in ship-types is not new, but is now more extensively used—e.g., bulk ore carriers. The United Steamship Company of Denmark uses a ship specially built on the roll-on, roll-off system to carry 1.4m bottles of Carlsberg Lager to the U.K. on each voyage from Copenhagen to Felixstowe. Early in 1969 Esso planned to put into service specially designed tankers carrying liquefied natural gas from Libya to Italy and Spain. Each ship is 674 feet long, weighs 37,000 tons and has a capacity of 250,000 bb of gas at a temperature of minus 260° F. A Swedish shipyard built a tanker to carry chlorine for a Norwegian company. With a capacity of 1,600 tons of chlorine, the highly automated ship will ply between Heroya and Maydown, Northern Ireland.

In April 1968 Scottish yards started work on six Danish-engined ships for Norwegian owners, all bulk carriers.

However, Denmark claims to be building the longest ship in the world, which at 349 metres will beat the previous longest by 3 metres. It is a tanker of 255,000 tons ordered by the U.S. Company Texaco from the Danish shipyard Odenses.

In early 1968 Esso ordered four super-tankers from two British shipyards, Swan Hunter (Tyne) and Harland and Wolff (Belfast). Each of 240,000 tons, the ships are the largest—330 metres long, 51 metres wide—to be built in the U.K. All will be delivered by 1970.

The resurgence of East Germany as an industrial country is largely due to the busy shipyards on East Germany's Baltic

Coast. In 1966 these yards turned out no fewer than 175 ships, totalling about 2.5m tons; in 1967 the figure had risen to 195, and in 1968 to 210. Since 1946 more than 2,900 East German-built ships have been sold to the U.S.S.R., often at prices 30% below the world market. Many of the ships have been made at Warnemunde's Warnow yards, East Germany's largest. East Germany's own state-controlled shipping line VEB (Volkseigener Betrieb) has 200 ships (one ship in 1951). In 1968 they carried 9m tons of cargo to 350 ports, while two 600-passenger cruise ships carried holiday-makers to Scandinavia, Scotland and Ireland.

SICILY

9,928 sq. m. Pop. 4.1m. Oil refineries are bringing much development to certain parts of this backward island, especially since the building during 1966-67 of associated fertilizer, chemical and petro-chemical plants in the Augusta-Syracuse area. In 1950 only 40,000 people worked for industrial concerns, apart from small handicraft factories. In 1968 industry employed 120,000 and indirectly gave work to many others in building and communications. Palermo and Milazzo in the north and Agrigento, Gela and Ragusa in the south, as well as Catania, 20 miles north of Augusta, are active and expanding centres of industry. Despite new opportunities emigration from Sicily accounts for more than a third of all emigration from Italy.

Land resettlement is a major part of Sicily's development, with farmers being taken from the drier, more sterile rain-shadowed areas of the centre and placed in new farms in the west. Some areas had been farmed for centuries without the land being given a year's respite. Again, some families are being moved from agriculturally congested regions. Apparently genuine efforts are being made to break the stultifying grasp of big landowners who, working through poor tenants, have done little to develop or improve their land.

SIERRA LEONE

27,925 sq. m. Pop. 2.5m. Japan is now buying Sierra Leone steel—1.1m tons annually for ten years. This means much expansion and building of new docks to accommodate large ore carriers. The first shipment of rutile, a source of titanium, was made in June 1967. There are proven reserves of 3m tons and estimated deposits of 30m tons of this mineral. Unemployment continues to be a problem with rising rural emigration. Among new factories opened in 1966-68 were those producing matches, metalware, knitted garments and confectionery. The FAO is assisting in a development plan for agriculture and in a five-year survey of fishing resources. With the completion of the Guma Valley HEP scheme the Sierra Leone Electricity Corporation intends to spend at least £3m during the next five years to improve the power supply in the western province. Sierra Leone's main supplier is Britain, 28%; Japan supplies 10.4% and the U.S.A. 6.2%.

SINGAPORE

224 sq. m. Pop. 2.1m. The earlier withdrawal of British forces from the Far East—1971 instead of the mid 1970s—will have serious repercussions in Singapore, since the military bases generate about a fifth of the republic's national income. Singapore already has a serious unemployment problem; in September 1968, 50,000 people were without work while on average a further 25,000 young people come on to the labour market each year. However, industrial production rose by 12% in 1967. To encourage further industrialization the government is offering generous investment incentives through tax relief. Foreign investment has come mainly from Japan, Hong Kong and the U.S.A. The British naval dockyard, said to be worth £3.75m is to be handed over to the government for a commercial ship repair yard. More than half the island's trade still results from entrepot activities but, long-term, as neighbouring countries develop their own industries and ports the value of re-export trade will gradually diminish. British trade in Singapore's competitive market has been declining, particularly in the face of aggressive Japanese competition.

SOMALIA

288,000 sq. m. Pop. 2.5m. Somalia has asked to join the East African Economic Community (Kenya, Tanzania and Uganda) because it feels it has a better chance of building a viable economy by co-operating with Black Africa rather than with Arab neighbours to the north. Somalia, in mid-1968, ceased to dispute land with neighbouring Kenya and Ethiopia. The country has a 1967-71 development plan but it is so modest that the Planning Ministry calls it "a collection of wishes wholly dependent on foreign aid". One aim is to increase the area of arable land from 13% to 13.5%. It is too early to say that militant Somali nationalism will not be disastrously revived.

SOUTH AFRICA, REPUBLIC OF

471,445 sq. m. Pop. 18.7m (Europeans 3.6m). After an exceptionally good harvest in 1966-67 the yields for 1967-68 reverted to more normal levels owing to early drought. Wool sales amounted to 266.5m lb (July 1, 1967—March 31, 1968) compared with 251.2m tons in the previous corresponding period. There have been some gloomy forecasts that gold production will rapidly decline in the 1970s unless there are new discoveries or an increase in the price of gold. In the 1968 budget the government decided to spend about £40m over eight years in assisting flagging gold mines, mostly by supplying better equipment. The output of gold in 1967 amounted to 30.5m fine ounces, worth 770m Rands (1.714 Rands = £1 sterling).

For the first time the South African sugar industry is exporting produce, mostly molasses to Japan. A white sugar refinery has been opened in East Transvaal and a synthetic fibre plant in Cape Town. A very large aluminium smelter was started in March 1968 at Richards Bay. South Africa is gaining about 40,000 immigrants a year, about 25% from the U.K. It should be noted that South Africa is emerging as the U.K.'s second best customer after the U.S.A., outstripping even Australia; exports to South Africa in 1967 amounted to £261.1m; the estimated figure for 1968 was £275m.

SOUTHERN YEMEN

112,000 sq. m. (approximately). Pop. 1.5m (Government-estimated). The People's Republic of Southern Yemmen was proclaimed when the South Arabian Federation, consisting of the former British colony of Aden and the protectorates achieved independence on November 30, 1967. The capital is Madinet al-Shaab, formerly known as Al Ittihad, outside Aden. Aden remains the main town together with its port complex (population, 25,000). Other towns are Sheikh Othman (30,000), Little Aden (9,300) and Mukalla (25,000). The future of this country is uncertain, but a number of light industries are growing up; they include factories producing aluminium pots and pans, cigarettes, perfumes, oil seeds and industrial gases. Salt was the main mineral mined for many years but production has greatly declined since 1966. Fishing would seem to provide Southern Yemen's best economic future.

SPAIN

196,700 sq. m. Pop. 32m. The second development plan, 1968-71, due to begin in January 1968 was postponed until April owing to inflation. Its principal objectives are a growth rate of 6% a year, with large sums being spent on transport and agriculture, to reduce imports. Almost 1m new jobs are to be created in industry and services while the farm labour force is expected to decline by 400,000. At the end of 1968 farming still employed a third of the labour force but accounted for less than a fifth of the national product. In 1967 18m tourists visited Spain and spent £430m and in 1968 the total was expected to be a little more than this; Spain hopes for 22m by 1971. At the end of 1968 Spain was the only country in Europe outside a trading group, although the EEC and EFTA take 36% and 22% respectively of Spanish exports. Britain is the fourth largest trading partner. Spain is seeking barter deals, for instance, wheat against Argentinian beef, the only meat Spain is short of.

Almeria is developing rapidly in tourism and in the cultivation of early vegetables. A new airport opened in July 1967 to move these vegetables to European markets. The success of the region can be measured by the price of land: £1,500 per hectare (2.47 acres) in 1964, £7,500 in 1968. This region now produces the earliest vegetables in Spain—potatoes, beans, egg plants, cucumbers and tomatoes. The once deserted coast is now attracting peasants from other less productive regions, especially the interior of Granada province and Jaen.

Now that Libyan methane is arriving at Barcelona the petro-chemical and fibre industries are expected to flourish; the demand for methane in Catalonia is expected to double within four years. Algerian gas is also to be imported—60,000m cubic metres in fifteen years, an annual average much higher than that of the British and French imports of Algerian gas.

The immediate objective after Barcelona is Bilbao to which gas may be supplied by pipeline from Barcelona. The ultimate aim is a pipeline network to supply natural gas to the whole of Spain.

The Ministry of Agriculture claims that since 1940 2.5m hectares have been reafforested in Spain at an average of 100,000 hectares a year. The tree-drive is typical of vigour in other fields: Spain manages to supply 80% of her own sugar needs and is producing an impressive number of ships, mostly relatively small ones; for instance, the Bilbao shipyards began work in mid-1968 on a hundred 100-ton fishing vessels for Cuba.

SPANISH AFRICA (Spanish Sahara, Spanish Guinea, Ifna, the Canary Islands)

120,000 sq. m. Pop. 1.4m. On July 15, 1968 Spain granted independence to Spanish Guinea, which consists of the verdant, volcanic island of Fernando Po, a few smaller islands, the larger, rain-forest mainland of Rio Muni and the coastal outposts of Ceuta and Melilla. Fernando Po has become remarkably prosperous on coffee, cocoa and bananas; two-thirds of the island's 60,000 population is made up of Nigerian labourers. Rio Muni is also prosperous, largely because of the large export subsidies and other grants from the Spanish government. Spain's other African colonies are also moving ahead, though at a slower pace. In the Spanish Sahara (40,000 nomads, 20,000 troops and officials), Spain is pouring £10m into the development of vast underground phosphate reserves, claimed to be the world's largest.

SUDAN

1m sq. m (approximately). Pop. 14.3m (increase 2.8%). As would be expected, development is relatively slow, but much is expected of the Gezira Scheme, a big cotton-growing project based on irrigation from the Sennar Dam. The Sudanese government describes it as the backbone of its economy. Big efforts are being made to increase production of coffee, tobacco, rice and sugar.

Two new dams have already extended the amount of irrigated arable land devoted to growing cotton and efforts are being made to increase cultivation of wheat, groundnuts, sesame and sugar cane. The Khashm El Girba dam irrigates

0.5m acres and the Roseires dam 3m acres. Shortage of skilled labour is an obstacle to industrialization, but several small industries are operating: shoes, soap, soft drinks, cement, sugar milling, and food canning factories. In 1968 a fertilizer plant, a paper mill and a sack factory commenced operations.

Foreign financial aid continues to contribute largely to the Sudan's development and trade missions are frequent. The number of trade, military and cultural agreements entered into by the Sudan with Communist countries after the 1967 Israel-Arab War may be indicative of a shift in Sudan's trading patterns. The U.K. maintains its position as leading supplier but the percentage dropped from 23.4% in 1965 to 18% in 1968.

SWAZILAND

6,705 sq. m. Pop. 400,000. Swaziland became an independent sovereign state on September 6, 1968; it was the last British colonial possession in Africa (excluding, of course, Rhodesia). The changes in Swaziland have been dramatic, many of them stemming from the initiative of the British-financed Commonwealth Development Corporation. These changes include the irrigation of 250,000 acres of land, the creation in the highveld of the largest man-planted forest—pine, eucalyptus and wattle—in Africa and the mining and export of iron ore with an assured market in Japan for years to come. Sugar, however, is the principal export, asbestos second. One of the most significant changes in agriculture is the growing interest of the Swazi in the cultivation of cash crops and the expansion of irrigation farming. Now that the communications have been vastly improved, electric power has been made available and the rail link to Goa on the Portuguese border has been completed, all that is necessary for a rapid rise in internal prosperity is a substantial increase in the flow of overseas investment capital.

One of the major benefits conferred upon the Swaziland government is the collection of customs and excise dues; they are gathered in by South African authorities and distributed by a given formula not only to Swaziland but also to Lesotho and Botswana for which countries South Africa performs a similiar service.

SWEDEN

173,436 sq. m. Pop. 7.8m. Sweden suffered financial difficulties during 1967-68 and had a substantial trade deficit. Nevertheless the nation's economy is sound, with increased earnings in iron ore, timber, paper, machinery and chemicals. Europe's largest fully computer-controlled cement factory was opened in May 1968 at Limhamm near Malmö; its capacity is 0.5m tons annually. In September 1968 a British Trade Week in Stockholm, with 1,800 British manufacturers taking part, was expected to stem the deterioration in the U.K.'s trade balance with Sweden; in 1967 U.K. sales to Sweden amounted to £225m, purchases from Sweden, £247m. As a result of plans to build a number of nuclear power plants in Sweden prospects for British manufacturers of nuclear equipment for the period 1968-78 are very bright.

SWITZERLAND

15,950 sq. m. Pop. 6m. Legislation introduced in March 1968 reduced by a further 5% the total foreign labour force, a step taken to lessen unemployment and to prevent overcrowding. The step has had detrimental effects, since it hampers industrial production, particularly in the building and metallurgical industries. Trade with EFTA countries has expanded, with exports accounting for 22% of the total and imports for 17% (1967). In contrast, the proportion of trade with the EEC declined.

The first nuclear power station in Switzerland, the underground generating plant at Lucens near Lausanne, started producing electricity in May 1968.

SYRIA

72,000 sq. m. Pop. 5.7m. Syria's progress is hampered by internal political troubles but some major products are developing. A vast high dam on the Euphrates will by 1972 double the nation's irrigated acreage and electrical output and treble the cotton crop, at present worth about £20m annually. The U.S.S.R. is paying 50% of the dam's cost and has also built power lines from Aleppo to the dam, constructed oil storage tanks at Homs refinery and is laying 500 miles of pipeline. Without financial help from Communist and Arab countries Syria's position would be desperate.

T

TAIWAN (Formosa or Nationalist China)

13,850 sq. m. Pop. 13m. Production has been expanding by at least 8% yearly, with investment in the period 1965-74 expected to reach £800m; much private capital is coming not only from the U.S.A., but from Japan and Australia. Income from tinned pineapples and tinned mushrooms—Taiwan is the principal exporter of both—was worth £14.3m in 1968. The sale of primary products accounts for about a quarter of the total export income, £200m in 1967. The island is now self-sufficient in most industrial products, and exports (mainly textiles, metals, machinery, chemical products and plywood) are running at £80m annually. Economically, Taiwan's main problem is to maintain exports in the face of growing competition from the light industries of other developing states. Small family businesses still have a significant influence on Taiwan's economy, but with other Asian countries, such as South Korea, already presenting a challenge in terms of cheap labour, there will be more urgent need for rationalization and better management. This applies to agriculture, too, since only 3,000 sq. m. of the land is arable. Among the country's government-run industries is the China Petroleum Company, which has petro-chemical complexes at either end of the island and a natural gas field at Miaoli in the north. The government-controlled Taiwan Power Company had, by 1968, brought electricity to 96% of Taiwan's population, the largest proportion in Asia. By mid-1969 the Tachia River power network will be supplying a quarter of the power through a mixture of HEP and thermal power generated by oil shipped from Kuwait. Between 1963 and 1968 the government's share of total industrial output had dropped from 68% to 31%. The country had 270,000 tourists in 1968.

TANZANIA

363,708 sq. m. Pop. 10m (including Zanzibar and Pemba, 340,000). Customs barriers were lifted in July 1968 but although Tanzania is a Union there is no sign of immigration barriers being removed. The country is in a state of hiatus and during 1966-68 it did not develop as rapidly as its neighbours. Progress with the five-year plan, ending 1970, fell far behind. Nevertheless, several large projects came into operation, notably the £5m oil refinery at Dar-es-Salaam. There is much diversity, too, with paper bags and sacks, suitcases, cellulose, paints, brewing, textiles, soap, matches, razor blades and shoes all recently established or expanded. A 1,060-mile eight-inch pipeline is being built from Dar-es-Salaam to the Zambian copperbelt town of Ndola by an Italian company. A Tanzanian mining firm has discovered rubies near Morogoro, about 120 miles from Dar-es-Salaam; the strike may prove to be one of the richest in Africa.

TEA

Tea is in over production, with world output growing by more than 3% and consumption rising by a mere 1%. At the same time production costs have increased steadily as prices declined. Various measures are being taken to promote the growth of tea blending and packing industries. International agreements are being made, too. For instance, in mid-1968 India and Ceylon decided on closer co-operation on the promotion and marketing of tea, on research and on the need to stabilize prices by means of a review of the existing auction machinery so as to strengthen the position of tea in world trade. The increased production is coming mainly from East African countries.

TELEGRAPHIC COMMUNICATIONS

The most important new development is the £25m submarine cable laid by Standard Telephones and Cables between Cape Town and Lisbon which will give South Africa, for the first time, direct telephone, telex, data and telegraph communications to almost all Europe. Extra facilities also connect South Africa to the U.S.A. The cable will be ready for operation in April 1969 and it supplements and largely replaces the high-frequency radio channels. About two-thirds of the equipment was made by Standard Telephones and Cables in South Africa, while the cable itself was made at Southampton. Eventually the new system will be extended to provide direct links with North and South America and the Middle East.

TEXTILES

The discovery of a man-made fibre which will make obsolete much of the present textile industry within ten years was disclosed in March 1968. Trademarked "Heterofol," the new fibres, developed by British ICI Fibre Research, can be made into fabrics without going through the traditional knitting and weaving processes and can be done very cheaply and with little labour. Basically, the new fibre has a different chemical as its core from the sheath around it. Many different "sheath-and-core Heterofilaments" have been made, ranging from those suitable for coarse sacking to fine wearing apparel. In all of these the melting point of the sheath is lower than the melting point of the core. If a mass of fibres, looking like cotton wool, is now heated to a temperature between the melting point of the sheath and the core only the sheath will melt, and on subsequent cooling, a strong physical bond is formed between any such fibres that were in contact during the heating and cooling process.

THAILAND

198,247 sq. m. Pop. 31.6m. Following the success of the first five-year plan during which total production expanded by a third, a growth rate exceeded in Asia only by Japan and Taiwan, the current programme 1967-71 places special emphasis on the development of rural areas and on diversification. The processing of foodstuffs still accounts for the major part of the manufacturing output but under the second programme increased emphasis is being placed on steel, cement, chemical fertilizers and tyres. A large paper mill will be in operation early in 1969 and industrial estates are being set up. The generating capacity of the Bumiphol HEP scheme, in operation since 1964, is to be quadrupled. In addition, a new £25m HEP dam has been commenced on the Nan River in north-west Thailand. Several small irrigation dams will add to the cultivable area, already increased by 1m acres through the Bumiphol scheme. The country has a growing tourist industry and a rising standard of living, as is seen by the increase in imports by an eighth in 1967. Thailand now has five motorcar assembly plants, all Japanese-run, and the steel industry was exporting in 1968. The extremely successful oil refinery at Sriraja wants to double its capacity to 65,000 bb a day by 1970. The five chemical fertilizer plants, three of them German-built, were producing to capacity at the end of 1968 and although Thai farms use only a fraction of the Japanese input, startling improvements have occurred in upland farms. Since 1958 production of tapioca and of hybrid maize has risen sixfold and eightfold respectively; the output of kenaf has increased 25 times to over 500,000 tons.

TIMBER

Forest products are among the fastest-growing exports of the developing countries as a whole and are the top foreign exchange earners of a number of Asian and African countries. In the period 1958 to 1968 exports grew from £120m to £365m and are expected to reach £625m annually by 1975. By 1967 the developing countries accounted for 16% of the world's forest products trade (8.3% in 1961). With only a fifth of their forest areas so far exploited much potential remains. Increases have been dramatic. Korea, for instance, increased her exports of hardwood plywood more than 100 times between 1962 and 1968 to 272,800 cubic metres.

The U.S.S.R. is the largest producer of timber, accounting for almost 20% of total world production. World forest production in 1967 was worth about £14,000m, including £5,500m in pulp products such as particle board, fibreboard, plywood and veneers. The world total of forested areas is 1,958m acres.

TOURISM

Tourism continues to expand more internationally and more dramatically than any other industry. OECD figures put the U.K. seventh among the 21 member countries in earnings from travel spending, after the U.S.A., Italy, Spain, France, West Germany and Canada. If Britain's large earnings from fares were included the country would be even higher in the list. Most international comparisons on travel are fruitless because of inadequate statistics. The British figures are based mostly on the International Passenger Survey, run by the Social Survey for the Board of Trade.

All the EFTA countries attract international tourists, though earnings are not always as significant as they are for Austria, where they equal one-third of income from direct exports. For 1967 the amounts were:

(In million dollars for better international comparison)

Britain	676	Denmark	220
Switzerland	634	Sweden	109
Austria	615	Norway	102
Portugal	258	Finland	50

Proportionate to population, Switzerland and Austria, longest established as tourist countries, lead the statistics of EFTA tourism and are challenged only in all Europe by Italy, 750m dollars and Spain, 700m; both the latter have larger populations.

Finland is concentrating its tourist traffic on the Saima Canal system, which runs partly through the bottleneck of Soviet territory separating the Gulf of Finland from Lake Ladoga, thus opening up a vast Finnish area containing at least 62,000 lakes. Starting points will be Helsinki, Viipuri (U.S.S.R.) or Leningrad (U.S.S.R.).

Denmark has a new tourist scheme, begun in 1966, for foreigners to stay on Danish farms. At the end of 1968 about 500 farms with a bed capacity of 2,000 were in the scheme with the number fast increasing.

Portugal is concentrating on the Algarve, the southern province, which has 75 miles of coastline facing due south and a climate more favourable than the French Riviera or the Costa del Sol, Spain. Algarve hotels work to capacity for nine months of the year.

Austria is developing summer-skiing tourism; an aerial cableway has been built near Kaprun leading to a large area of perennial snow around the Kitzsteinhorn, suitable for skiing in summer at a height of 10,000 feet. At the end of 1968 Austria had no fewer than 1,850 aerial cableways and ski lifts. With a network of new alpine roads it is now possible to drive into the Dachstein region, the Gesause mountains in Styria, and the Karawaken Range, separating Carinthia from Yugoslavia. Two new national parks have been established in Lower Austria on the Danube, while in 1968 a fourth was added in Geras. (The other one is Vienna Woods.)

Sweden now has sixteen national parks, planned to attract summer campers, all developed since 1961.

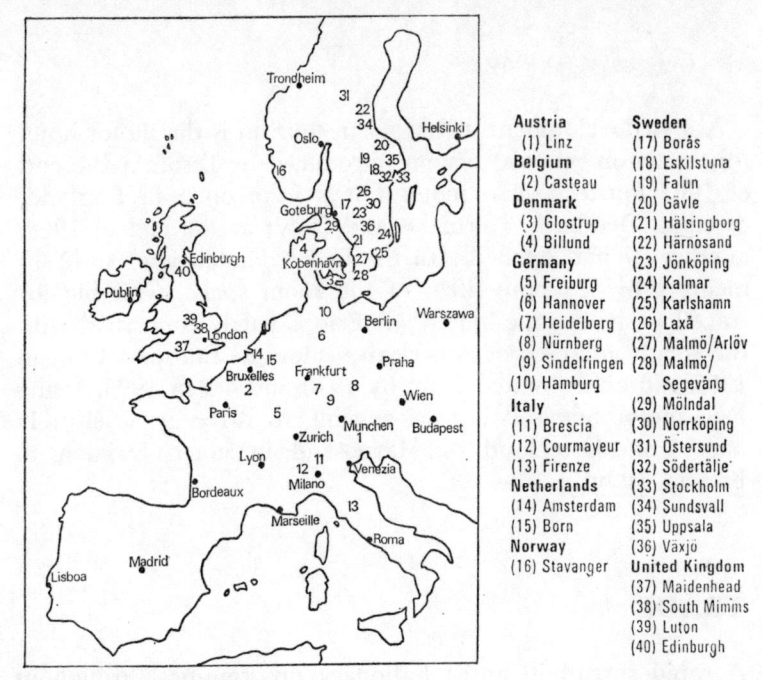

Austria	Sweden
(1) Linz	(17) Borås
Belgium	(18) Eskilstuna
(2) Casteau	(19) Falun
Denmark	(20) Gävle
(3) Glostrup	(21) Hälsingborg
(4) Billund	(22) Härnösand
Germany	(23) Jönköping
(5) Freiburg	(24) Kalmar
(6) Hannover	(25) Karlshamn
(7) Heidelberg	(26) Laxå
(8) Nürnberg	(27) Malmö/Arlöv
(9) Sindelfingen	(28) Malmö/
(10) Hamburg	Segevång
Italy	(29) Mölndal
(11) Brescia	(30) Norrköping
(12) Courmayeur	(31) Östersund
(13) Firenze	(32) Södertälje
Netherlands	(33) Stockholm
(14) Amsterdam	(34) Sundsvall
(15) Born	(35) Uppsala
Norway	(36) Växjö
(16) Stavanger	United Kingdom
	(37) Maidenhead
	(38) South Mimms
	(39) Luton
	(40) Edinburgh

15. Esso Motor Hotels in Europe

In Norway 10% of the working population depends on the tourist trade for a living, but summer traffic is decreasing. The autumn is very quiet and winter sports tourism is not making serious headway. The Norwegian Regional Development Board has selected Vossevangen as a pioneer planning project to develop it into an all-year tourist centre by providing modern facilities and attractions.

Britain expects 5m tourists by 1970 (3.5m in 1967) and a direct tourist income of £500m. At the beginning of 1968 there were about 43,000 hotels and boarding houses.

The Greek government in 1968 engaged Litton Industries Inc. of California to plan and largely supervise an 830m dollar programme to develop tourism (and to some extent industry and agriculture) in the western Peloponnese and in Crete. For Crete, Litton intends to raise tourist capacity from 60,000 to 620,000; in the Peloponnese, Litton proposes to build three new airports, develop five industrial centres and five harbours.

A new development in European tourism is the motor hotel (distinct from motels) system introduced by Esso. At the end of 1967 fourteen Esso motor hotels were open in England, Sweden, Denmark, Germany and Italy; at the end of 1968, another 27 had opened. (In the U.S.A. motel-type establishments provide about 40% of the room space available for travellers, in Europe only 4%.) Esso is partly concerned with the steady increase of American visitors to Europe—1.4m in 1965 and an estimated 2.5m by 1970 and 4.5 in 1975. Using Esso motor hotels it is now possible to drive at a leisurely pace from Östersund or Härnosänd in north Sweden to Brescia, Italy.

TRADE

A rapid spread in anti-inflationary programmes throughout the world had significant effects on the momentum of world trade between 1966 and 1968. World exports in 1967 increased by only 5% compared with almost 10% in 1966 and, in real terms, the improvement for 1967 was less than half the average expansion achieved between 1960 and 1966. The decline in the rate of growth is a reflection of relatively lower levels of economic activity in important areas of the world, notably Western Europe.

The gap between the rate of expansion of the trade of industrialized and other countries is likely to continue. One reason for this is the trend of primary commodity prices in which the developing countries are so largely interested. The purchasing power of primary producing countries is likely to continue to be subdued, with notable exceptions such as the oil producers of the Middle East, North Africa and Latin America. Any slowing down of the growth of world trade owing to low commodity prices is likely to be more than offset by the continuing expansion of trade in manufactured goods, where two tendencies are at work, each pulling in the same expansionist direction. The first is the gradual disappearance of narrow economic nationalism through the formation of groups, such as the EEC and EFTA; the second is the moderating, but still considerable, rate of economic growth. There was a danger that these groupings might develop an economic nationalism of their own. To test and avert this was one of the objectives of the 1967-68 series of multilateral tariff negotiations held under the General Agreement for Tariffs and Trade (GATT). This is the Kennedy Round, so called because it was enacted under the late President Kennedy, under which the U.S.A. was able to offer across-the-board tariff cuts of up to 50% under a revised version of the Trade Expansion Act.

TRANSPORT

AIR. An airline executive told the compiler of this book that "geography has been reduced to time, not distance". Certainly every new advance in transportation has eliminated geographical barriers and stimulated new areas of trade. The jet aircraft is accomplishing these results. Goods can now be moved faster by jet from New York to London than they can be shipped by ground transportation to Cleveland. A Philadelphia distributor can deliver his product to New Delhi in thirty hours. The elimination of the time barrier is creating new markets for many products. Fresh strawberries in winter were unkown in Sweden until recently. Now Californian strawberry farmers have the fruit in Stockholm markets three days after picking. Computers are frequently air-freighted. Since they are leased at rates of up to 1,000 dollars a day a manufacturer is losing money every day one is in transit. Shipped by jet from the U.S.A. to Europe, a computer can be delivered, installed and earning money 36 hours after leaving the factory. Many manufacturers are finding it more economical to shop by air because they can centralize distribution and eliminate the cost of maintaining regional warehouses. An American refrigerator manufacturer who until 1966 kept stocks in all his outlets in South America now supplies them by air from a warehouse in Miami. Many goods not usually associated with air transport are now so carried. Ten-ton rotor turbines from generators are now often air-freighted thousands of miles for overhaul. Before the first jet freighters were introduced in 1964 the high operating costs and the small loads carried by piston aircraft made air cargo rates prohibitive and most air cargo was emergency in nature. Bulk use of air freight has become a reality only since the advent of the larger jets which, because they are relatively less expensive to operate, have enabled the airlines to cut cargo rates. (Even so rates in 1968 were ten times more expensive per ton-mile than marine rates, seven times that of rail.)

For the air cargo business a family of jumbo jets will be operating by 1970. The first, Boeing's 747, will carry 110 tons of cargo. An even bigger one, Lockheed's L-500, will have a 150-ton capacity. Both will carry highway truck-trailers—a development of the container system. With increasing traffic every major airline in the U.S.A. and many elsewhere have built or plan to build new air-cargo terminals, most of them automated and run by computers. With the system installed in 1968 at Pan American's cargo terminal at Kennedy Airport, New York, two can load 90,000 lb of freight in less than half an hour. When freight was manually loaded and unloaded freight-handling costs were up to 3 dollars per 100 lb; now they are down to 40 cents per 100 lb. The jets and their associated equipment have transformed the geography of transport.

CONTAINER TRANSPORT. The advantages of containers have been slow to cross the Atlantic from the U.S. to the U.K. Widely developed in the U.S.A., this form of bulk transport provides a highly efficient and flexible trading system, benefiting both manufacturers and ship-owners. Goods are handled in unit form (containers are of standard lengths up to forty feet) resulting in reduced costs—a crane can handle a container a minute—smaller losses and fewer claims for damages. Mechanized handling allows cargo to be loaded and unloaded in hours rather than days. It would be difficult to over-estimate the dramatic short-term increase in container transport or its long-term possibilities. In Britain in the sixteen months ended May 30, 1968 there was an increase of 400% in tonnage carried in rail containers—in 5,000 containers a week. At the end of 1968 Britain certainly led the world in freightliner technology if not in freight volume. The steady conversion of European railway systems to freightliners and the growth of seaborne container services from British ports will all help it move towards a target of around 50m tons a year or over 10% of the country's total freight movement, excluding fuel and steel, by the late seventies. For the service to Australia insulated containers are being used for perishable products and these will be refrigerated by plant on the ship. Containers are expensive. A 20-foot steel one costs £500, a similar aluminium clad one £600 and a refrigerated container £1000.

Much more capital will have to be invested in Britain's ports before full rewards can be reaped. In 1968 the Port of London Authority spent nearly £8m on additional berths and warehouses specifically for unit transport. By the end of 1968 Tilbury had 6,000 more feet of dock space for containers than was available in 1966. The National Ports Council is developing Liverpool (£40m), Bristol (£29m) and London (£25m) for containers. An inland terminal at Birmingham now caters for export container traffic and the distribution of imported merchandise. Efficient communications with industrial centres are essential. The fact that about 30% of all U.K. trade passes through London is not necessarily an argument on which to base claims for attracting more cargo into a port which, with more than 19,000 sailings a year, is already congested. As the cargo liner evolves into a container ship there will be fewer reasons why it should not dock where the turn-around is fastest; Bristol and Southampton can both put forward good cases. The advent of liner trains, reluctantly agreed to by some unions, has certainly added to overall transport efficiency. An outstanding instance is the Cardiff-Sheffield freightliner, the greater part of which is occupied by the steel traffic of one firm. This company has switched practically all its trunk road movement between

Cardiff and Sheffield to rail. The Cardiff-Hull freightliner is organized almost exclusively for Scandinavian export steel.

The latest and most revolutionary development is the LASH (lighter-aboard-ship) carrier. A new type of vessel of about 45,000 tons, it stores its cargo in 73 lighters or barges capable of carrying 400 tons each. Without docking, the ship swings the lighters overboard for towing to their destination. It will be possible, during 1969, for a company in Basle to load a lighter and despatch it direct to Chicago or many other inland destinations.

FREIGHT SERVICES. New through-freight services between Britain and Europe and more exotic destinations are proliferating rapidly. In January 1968, Conemar, an international freight company, began an overland service for British exporters to Japan. Another London-based firm is running shipments on an overland container service across the Soviet Union to Yokohama. Both firms are using the Trans-Siberian Railway. In the two years 1966-68 dozens of other through services have been instituted. The 1,000 shipping and forwarding agents in Britain play a key part in the nation's economy; the six biggest firms are estimated to handle exports worth £400m annually. Gentransco advertises fifty weekly departures to 24 cities. More than anything else rapid technological changes in the methods of conveying freight, especially containers, are causing radical changes to the structure of the business. Britain now has three major depots for loading and unloading of "groupage services"—in Hull, Manchester and in the 35-acre, £1.5m London International Freight Terminal at Stratford.

RAIL. The long-projected and costly Zambia-Tanzania Railway may be a step nearer fulfilment following the signing of an agreement between China and Zambia-Tanzania late in 1967. China is said to be prepared to finance and build the railway, which would be the third biggest development project in Africa, after the Aswan Dam and the Volta River HEP scheme. Despite an expensive Anglo-Canadian survey and other surveys before it there must still be a detailed engineering survey. Construction itself would take about eight years. Such a railway would enable Zambia to become independent of white-ruled countries—Rhodesia, Mozambique, Angola—and would end economic ties with the white South. For Tanzania it would open up the fertile southern wilderness of the country as well as untapped mineral resources.

In Western Europe air traffic is getting increasing competition from railways. Across the Continent the Trans-Europe Express is widening its services. The most important in 1967-68 was the addition of the *Rembrandt* between Amsterdam and Munich. TEE trains cover all six EEC countries and provide better than jet-time on trips of 250 miles or less. The network has become so popular, since it provides convenience, luxury and speed, that passengers need to book well in advance.

U.S. railroads lost about 400m dollars on passenger traffic in 1967.*

ROADS. In spring 1968 the new Yellowhead Pass route through the Canadian Rockies was opened. The highway, 150 miles north of the Rogers Pass road, from Kamloops to Jaune Cache, is 277 miles long and follows an old trail parallel to the Canadian National Railway. It shortens the route from Edmonton (Northern Alberta) to the coast of British Columbia and its gentle gradients will attract heavy traffic from Calgary in Southern Alberta. The new road enables motorists to make a round trip from the Pacific Coast through the Rockies using the Rogers Pass route, opened in 1960. The new road cost £670,000 a mile in some places.

Despite increased rail and air freight, in 1967 trucks moved 80% of all loads in the U.K.—i.e. 1,500m tons of goods.

---

* In a letter to the author, B. F. Biaggini, President of Southern Pacific Railroad Company, notes that "the long-distance passenger train in this county has lost its purpose in the light of very evident public preference for other modes of travel".

TRINIDAD AND TOBAGO

1,864 and 116 sq. m. respectively. Pop. 1,050,000. The country has become excessively dependent on the oil industry, but the supply of crude oil from known resources could be exhausted within eight to ten years. Seismic surveys are being carried out to extend exploration to large areas off the coast of Trinidad. The high birthrate of 38 per 1,000 poses a threat to economic well-being; the government in 1968 started a family planning programme to reduce the birthrate to 19 per 1,000 in ten years. Venezuela has now replaced Saudi Arabia as the main supplier of crude oil for refining; between 1966-68 Saudi Arabia's oil exports to Trinidad fell by £27m, while Venezuela's rose by £15.6m. Sugar and asphalt exports have dropped but tourism is compensating for losses. New factories opened in 1967-68 included two car assembly plants, domestic appliance and tyre factories. In 1967 the U.S.A. took 41.3% of Trinidad exports, U.K. 13.5% and the EEC countries 5.8%.

TUNISIA

45,000 sq. m. Pop. 4.5m. This country, with its high birthrate (2.2%) and constantly falling death rate, has become prosperous in the ten years since it promulgated its first constitution (June 1, 1959). Processing of local raw materials—minerals, wool, leather, food, vegetable oil—has developed rapidly since 1966. A new sugar refinery at Beja has a capacity of 1,850 tons a day and twenty major flour mills are now in operation (ten in 1966). A new factory at Kasserine processes cellulose from local esparto grass. During 1966-68 two wool factories in the Sousse region and twenty fish-canning factories opened. At Gabes there is a phosphates plant, at Sfax a glassworks, at Megrine a tractor and agricultural equipment assembly plant and an electrical equipment plant, and at Menzel Bourguiba a steel complex. A nuclear reactor at Gabes, scheduled for completion in 1970, will produce 20,000 cubic metres of desalinized water a day.

Under the new ten-year plan agricultural production is expected to rise by 5.5% annually. The basis of the government's agrarian reform policy is the formation of agricultural units, which will be operated as co-operatives to consolidate small peasant holdings and to exploit formerly foreign-owned lands. By the end of 1968 a further 2,000 sq. m. had been transferred to the co-operatives, which now involve 100,000 farmers (90,000 in 1965).

Tourism is of vital interest in the country's future and already new beach resorts and hotels are attracting Europeans.

TURKEY

294,502 sq. m. Pop. 33m. Turkey is making steady progress under a series of development programmes designed to establish self-sufficiency before 1980. In 1967 industrial output increased by over 12%, the main successes being in the tyre and glassware industries—where production rose by 50%—iron and steel, woollen yarns and fabrics, and cement.

Fragmentation of land is a major problem; farms are very small, the majority being less than 25 acres and because of size and remoteness much of Turkish produce is still consumed on the farm. Only a tenth of the total output is sold abroad. In recent years food production has only just kept pace with demand—the population is increasing by 3% annually—and wheat and vegetable oil have been imported from the U.S.A. Nearly three-quarters of the working population is engaged in industry, easily the highest proportion in Europe. It is not generally appreciated that the potential for HEP and irrigation is the third best in Europe.

In 1967 there was a decline of a fifth to about £35m in remittances from Turkish workers abroad, particularly in West Germany where the number of foreign workers fell steeply. Much emphasis is being given to expansion of the tourist industry; the government estimates an increase of a third annually.

U

UGANDA

93,381 sq. m. Pop. 7.6m (including 9,000 Europeans). In September 1967 Uganda became a republic; the kingdoms of Buganda, Bunyoro, Ankole and Toro were abolished and Uganda was divided into eighteen administrative districts. Production of coffee, the country's leading export, reached 2.55m bags in 1967-68, with an export quota under the International Coffee Agreement of 2,379,000 bags. The second five-year plan (1966-71) appears to be succeeding in its aims to diversify the economy in order to lessen dependence on coffee and cotton. The variety of new or extended projects ranges from bicycles, cement, batteries, chipboard and pottery, to wire rolling mills and superphosphate fertilizers. Improved roads and railways are planned for 1969-71.

UNITED ARAB REPUBLIC (Egypt)

386,110 sq. m. Pop. 31m (increasing by 2.6% annually). The Israel-Arab War of 1967 with the consequent closure of the Suez Canal has deprived Egypt of her main source of income; at the time this book was published no re-opening was in sight. In any case some of the economic damage will be permanent since world shipping now classes the canal as "unreliable". Many large tankers now being built will be unable to use the canal.

New industries being developed are mainly canning of sea foods, petro-chemicals and methane. Development of agricultural co-operatives has been stepped up since 1966, and in 1968 fresh drinking water became available for the first time to every small village. Already the Aswan High Dam has changed the social and economic pattern of the region of Aswan. The small town of 50,000 has more than quadrupled. It will become an industrial centre comprising an iron mill, chemical fertilizer factory and other industries.

The New Valley Scheme is proving effective; the population has doubled to 100,000 since 1966 but the main effects will not be seen until 1970.

Economically, the United Arab Republic is so heavily in debt to the Soviet Union, Poland and East Germany for armaments that the cotton crop has had to be mortgaged in repayment. It is difficult to see how its overseas trade can be much more than barter dealing.

UNITED KINGDOM

93,053 sq. m. Pop. 54.745m. Owing to a series of setbacks—strikes, inflation, higher taxes, runs on the pound sterling, devaluation—the U.K. had two difficult economic years between 1967-68 and other aspects of its geography were no more encouraging. Further restriction of migrants, this time of Kenya Asians in early 1968, and difficulties of integration of white and coloured communities brought problems of human geography. A further difficulty has been the task of competing in world markets with the countries of the EEC, the U.S.A., Japan and those of Eastern Europe. Imports still exceed exports—by more than £750m in 1967—but there is hope for improvement. British goods were, in 1968, prominent in some fields of foreign markets; for instance, English toys dominate the French market. Since 1967, when a further British attempt to join the EEC was rebuffed, many British manufacturers have set up factories in Common Market countries. For instance, British Titon Products set up a £9m

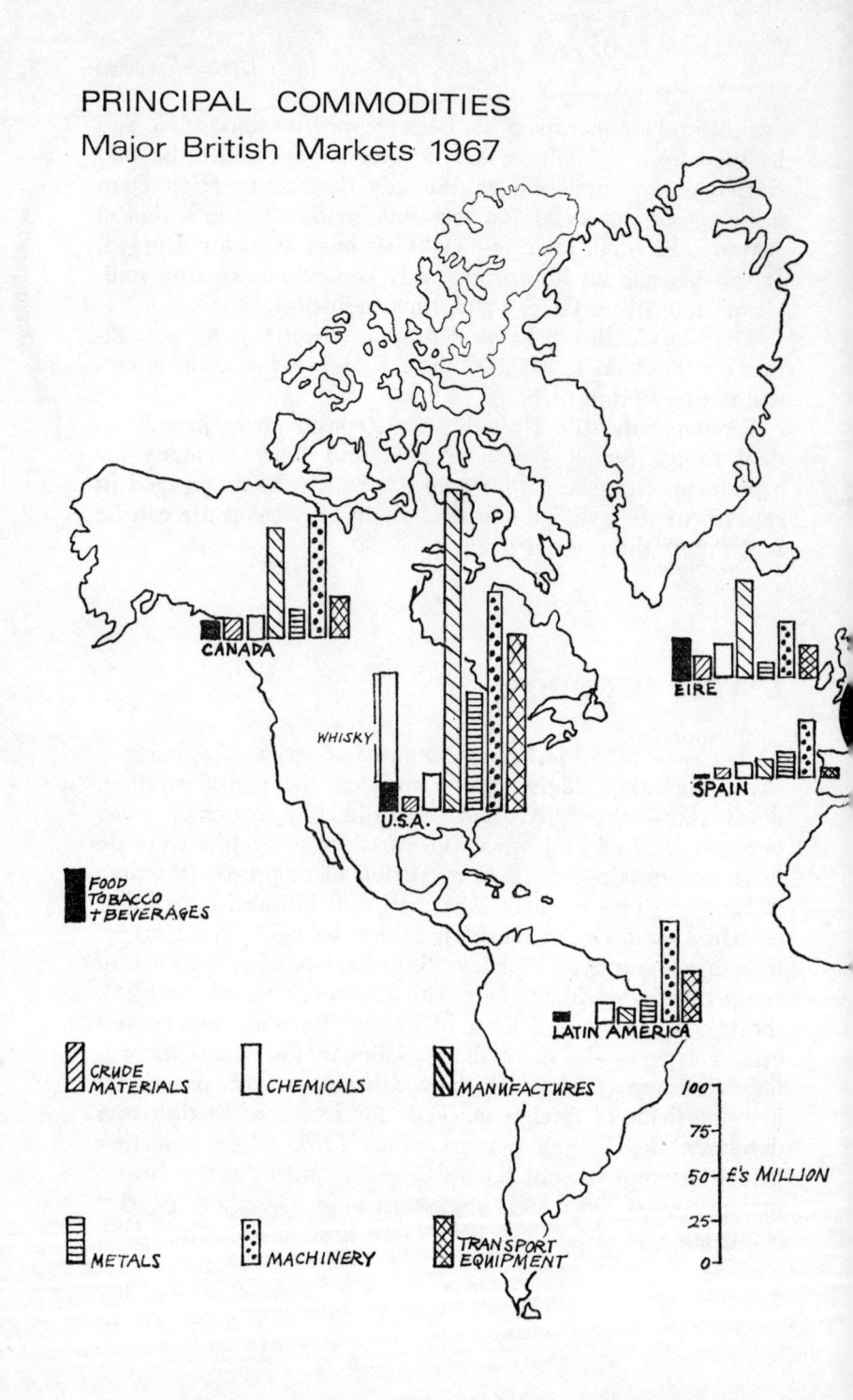

PRINCIPAL COMMODITIES
Major British Markets 1967

16. Major British Commodity Markets in 1967

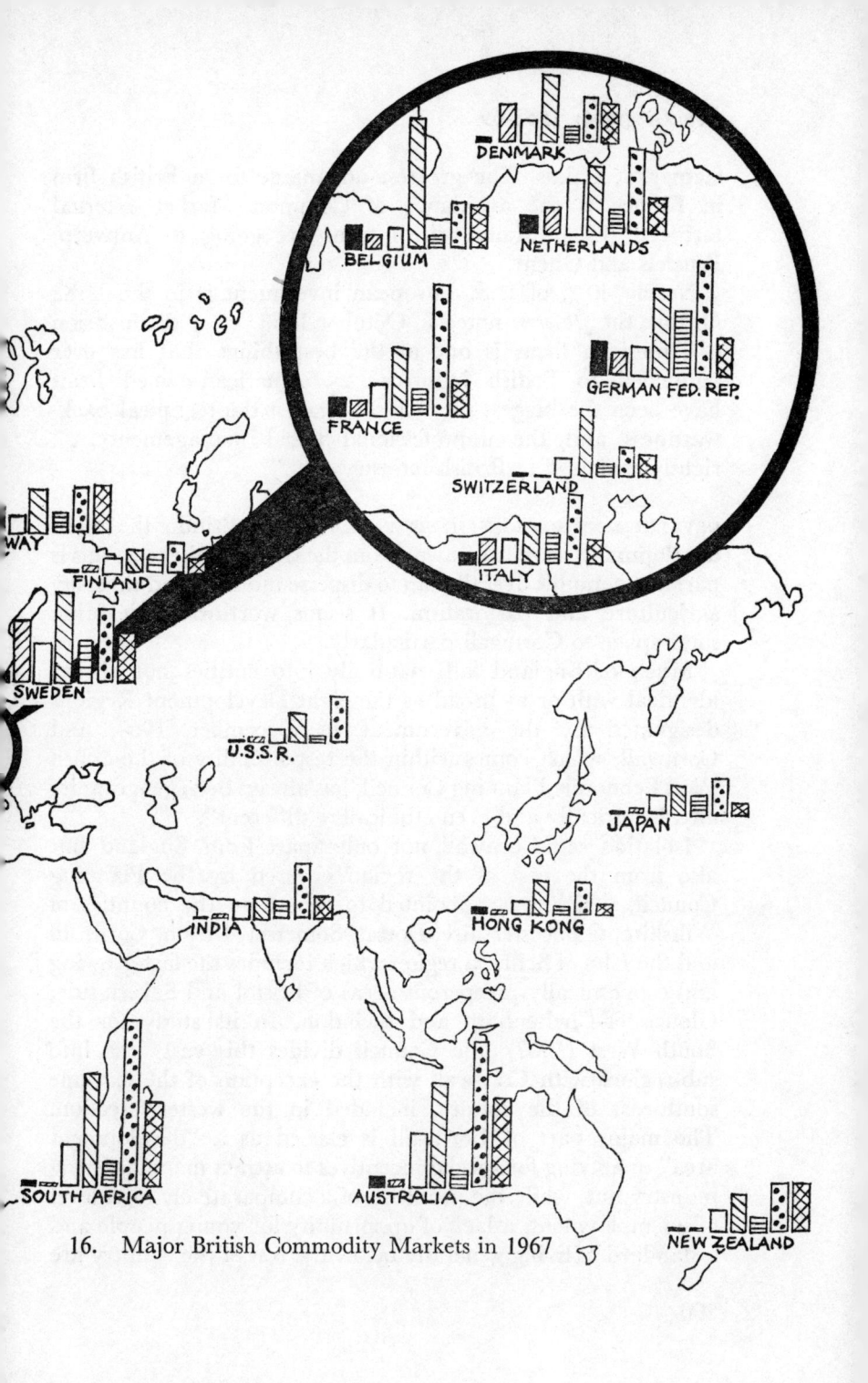

factory at Calais. The greatest advantage for a British firm in France is the avoidance of Common Market external tariffs of 15%. Many British firms are going to Antwerp, Brussels and Ghent.

Nearly 40% of U.S. European investment is in the U.K. Of this, the *Observer* noted in October 1966 ". . . the invasion of American firms is one of the best things that has ever happened to British industry . . . American-owned firms have been the biggest single force against the technical backwardness and the unprofessional tribal management . . . rightly criticized in British industry . . ."

DEVELOPMENT REGIONS: CORNWALL. Within Britain the main developments have been away from the traditional areas; this is part of a complex overall plan to disperse industry and diversify agriculture and pastoralism. It seems worthwhile devoting some space to Cornwall particularly.

Much of England falls naturally into entities not always identical with or as broad as the eight Development Regions designated by the government in December 1964, and Cornwall, which comes within the responsibility of the South West Economic Planning Council, has always been geographically, historically and even ethnically "different".

Isolation sets Cornwall not only apart from England but also from the rest of the region covered by the Planning Council, which was appointed to report on the counties of Wiltshire, Gloucestershire, Dorset, Somerset, Devon, Cornwall and the Isles of Scilly, a region which includes the fast-growing and economically prosperous areas of Bristol and Severn-side, Gloucester-Cheltenham and Swindon. In its study for the South West (1967), the Council divides this vast area into sub-regions with Cornwall with the exception of the extreme south-east of the county, included in the western section. The major part of Cornwall is classed as a "development area" qualifying for special incentives to attract manufacturing industry but, while the problems of a comparatively high level of unemployment, a lack of opportunity for young people and a standard of living generally below the rest of the country are

United Kingdom

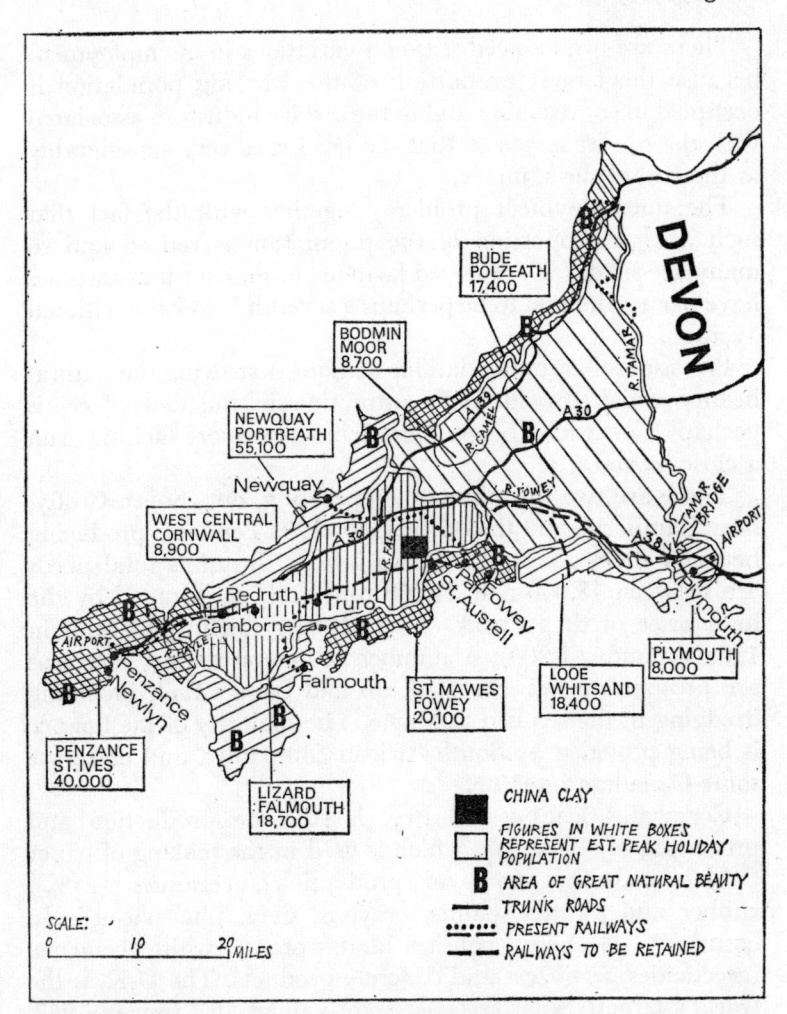

17. Main Economic Activities in Cornwall

shared by all these areas, their solution in each case must start from a basic consideration of each region's special needs. With employment in farming, forestry and fishing at nearly twice the level for the U.K. as a whole, the self-employed form a higher proportion of the labour force than in any other region, accounting for about a fifth of the working population.

There are pronounced seasonal variations in unemployment because the largest proportion of the working population is occupied in construction and in the service industries associated with the tourist season so that the level rises very considerably at the end of the summer.

The unemployment problem, together with the fact that such a high proportion of the population is retired and so many are small self-employed farmers, has meant that incomes have been estimated to be perhaps a seventh below the national average.

Provision of accommodation, without destroying the natural beauty which provided the attraction in the first place, is perhaps Cornwall's biggest problem. Transport facilities run a close second.

There are two tin mines now operating, one, South Crofty, near Camborne and the other, Geevor, at Pendeen, producing between them about 1,300 tons a year. Britain's total needs are between 18,000 and 21,000 tons and, encouraged by the high price of tin (a peak of £1,610 per ton in 1965 and in 1968 around £1,300), a number of major mining concerns are prospecting between Redruth and Land's End, including dredging in the sea bed at Hayle. The majority of the finance is being provided by South African companies, and there are some Canadian interests.

Cornwall's leading industry, is still the production and processing of china clay, which is used in the making of paper (which consumes 65% of production), ceramics (25%), rubber and plastics, paints, crayons, dyes, pharmaceuticals, cosmetics, cleaners, polishes and sprays, white cements, insecticides, fertilizers and concrete products. The U.K. is the world's largest exporter (sales were valued at £16m in 1967, three-quarters of total output) and the port of Par, the main outlet which handles over 900,000 tons of raw materials annually, has the reputation of being the busiest port for its size in the U.K. Par is, however, limited by its size and can only handle vessels of up to just over 1,000 tons, and a recent development has been the proposal to extend the use of the port of Fowey which can handle vessels up to 10,000 tons.

CUMBERLAND. If the forecasts of statisticians are only partly correct about the increase of population then anxious eyes may be turned towards Cumberland in the future. Already eager to attract new industry and population growth local authorities in Cumberland have redoubled their efforts to improve amenities in the area. Improved roads will soon make the Lake District much more accessible to millions of people and a marina at Workington is giving access to Solway Firth. Among recent industrial advances have been the completion of a £5m pulp and packaging mill at Workington, a shoe manufacturing company at Lilly Hall, with another similiar factory planned; Courtaulds will site new textile spinning mills in the same region. A £6m plant is being built at Seaton, also for fibres. The population of Cumberland, 300,000 in 1968, is expected to increase to 450,000 in the next twenty years.

SCOTLAND. The special problems of the Central Borders were recognized in the White Paper on the Scottish economy. Action has begun and the report of a development study commissioned by the Secretary of State for Scotland was published in April 1968.

The Central Borders (population 73,000) comprise the counties of Roxburgh, Selkirk and Peebles, with small corners of Midlothian and Dumfriesshire. They are mostly sparsely populated upland country, but contain the woollen textile towns of the Middle Tweed valley, of which the largest are Hawick and Galashiels. The approximate centre, St. Boswells, is about 25 miles south of Edinburgh.

The White Paper proposed a development strategy for the whole of Scotland, and set the Borders' problems in a national context. Prolonged emigration has not only caused much rural depopulation, which with increasing mechanization and the falling demand for agricultural labour is not in itself economically serious, but it has also undermined the population and employment structure of the main towns. Without intervention there is no possibility of existing industry being able to renew its rapidly ageing labour force or modernizing effectively, or of new industry being attracted to bring much needed diversification to employment. Most migrants leave Scotland altogether—few go to Central Scotland—and to give the Central Borders a reasonably healthy population structure, and to provide enough labour for existing industry to survive and for new industry to be attracted, now calls for the introduction of about 25,000 more people by 1981, bringing the total population to nearly 100,000.

A start has been made by expanding Galashiels, the most centrally placed of the textile towns, eastwards towards the nearby village of Darnick. It was proposed to do this in a way that would speed up the improvement and re-alignment with a major new crossing of the Tweed of an important road linking Galashiels with other towns and with the A.68, the fast trunk route to Edinburgh and the south.

The consultants propose that about half the balance of the 25,000 incomers should be distributed among the existing towns, and that 10,000 should form the basis of a strategically sited new community with a major industrial estate at St. Boswells on the A.68.

Grangemouth, Scotland's only major oil refinery, is now fourth largest in the U.K. (ninth in 1967). It has been expanded because of additional petro-chemical facilities. The new complex will produce 130,000 tons a year of orthoxylene and 100,000 tons a year of paraxylene; the latter will be shipped mainly to Europe for polyester fibre production. The crude oil terminal at Finnart on the west coast of Scotland is being expanded and will be pipeline-linked with Grangemouth (57 miles) by the end of 1969.

SOUTH-EAST ENGLAND. With 17m inhabitants, an area of 10,000 sq. m. (the largest English region in size and population) the South-East contributed in 1968 about one-third of the country's visible exports. The population is expected to grow by 2m by 1981. The South-East Planning Council announced in November 1967 a long-term strategy advocating development in the form of corridors or axes, following major lines of transportation outwards from London. (See sketch map.)

United Kingdom

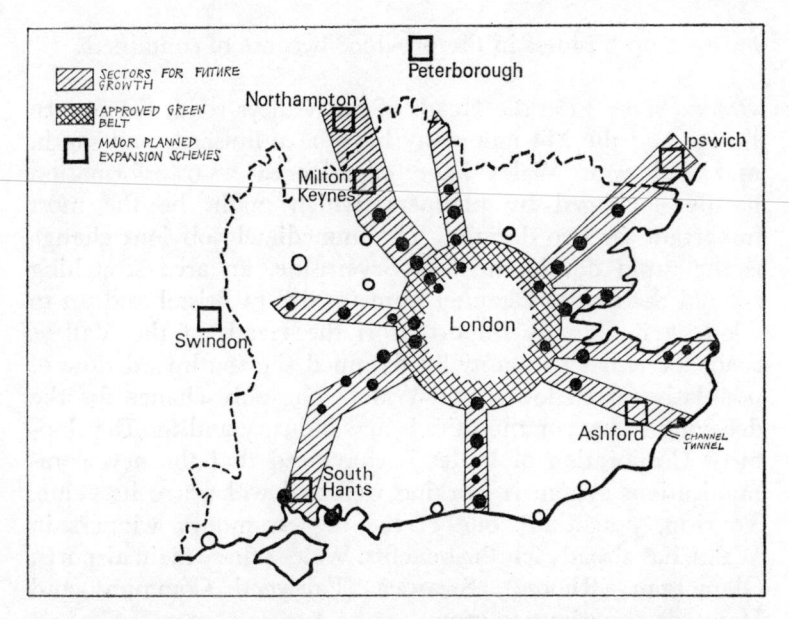

18. Strategy for the Development of South-East England

ULSTER. The success in attracting new industry to Northern Ireland has been such since 1966 that the once huge pool of skilled labour is evaporating. Many factories have opened, notably one for Rolls-Royce and another for Goodyear Tyres. Standard Telephones and Cables have 5,000 employees in five factories. Most incoming industry has crowded round Belfast and Irish Sea centres of communications. The linen industry has stabilized itself but its trade with 135 countries is subject to many outside influences and it employs only 30,000 workers compared with 58,000 in 1950. Other factories have opened at Ballynure (cheese), Ballymoney (cotton textiles), Enniskillen (pork) and Cookstown (cement). There are probably few countries in the world, certainly there is no other part of the British Isles, where the whole concept of container transport has had a more fundamental effect than in Northern Ireland. It enables manufacturers to compete on even terms with mainland competitors; the N.I. Ministry of Commerce claims that at least 200 new manufacturers have set up business in the province because of containers.

WALES. Since 1966 the Heads of the Valleys road, the Severn Bridge and the M4 motorway have been finished, and south, mid and west Wales have experienced a transformation hardly envisaged by planners, which might be the most important for two decades. The immediately obvious change is the rapid development of Severnside, an area stretching around the Bristol Channel from Cardiff to Bristol and up to Gloucester. Equally important is the Heads of the Valleys road, for it has substantially dammed the southward flow of population from lower mid-Wales. The only chance for the decaying valley communities is new industry and the Development Corporation of Wales is convinced that the new communications system is working well and will prove its value. Tourism, potentially one of the biggest money winners in Wales, has already felt the benefits. Wales's three main airports, Glamorgan (Rhoose), Swansea (Fairwood Common) and Hawarden continue to grow.

ALUMINIUM. It was announced in July 1968 that three new major aluminium smelters are to go ahead in Britain. Alcan are building at Lynemouth in Northumberland and Rio Tinto/British Insulated Callender's Cables at Invergordon and Holyhead. The existing aluminium smelting capacity in the U.K. is 38,000 tons a year. The Holyhead and Invergordon smelters will each have an initial capacity of 100,000 tons a year and the first stage of the Lynemouth smelter will produce 60,000 tons a year. All will be in production in 1971. The additional production of 260,000 tons in the early 1970s will be used to meet the expected rise in the use of aluminium in the U.K. and after allowing for the import of necessary raw materials it should reduce Britain's aluminium import bill by £40m a year. All this is of major importance.

FARMING. The U.K. is the world's largest importer of food, the bill for 1967 came to over £1,560m, a quarter of total imports. A third of this consisted of tropical products but it is

United Kingdom

estimated that additional home output could save £200-£300m a year. Overseas sales of farm produce in 1967 amounted to £125m, compared with £90m in 1960, or more than double this figure if the definition is stretched to cover such items as whisky and beer. However, it must be noted that the U.K.'s share of overseas markets is declining in the face of positive policy which is being pursued by such countries as Denmark, the Netherlands and Canada. Nearly all Britain's competitors are surplus producers geared to exporting. In contrast, much of Britain's trade is opportunist, with exporters taking advantage of temporary demand.

The total output of cereals has risen from around 8m tons on slightly over 7m acres in 1957 to 14m tons on 9m acres in 1967. Barley acreage is 2.5 times greater than in 1957 and output has trebled. Oats acreage is only two-fifths of the 1957 level and production has halved. The wheat harvest has risen by about two-fifths with only a slight increase in acreage. The average yield of wheat per acre in the ten years to 1963 was just under 28 cwt; in 1967 it was 32.5 cwt and a yield of 2-2.5 tons is not uncommon. However, continuous and intensive cereal cropping, without growing break crops, has now resulted in widespread diseases and a standstill or even a decline in yields. Some agronomists are warning of "dust bowls". A number of farmers are finding it impossible to return to the rotation system because of increasing land prices, shortage of labour, the heavy cost of machinery and rising costs. Increased pressure on profit margins has led many to economize on fertilizers. Only patient research can solve the many practical problems.

British food production, overall, dropped alarmingly in 1968. In 1965 the increase was 8%, in 1966 only 2%; in 1967 and 1968 it was static. With increased demands this is, in effect, a drop. Farmworkers are leaving the land at the rate of 27,000 a year; more and more farmers have reached the stage where they can no longer substitute machines for men. The number of farms in 1967 which made less than £1,000 rose by 28%; another 9% made less than £500 and 4% showed a loss.

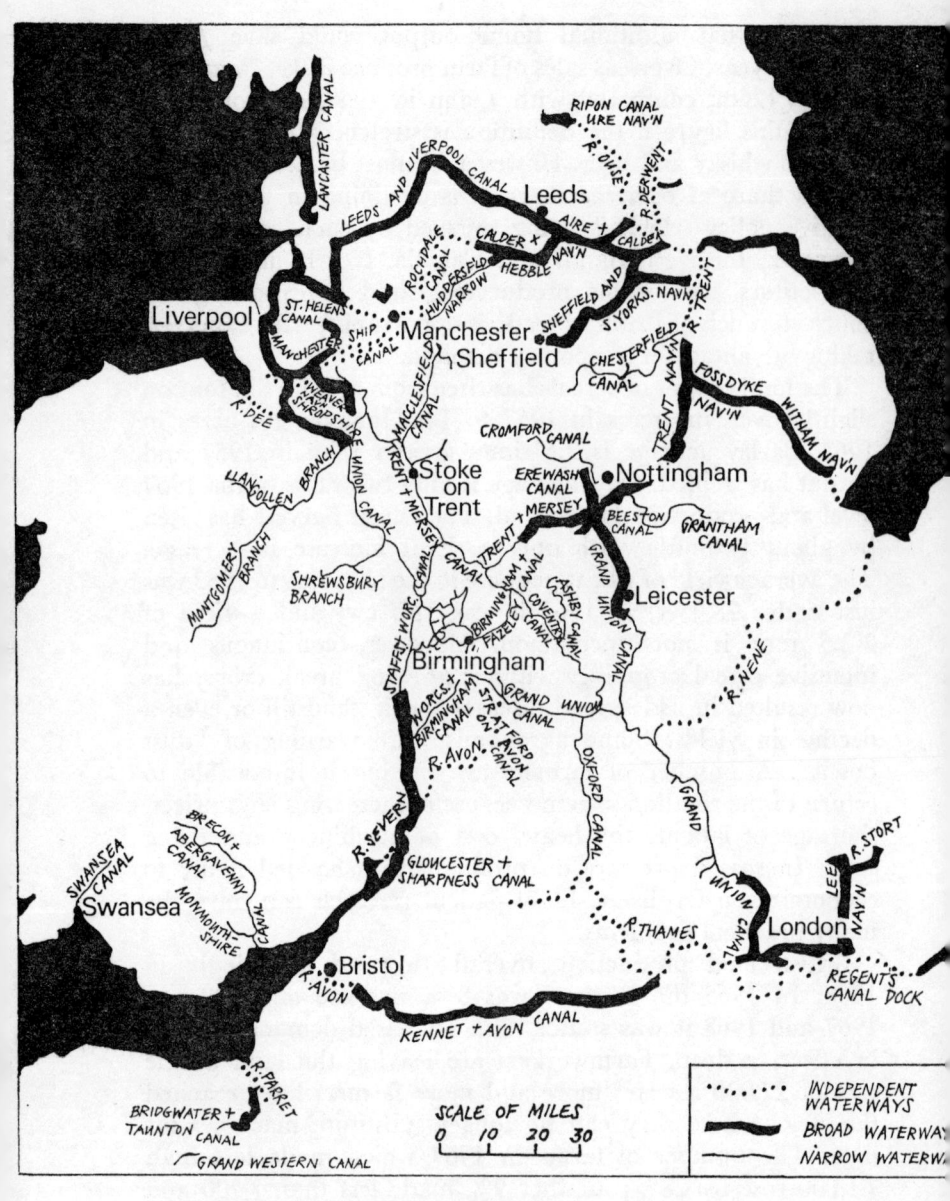

19. Canals in England and Wales

United Kingdom

INLAND WATERWAYS. The Waterways Board has been concerned with checking the deficit on operations and in evolving a policy of future management. Success has been achieved by approaching the waterways as a multi-purpose undertaking, developing them as an organized entity and attempting to make them pay their way as a whole. Every possible use—transport, water-supply, pleasure boating, angling and general amenity—has been considered and exploited. The gradual decline in freight transport each year (about 10m tons were carried in 1962, 7.3m in 1967) has been accompanied by a corresponding fall in toll income, though progress has been made in sales of water to industry, agriculture and to public authorities. Docks and warehouses are proving profitable enterprises. The Board has decided that eight waterways contribute on a significant scale to transport in Britain and "show promise of a reasonable financial performance". They are:

Aire and Calder Navigation (including the New Junction Canal).
Calder and Hebble Navigation (Greenwood Lock to Wakefield).
Sheffield and South Yorkshire Navigation (Rotherham to Keadby).
Trent Navigation (Gainsborough to Nottingham).
Weaver Navigation.
Lee Navigation.
Gloucester and Sharpness Canal.
River Severn (Gloucester to Stourport).

The omission of Lower Grand Union Canal, Caledonian Canal, Crinan Canal and the Fossdyke should be noted. All these canals lose heavily though carrying a substantial amount of commercial traffic. The waterways can never be what they were a century ago (30m tons of traffic in 1865) but there seem to be good prospects for a healthy recovery.

PORTS. British ports may be able to shed some of the handicaps that have left them far behind their Continental opponents, with a technological revolution following on research and marketing techniques. In the past British ports have been passive, serving simply as points of contact for shipowners, importers and exporters. Despite improvements such as containers, and roll-on, roll-off vehicles—poor road communications, inferior management and disastrous labour relations still make ambitious development difficult. (At London and Liverpool motorways are sited on the far side of already congested city areas from the docks; Southampton has no motorway near; Hull is far out on an unbridged and untunnelled estuary.) Britain has no swelling port industrial complex to compare with Rotterdam-Europort or Antwerp, no world-class steel works on natural deep water and no deepwater ore facilities on the east coast. Britain had lost, by 1968, the first round for the main container trade between Europe and America. However, the new techniques do give Britain breathing space to become more competitive. (See *Transport*.)

RECLAMATION. Britain now loses about 50,000 acres of agricultural land annually, roughly a tenth for water conservation. The twelve major reservoir schemes in progress in mid-1968 will remove another 35,000 acres in the south-east alone. The country's over-riding need for water—expected to double by 2000—is undeniable, but many geographers feel it should not be satisfied at the expense of farmland. Since 1920, while the U.K. has satisfied its water requirements and sacrificed untold acres in the process, the Netherlands has assured its supply and in doing so added 10% to the cultivable land. The situation is changing as it is realized that it would be as cheap or cheaper to get the extra water by putting up tidal or estuarial barrages. One way in which the U.K. could get most of the water needed during the next forty years would be to trap it in the Wash, Morecambe Bay and Solway Firth. Land reclamation would be a subsidiary object but the Wash scheme would reclaim 40,000 acres. Northern England's prospective water deficiency might be made good by thirty inland reservoirs of which ten would be in national parks. In the south-east there is the even more interesting project of storing water in the chalk substratum, as is done in Brighton.

TOURISM. Since 1964 the number of visitors to Britain has increased by more than 50% and approached 4.5m in 1968. About a fifth of all trips and all spending are by business visitors. About a quarter of all visitors to Britain are from North America, another quarter from the Overseas Sterling Area including the Irish Republic; over 1.5m come from Western Europe.

ZINC. A £15m smelting and chemical complex, the largest of its type in the world, was opened in July 1968 at Avonmouth. With a planned capacity of 120,000 tons a year it is owned by the Imperial Smelting Corporation, the only producer of primary zinc in Britain.

UNITED NATIONS

There is strong feeling that the "mini-states" members of the U.N. are causing obstructions to its efficient working. The mini-states are those with less than 1m population—such as Cyprus, Iceland, Trinidad-Tobago, Congo-Brazzaville, Guyana, Gabon, Kuwait, Luxembourg, Malta and Gambia. All these countries together pay 0.33% of the U.N. budget, compared with the U.S.A. (30%), the U.S.S.R. (17%), the U.K. and France (7% each). The Secretary General in mid-1968 said the time had come for a close examination of the criteria of admission for new members. But none of the stronger nations wishes to offend the new African and Asian countries, who form about half the membership of the General Assembly. The more experienced African diplomats regret that the gates were opened to all the new countries emerging from colonial rule. Mr. Ahmed Aba Miske, Mauritanian ambassador to the U.N., said in *Jeune Afrique*, in 1967, that the nearly forty votes of the African countries at the U.N. are an anomaly. "We are the group which represents the least but which has the most votes." He suggests that the ultimate solution for

Africa lies in federation—a process that is happening, at least economically, for instance, the East African Economic Community.

UNITED SOVIET SOCIALIST REPUBLIC

8.6m sq. m. Pop. 240m (estimate of Nikolai Mikhailov, the Soviet geographer). The most interesting new geography of the U.S.S.R. concerns Siberia. The popular image of Siberia is perhaps that of a remote, barren wasteland, unproductive and mainly ignored. The relative inaccessibility of this vast tract of land together with its sparse population huddled around the Trans-Siberian Railway would seem to give additional support to such an analysis. To dismiss Siberia as insignificant is to take too superficial a view of the region's contribution to the Soviet economy, in agriculture for instance. Moreover, it ignores the potential wealth which is being derived from the exploitation of immense quantities of mineral deposits and the harnessing of natural power resources.

Siberia is rich in coal, iron ore, oil, natural gas, timber and diamonds, while at the same time the scope for HEP power is unlimited. When all the power stations under construction—more than thirty of them—go into operation by 1971, Siberia will be producing more electric power than any Western country. The abundance of cheap power is paving the way to a rapid expansion of industry; a number of aluminium plants are already operating, in Bratsk, Krasnoyarsk, Irkutsk and another in the Kuznetsk coal basin. Iron and steel production is expanding. Novosibirsk on the Ob (1.090m) now produces as many machines as did all Russia before 1917. Krasnoyarsk, on the Yenisei, has turned into a major machine building centre, providing river boats, bridge cranes, combines, household equipment. The Tyumen region, on the lower Ob, by 1970 will be producing as much oil as the whole of Azerbaijan. In the Yakutia taiga rich diamond fields were found in 1967 and some mining was in progress in 1968. Three-quarters of all the cities east of the Urals are new. Some of these cities, such as Nirilsk, have grown up on permafrost, the buildings being erected on special reinforced concrete piles driven into the ice.

Remarkable changes have also occurred in the development of the extreme north. Along the formerly impassable coastal waters there is now a regular North Sea route, kept open by ice-breakers. The city of Kirovsk has become a world centre for the production of apatite fertilizer; research institutes here are studying the ocean floor and the aurora borealis. On the Kila Peninsula, 90% of the inhabitants are city dwellers.

The Soviet far north-east was once a more desolate region than Siberia. Today in areas such as the Chukotka Peninsula beyond the Arctic Circle modern industrial enterprises have been built and an atomic power station was due for completion late in 1968.

The new distribution of industry has caused new lines of communication; the overall railway mileage has doubled since 1958. The Turksib (Turkestan-Siberian) Railway connects Central Asia with Siberia across thousands of miles of desert. The South-Siberian trunk line passes through a vast area from the southern Urals to the Kuzbass and the Yenisei and beyond. The area of tilled land has increased everywhere, especially in the large area of steppes beyond the Urals in northern Kazakhstan and south-west Siberia.

Progress has been hampered to some extent by high transport costs, by an inability to attract labour from European Russia and, most significantly of all, by insufficient capital. Hence, the establishment of closer relations between the U.S.S.R. and Japan becomes particularly important. Trade between the two has risen rapidly in the past few years, and there has been an ever-increasing flow of Japanese tourists. Now there are hopes of an inflow of Japanese investment to help in the opening-up of Russia's provinces. Japan requires raw materials for its highly industrialized economy. In return, Japan would be expected to supply capital, machinery and technological assistance. Discussions on possible Japanese co-operation in various projects have been held intermittently since 1966, although few definite conclusions have been reached. The projects under consideration include the development of a copper mine in Udokan; of potassium salt resources in the Urals; of phosphate rock near Lake Baikal; of natural gas on Sakhalin Island, north of Japan; and the construction of a 5,000-mile pipeline from the Tyumen oilfields in western Siberia to the port of Nakhodka on the Sea of Japan.

A lack of adequate communications and difficulties in coping with extremes of temperature are two of the physical factors which have so far frustrated attempts at reaching agreement; the copper deposits at Udokan, for example, are reported to be capable of yielding 40m tons annually for centuries, but they are located 400 miles north of the Trans-Siberian Railway at a height of 5,600 feet above sea level where the average temperature is $-35°C$. What is proving even more of a hindrance, however, is the failure to agree over methods and terms of finance. The Russians claim that Japan, as a principal beneficiary of the copper project, should supply half the requisite funds, estimated at 1,450m dollars. Of this sum, Japan is willing to contribute around 400m, a figure which reflects a reluctance among Japanese concerns to enter into joint ventures involving large-scale finance over a long period. The original Russian stipulation was for repayment over twenty years by means of 10-12m tons of oil each year, but these terms have since been modified.

Compromise on these, as on the other projects, would seem inevitable. Siberia is probably the most promising area in which socialist and capitalist interests could co-operate to the economic advantage of both parties.

Nearly all the rivers of the far south have been brought under control in one way or another, from the modest Salgir in the Crimea to the Kura in Transcaucasia and the Syr-Dariya in Central Asia. In many regions of the Byelorussian Polesie and the Georgian Kolkhida swamps have been turned into fertile ploughlands and the mountains skirting the Black Sea have been covered with tropical plantations. Forest strips are being grown in the open steppes, changing the whole face of some regions. Important shifts have occurred in the distribution of crops in arable zones; wheat has migrated further north into the non-chernozem zone, sugar beet has travelled from the Ukraine to the Far East, vegetable gardens have sprung up around cities, apple orchards have spread to the Urals and Siberia.

Much of the increased production noticeable in the Soviet Union can be attributed to the economic reforms first implemented in 1966 under which factories and other enterprises, formerly subject to strict state control, now have a degree of financial and administrative independence. By April 1968 about 10,000 enterprises (accounting for around 50% of industrial output) were operating on a profit basis. Apart from industry the new reforms are being applied to the transport system and to a large part of the distribution network.

At Toghatti, a Detroit-like city on the Volga, a great Fiat car factory has been completed as the hub of a plan to boost passenger-vehicle output to 800,000 in 1970 (200,000 in 1965).

Agricultural output has risen by only 1% for each of the years 1967 and 1968, a disappointing result considering the increased mechanization. The grain harvest of 1967 was only 148m tons (172m in 1966) but sugar beet and vegetables increased in volume. The cotton crop for 1967 was 6m tons, despite weather difficulties. In 1968 the U.S.S.R. was expected to be the only major producer with a large exportable surplus of the better quality cottons.

British trade with the U.S.S.R. benefited from large orders in 1967, for clothing and footwear and machine tools, but in 1968 Finland displaced Britain as Russia's principal trading partner in the West.

UNITED STATES OF AMERICA

3,548,974 sq. m. Pop. 200m. The most interesting new American geography is taking place outside the nation's borders—a reaction abroad to the technology gap which is widening

20. Agricultural Areas of the U.S.A.

between the U.S.A. and the rest of the world. Western Europe in particular fears that it is falling victim to American economic conquest. This is exaggerated since in no European country do U.S.-owned firms account for more than about 6% of total business. But American activity is concentrated in a few high-technology industries which shape economic life such as oil, vehicles, chemicals, electronics and computers. U.S.-owned or U.S.-controlled companies sell three-quarters of all computers in Europe; the oil industry is 40% U.S.-owned in the U.K. and West Germany. Similarly, American companies account for a third of European motor-car sales, 35% of the British tyre market, 40% of France's tractors and farm machinery, 70% of its sewing machines, 75% of its electrical and statistical machines, 90% of its synthetic rubber.

The size of the U.S. home market, more than six times as large as that of any one European country, gives American industry a base for mass production and sales. Also, the U.S.A. spends about ten times as much per capita on research and development and four times as much altogether as Europe (25 billion dollars in 1967). However, it is erroneous to believe that the U.S.A. is exploiting Europe; it is merely taking fair advantage of the Continental practices which divide Europe's markets, restrict competition, protect inefficiency and which fail to meet American sales methods. For instance, Britain had the world's first nuclear power stations but at the end of 1968 had sold only three abroad while the American company, General Electric & Westinghouse, had sold twenty.

CALIFORNIA. California remains America's richest and most populous state—20m in August 1968. While agriculture is the state's most important single industry, manufacturing is the most rapidly expanding part of the economy. The aerospace industry, in particular, has orders for a decade in advance. The heavy demand for aircraft is a factor in the growing demand for aluminium. The industry's capacity is being increased by half and by 1972 output should reach 1m tons—a sixth of the U.S.A.'s capacity. The steel industry in the west, which does not depend on the car industry, is much more prosperous than anywhere else in the country.

CONSERVATION. At the present rate of cutting it will take only fifteen to twenty years for the last stand of unprotected redwood forests to fall. They once covered 2m acres but at the end of 1968 only 295,000 acres were left. Since redwoods grow only in the temperate, foggy climate of northern California and southern Oregon efforts are being made to create a large national park to preserve the oldest trees; areas quoted range from 90,000 acres to 43,234 acres. Conservationists have been able to stop a plan to build two dams that would have flooded both ends of the Grand Canyon and drowned vast areas of redwood forests. (Redwood timber is rotproof, termiteproof, non-warping, almost weatherproof, is easy to work and retains paint.)

POVERTY. About 280 of the 3,100 counties in the U.S.A. are critical hunger areas and hunger problems exist in another 1,033 counties; 30m people are involved. The report, *Hunger, U.S.A.* (April 1968), produced by the Citizens' Crusade Against Hunger, states that 10m Americans are chronically under-nourished and according to the Office of Economic Opportunity, a government department, the poor make up 15% of the nation's population. Two in every three poor families are white and of the 11m rural poor, 9m are white. No region has a monopoly on poverty but the south comes closest. Virtually half the nation's poor live in the sixteen southern and border states yet this area holds less than a third of the U.S. population. Since 1940 more than 4m Negroes and uncounted poor whites have left the south to seek a more rewarding life in the north and west, but few have found it. The number of American poor has declined in absolute numbers from 34m to 30m (June 1968) but many experts believe that the nation may be reaching an irreducible minimum under existing programmes.

TRADE. An alarming fact of U.S. economic life is the deterioration of the nation's traditionally healthy trade surplus; in

United States of America

March 1968 the surplus gave way to a deficit of 157.7m dollars, the first since 1963. A major factor is that a wide range of U.S. goods have become less competitive since 1965, though the country retains its competitiveness in capital goods such as heavy machinery and food. Foreign consumer goods and industrial materials are increasing rapidly in quantity. In 1967 foreign cars worth 877m dollars were sold, but car exports amounted to only 294m dollars. Remarkable foreign progress has been made in the bicycle, motorcycle, radio, television, phonograph and tape-recorder markets. (In 1960 foreign tape-recorders worth 96m dollars were sold in the U.S.A.; in 1967 the figure was 368m dollars.) The National Export Expansion Council believes that one remedy is for an increasing number of firms to break into overseas markets; at the end of 1968 only 15,000 of the 400,000 American manufacturers and business firms were engaged in export. Some industries, such as steel, demand protection. In 1967 steel worth 1.4 billion dollars was imported, nearly all from Western Europe and Japan; this was 720m dollars more than exports.

British sales to the U.S.A. represent about a tenth of total U.K. exports, nearly twice as much as is sold to any other country. Machinery, whisky, cars, iron and steel, aircraft and chemicals prospered more than others between 1966-68.

MAIN U.S. EXPORTS AND IMPORTS
(expressed as a percentage of total)

Exports
Machinery 25
Grain, food and livestock 15
Manufactured goods 12
Chemicals 9
Vehicles 8
Tobacco, oilseeds and cotton 6
Aircraft 4

Imports
Food and livestock 16
Crude materials 13 (timber, rubber, phosphates, copra)

Machinery 10
Petroleum and products 8
Vehicles 7
Non-ferrous metals 6
Iron and steel 5

TRANSPORT. If the demand for transportation in the U.S.A. continues it will double by 1980 and again by the year 2000. In 1968 there were 100m motor cars. The transport system generally (June 1968 figures) accounts for one-fifth of the output of goods and services, provides one job in seven, has 57% of the world's passenger vehicles and, discounting Communist countries, half the world's rolling stock. A Department of Transportation, created in October 1966, is trying to bring system to U.S. transport, which has been greatly complicated by rapid urbanization—85% of the population is found on 2% of the land. Frequently a new freeway built to carry 100,000 cars a day no sooner opens than it is inundated with twice as many. Airlines have grown so rapidly that in 1967 they accounted for much more inter-city traffic than buses and railways together, but terminal facilities are grossly overloaded. Rail is being considered, however, as the most efficient way of getting people into and out of big cities; one lane of a freeway can move only 2,400 persons an hour, a train 30,000. San Francisco in 1966 began to build the nation's first wholly new rail transit scheme in sixty years and Washington in 1968 began another. 160-mph trains (similar to Japan's Tokaido Line) will be operating by 1970 between Boston and Washington, the nation's most crowded corridor.

In January 1968 the U.S. Supreme Court approved the merger of the Pennsylvania and New York Central railroads. This decision was a victory for railroads all over the nation, since it approved the transport philosophy that railroads must combine, that they must grow in size and decline in number if they are to serve their customers and survive. The new amalgamation, Penn Central, operates on 40,000 miles of track in fourteen states and two Canadian provinces; it runs 4,200 locomotives, 195,000 freight cars and 4,937 passenger cars. It is certainly the prototype of the U.S. railroad of the future. The Norfolk & Western and Chesapeake & Ohio will merge in 1970; both have already absorbed several small companies.

URANIUM

After the uranium boom of the early 1950s interest declined as a result of the decision of the U.S. Atomic Energy Commission to restrict its demands to limited contracts with domestic suppliers at an agreed figure of between 7 dollars and 8 dollars per pound until 1968 and to ban imports. It appeared at that time that any uranium produced at a price exceeding 10 dollars per pound would not be marketable, even had there then existed a commercial market. In 1967, however, it was realized that assessments of nuclear demands for uranium for the next thirty to fifty years had been based on two serious errors of judgment. The rapid acceleration in consumption of uranium concentrate was unforeseen and the time-lag between discovery of ore and commercial production had been continually under-estimated; financial preparation for mining (20m dollars) and the great engineering difficulties could involve ten years. In July 1967 the International Atomic Energy Agency reported that known world deposits of uranium on land are adequate for known nuclear requirements. Uranium shortage has led to new mining rushes, notably in the Elliot Lake area, north Canada. The future is uncertain since power stations of the 1980s will re-use perhaps as much as two-thirds of their uranium intake.

However, man is not likely to run short of uranium for nuclear power installations; the sea is a virtually limitless reservoir. It has been found that the Norwegian Current carries about 250,000 tons of uranium annually. More than 1m tons pass through Florida Strait and another 1m through Japan Strait yearly. The uranium can be extracted but this is not yet economic. Since March 1968 the British

Nuclear Energy Society has been examining a "tidal trap" plan for uranium extraction.

URBAN DEVELOPMENT

(An urban population is generally taken to be a community of 20,000 or more inhabitants.)

The complexity of today's urban problems demands a multi-disciplinary approach, including economics, sociology, and demography. A multiplicity of official agencies, professional institutes, academic bodies and others are now concerned with urban geography. WHO's Technical Report No. 227, 1966, states that the metropolitan problem is perhaps the greatest single problem facing man in the second half of the century. A U.N. report, September 1966, shows that urban growth is increasing most rapidly in Africa, Asia, Latin America and the U.S.S.R.; it is very much less in Europe, for two reasons: (a) at 0.9% the average annual rate of population increase is half the rate for the world as a whole; (b) much of its urban development had already taken place by the end of the nineteenth century.

Region	Urban population as a percentage of total population 1967	1975 (estimated)	Average rate of increase per cent of total population 1967	Average rate of increase per cent of urban population 1967
Europe	41.9	44.3	0.6	1.2
U.S.S.R.	53.2	61.7	1.2	(estimated)2.9
Asia	18.4	21.8	1.9	3.8
Africa	15.5	19.3	2.5	5.0
Latin America	38.2	48.3	2.9	5.8

Urban Development

The processes of urban redevelopment in the U.K. and U.S.A. are intricate and difficult to define; the aims and policies have different emphases in the two countries. In the U.S.A. the process has been affected, more than in the U.K., by the weight of political and commercial interests vested in the city centre, interests that must be maintained to keep the city solvent. In some cities, therefore, urban renewal schemes have been based on recovery of the former attractions of the centre. In the U.K., replanning and rehousing is based on slum clearance. The U.K. is more concerned than is the U.S.A. with the creation of new towns.

40% of the British population lives in the seven conurbations: Greater London, South-East Lancashire (Manchester), West Midlands (Birmingham), West Yorkshire (Leeds-Bradford), Central Clydeside (Glasgow), Merseyside (Liverpool) and Tyneside (Newcastle). There is a possibility that south-east Lancashire and Merseyside will coalesce to form a built-up area of 600 sq. m. (Greater London is 722 sq. m.) Similarly 40% of the U.S. population lives in the north-eastern states. But because of the strictly limited amount of arable and pastoral land the U.K. has a much greater need for urban control.

Many planners are asking if new urban centres can exist without a centre; Los Angeles, for instance, comprises seventeen surburbs without a centre. Birmingham, the British city ahead of all others in its redevelopment, seems to have failed as an experiment. Its centre has been half reconstructed since 1945, but speculative development is slowing, the £25m ring road is known to be incapable of taking the build-up of traffic and the main commercial centre is not paying its way. In Britain, despite the flight to the country, 60% of the population lives in urban tracts with over 250,000 population. Regardless of the planned growth of new cities, Dr. G. M. Lomas, of the faculty of Commerce and Social Science, Birmingham University, believes that in the year 2000 the existing cities will still house the greater part of the population. The Registrar General forecasts that in that year, the U.K. will have an additional 18m people.

It should be noted that highly industrialized and developed countries build new dwellings at a rate of six or seven per 1,000 inhabitants. The underdeveloped countries need a rate of at least 11 per 1,000 inhabitants, but do not necessarily attain it. Housing is a very large consumer of a country's investment resources, accounting for 50% of total investment in construction. In the U.K. the total cost of £85.5m (1966) of a new town of 80,000 inhabitants housing accounted for 45%.

The "new towns" have established themselves as worthwhile enterprises and have become symbols of a profound new approach to the whole problem of urbanization, but with the co-existence of the population growth problem, the land use, regional and traffic problems, plans for 1970 and beyond can only be uncertain and experimental. In 1970 the master plan for the 250,000-population city of Milton Keynes, Buckinghamshire, will be published. (See *Cities*.)

URUGUAY

72,180 sq. m. Pop. 3m. The year 1967 was a difficult one for Uruguay, with agriculture severely hit by poor weather and business activity declining. With unchecked inflation, prices rose 135% in 1967 and in October 1968 the estimated increase for that year was 180%. Meat and wool make up four-fifths of all exports so fluctuations in world trading drastically affect Uruguay. During 1967, through drought, the country lost 1m cattle, 1.5m sheep and almost all the wheat crop. In some places up to 20% of the working population was jobless during 1968. Wool accounts for more than 75% of Uruguay's exports to the U.K. Despite foreign assistance, the outlook for Uruguay is poor. (See *Aid*.)

V

VENEZUELA

352,051 sq. m. Pop. 9.5m. Conditions in the oil industry have an overwhelming effect on the economy and marked strengthening (following a general depression in 1966) is directly due to oil production. Venezuela is the third largest producer and the leading exporter, but the industry has some long-term problems. The enforcement of clean air regulations along the eastern U.S. coast, the main outlet for Venezuelan oil, will make it essential that the sulphur content of oil be reduced, and this will add to the cost of production. Two sulphur extraction plants are being built; one, when completed in 1970, will be the largest of its kind in the world. To avoid excessive dependence on oil much is being done to increase investment elsewhere, particularly in the interior. The greatest potential development is in petro-chemicals; inexpensive HEP will assist their development. The most important complex is at El Tablazo. Development of the iron and steel industry is proceeding through exploitation of iron ore deposits in the Guayana region. The U.K. spends about £70m on Venezuelan products, mostly oil.

Large-scale efforts are being made to bring relief to the *barrios*, the mountain-side slums of Caracas, in which live 0.5m of the capital's 2m people. Less conspicuous are the economic, educational and social needs of the *campesinos* (the small farmers), and the fishermen. 200,000 Venezuelans depend on fishing living, in isolated villages along Venezuela's 2,200m coastline. The plan is to give more opportunities in agriculture, fishing and rural industries to check the steady drift to the capital.

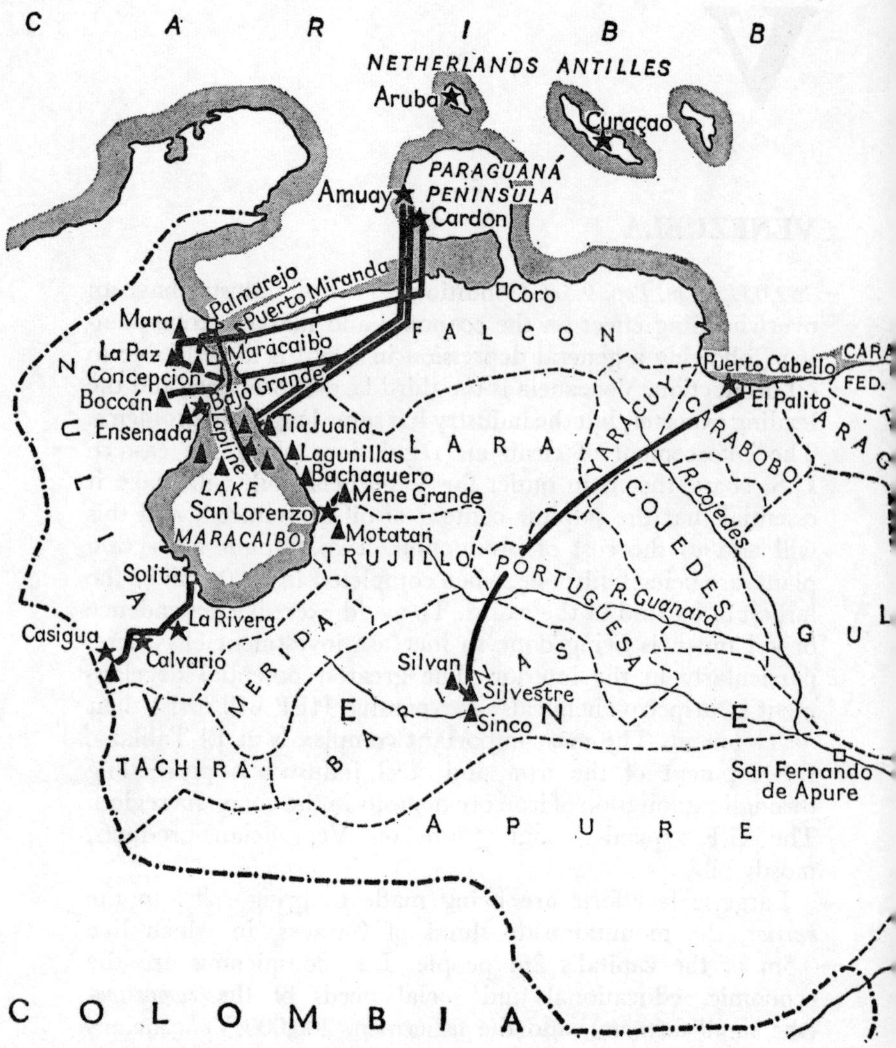
C A R I B B B
NETHERLANDS ANTILLES
Aruba
Curaçao
PARAGUANÁ
PENINSULA
Amuay
Cardon
Coro
Palmarejo
Puerto Miranda
Mara
La Paz
Maracaibo
Concepcion
Bajo Grande
Boccán
Ensenada
Lapline
Tia Juana
Lagunillas
Bachaquero
Mene Grande
LAKE
MARACAIBO
San Lorenzo
Motatan
FALCON
LARA
TRUJILLO
Z U L I A
Solita
La Rivera
Casigua
Calvario
MERIDA
TACHIRA
BARINAS
PORTUGUESA
R. Guanara
COJEDES
R. Cojedes
YARACUY
CARABOBO
ARAG
Puerto Cabello
El Palito
CARA
FED.
Silvan
Silvestre
Sinco
V E N E
GU
San Fernando
de Apure
A P U R E
C O L O M B I A

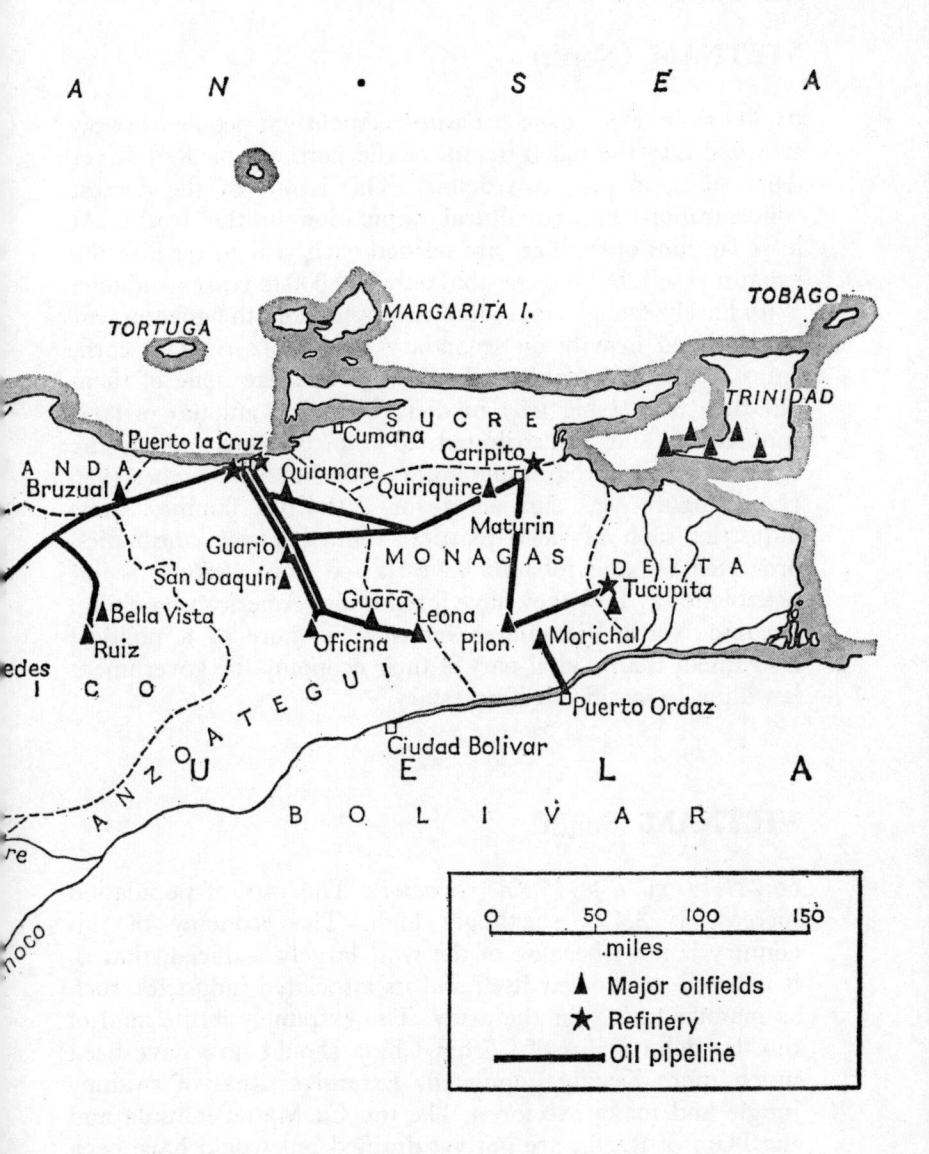

21. The Venezuelan Oilfields

VIETNAM (North)

63,000 sq. m. Pop. 16.6m (estimated). About 9m people are now crowded into the 6,000 sq. m. of the northern or Red River delta (it is, in fact, two deltas). This is one of the densest concentrations of agricultural population in the world. At least 1m tons of fertilizer are needed each year to fertilize the exhausted soils but it seems that only 200,000 tons are available. With barely enough rice to feed its population, the government has counted heavily on secondary food crops such as corn, yams, beans and manioc; the Vietnamese like none of them but they play a big part in diet. The total amount of land confiscated and redistributed to the peasants under the agrarian reform programme is uncertain but a December 1966 Hanoi figure was 2m acres for 2,104,100 families. New industries such as steel, plastics, refined sugar, antibiotics, processed tea and tobacco have started since 1966; it is impossible to say how they have fared under American bombing. Because North Vietnamese industry is more of a political instrument than a vital part of their economy the government is willing to sacrifice it if necessary.

VIETNAM (South)

66,281 sq. m. Pop. 16.8m (estimated). The rate of population increase is 3.4%, startlingly high. The economy of this country is now, because of the war, largely artificial, that is, it is based on the war itself and its associated industries, such as manufacturing for the army. The extremely fertile land of the flat delta plains of Cochin China should now have been much more heavily populated. Extensive areas of swampy jungle and mangrove forest, like the Ca Mau Peninsula and the Plain of Reeds, are not yet drained but would have been but for the war. The country's considerable agricultural riches are most abundant in South Vietnam and as a result of the country's division in 1954 hard-pressed North Vietnam is barred from the southern "rice bowl" from which, until division, it imported 250,000 tons of rice annually. Since 1963 intensification of the war has made it increasingly difficult for the peasant to harvest his crops, still more difficult for him to ship his surplus to the cities, and impossible to open new lands to cultivation. (In 1967 South Vietnam had to import 200,000 tons of U.S. rice to feed urban areas.) Many big rubber plantations have been bomb-devastated or closed down because of production difficulties. The sugar, plastics, glass, pharmaceutical and rubber industries have declined but cotton textiles have increased. The principal food industry is preparation of nuoc mam, the fish sauce.

VOLCANOES

The Belgian geologist and vulcanologist, Haroun Tazieff, believes that there is an imminent prospect of "unheard-of volcanic catastrophes". In a report to UNESCO, in October 1967, he says that such places as Naples, Rome, Oakland, Portland, Seattle, Mexico City, Bandung, Sapporo, Catania and Clermont-Ferrand are threatened. Tazieff claims that there are no grounds for supposing that present calm signifies the end of a volcano's activity and that there is really no such thing as an "extinct" volcano. (On March 30, 1956 the supposedly extinct Mount Bezimianyi, on the Kamchatka Peninsula, exploded, destroying 400 sq. m. of forest.) He also points out that some mountains are thought to be innocuous until they erupt as volcanoes. (In January 1951 Mount Lamington, New Guinea, an "ordinary mountain", erupted, killing 3,000 people and destroying 250 sq. m. of country.) Tazieff writes: "Governments, whether 'advanced' or 'developing' are not worried because of ignorance . . . A few more examples like Krakatoa (East Indies), St. Pierre de la Martinique (West Indies) or Pompeii will probably be necessary before the decision is made to set up observatories which would make it possible to forecast the awakening of 'extinct' volcanoes and the opening of fissures from which ignimbrite flows escape." (Ignimbrite is magma supersaturated with gas which spurts up and spreads out at speeds of 180 mph. Such waves were once common but only one has occurred in historic time—in Alaska in 1912, where the solidified magma is 330 feet high.) An important step was, in August 1966, the development of the telechromatograph, which carries out continuous and automatic sampling and analysis of volcanic gases and transmits the results to a recording meter at a safe distance from the crater.

Merapi, a volcano in central Java, erupted early in October 1967, destroying rice fields and sugar plantations.

W

WATER

The threat of water shortages has, naturally, become more acute and desalting has become more urgent and more widespread. Israel is the first country in the world where desalted water is making an economic impact. A kibbutz in the western Negev obtains by this means 125,000 gallons a day for agriculture and the town of Eilat, on the Red Sea, secures its daily needs of about 1.5m gallons by extracting it from the sea. At the Negev Institute for Arid Zone Research a process of electrodialysis has been devised which depends on electric power to force water through a membrane which retains the salt. Another process uses a membrane of cellulose acetate and a hydraulic pressure of 600 lb per square inch simply to squeeze the salt out of the water. A third process freezes sea water and separates the ice, consisting of pure water, from the resulting brine. Several other systems are in operation. Professor Y. Dostrovski, Director General of Israel's Atomic Energy Commission, says: "We are the only country in the world that has both an electricity grid and a national water distribution system. Thus the large quantities of electricity and water produced by an atomic plant can be widely and efficiently distributed and used economically."

WEATHER

Weather research has become highly sophisticated through such aids as the weather satellites, Tiros, Nimbus and Essa 1 and 11. Weather control is also developing. The U.S.A.'s boldest single weather-control plan, Project Stormfury, is designed to find out if the wind strength of hurricanes can be reduced by seeding their centres with silver iodide crystals. The Russians use anti-aircraft guns over the mountains of Georgia, the northern Caucasus and Armenia, to pump silver iodide into storms until they subside. They claim to have cut crop loss from hail to a tenth of the usual loss. In one trial crop loss was reduced to 3% in protected areas compared with a 19% loss in adjacent unprotected fields. However, it is realized that it might not be safe to tamper with natural forces. To destroy a typhoon threatening Kyushu, for example, might indirectly deprive a drought-ridden corner of Asia of rain. Scientists are already using computers to set up atmospheric models on which the effects of man-made weather changes can be calculated in advance. The director of IBM's Advanced Space Studies suggests a satellite programme that would post meteorologists in the sky, together with two unmanned platforms equipped with complex weather-probing devices.

WEST GERMANY

95,744 sq. m. Pop. 59.7m (including West Berlin, 2.2m). Economic setbacks in 1967 and 1968 affected such industries as coal, steel, textiles and railways and led to higher unemployment in some areas, notably the Ruhr, where an industrial redevelopment plan has been specifically designed to encourage the establishment of a variety of new enterprises. Because the coal industry's output of 135m tons in 1967 is to be reduced by 30m tons between 1968-70 new jobs must be found for 40,000 miners.

In January 1968 West Germany claimed to have become the atomic leader of Europe. Among the nation's accomplishments is the launching of the third civilian atomic-powered merchant ship, *Otto Hahn* (following the U.S.A.'s *Savannah* and the U.S.S.R.'s *Lenin*). The 15-megawatt test reactor at the Juelich Atomic Research Centre is producing electricity using a German-patented fuel system that promises a new low in operating costs. At Karlsruhe, the nation's principal research centre, a 300-megawatt prototype fast breeder reactor, which generates its own fuel, has been developed. It is being built in Aachen, with West Germany contributing 70% of the cost and Belgium and the Netherlands the rest.

Of more immediate importance to German industry is the construction of the country's first practical reactor-driven electric power plants; when completed in 1972—at Stadersand, north Germany, and near Hoexter on the Weser—they will be the two largest power stations in Germany.

Hamburg has opened a 16m dollar "Overseas Centre" to speed container shipping; it hopes to attract 0.5m tons of cargo annually. Hamburg now handles about a third as much cargo as Rotterdam, mostly as the Common Market's chief oil, grain and general cargo port. Its harbour can deal with 320 ocean-going ships at a time. The government has agreed, under pressure, to build the long-disputed 75-mile North-South Canal to link Hamburg with Europe's major canal systems. During the decade 1968-78 Hamburg plans to meet Rotterdam's superiority in handling the new super-tankers by building a 125m dollar harbour extension where the shallow Elbe meets the North Sea, thus enabling deep-draft tankers to send their oil to Hamburg via pipeline.

Germany's exports are concentrated to a large extent in the fastest growing markets of the industrial nations, whereas a far greater proportion of the U.K.'s trade has traditionally been with countries in the sterling area.

Much of Emsland, a broad marshy area near the Dutch frontier and formerly Germany's poorest province has been reclaimed and cultivated. About 250,000 acres have been turned into valuable farmland with high yields. Since 1966 more than 100 new factories and plants have been set up. Papenberg has developed into one of the nation's most important vegetable growing areas; Cloppenburg is a major egg market. Emsland contains important mineral resources, especially oil. On the outskirts of Lingen a new super-refinery is producing 3m tons of oil annually.

WINES AND VINES

During the period 1958-68 wine consumption has risen by about 25% annually in Britain. Increase, to lesser extents, is noticeable in many other countries, with consequent expansion of viticulture. In 1966-67 the total area was about 25.3m acres, with Italy, Spain and France accounting for half. Turkey, Algeria, Portugal, Yugoslavia and Greece together amount to more than a sixth of the total. During the period 1948-64, when the total area under vine increased by about 18%, expansion was most marked in the U.S.S.R., Turkey, Spain and Latin America. In France and Italy annual wine consumption exceeds 22 gallons per person. International trade in wine involves only a small proportion of the total production; in 1967 this amounted to 600m gallons, France being the main exporter. Major buyers include the U.K., West Germany, the U.S.A. and the U.S.S.R. The value of U.K. imports during the two years 1966-67 averaged almost 10s per head of population.

WOOL

Since 1945 the output of wool has expanded at only half the pace of fibre output as a whole. Competition from synthetics has had a considerable effect on wool in the carpet trade and in the 1960s wool's share of the market in apparel fibres has also dropped—from 10% to 8% in the four years 1964-68. Wool producers are likely to face still more diverse competition. Australia, New Zealand, South Africa, Argentina and Uruguay account for 83% of the total exports; Australia's share is half the world's total. New Zealand and the U.S.S.R. have achieved the greatest increases in output in recent years. The average yield of wool per sheep is greatest by far in New Zealand—12.1 lb. The Australian average is 10.5 lb, South Africa's 8.6 lb. Britain's leading position as a consumer of raw wool—368m lb in 1967—is threatened by Japan's 367m lb.

Wool

Australian scientists have discovered how to get more wool from a sheep fed a subsistence diet. This is important in a country which relies on wool for its major export and where many sheep have died in droughts. The CSIRO, by introducing small quantities of protein directly into the fourth stomach of the sheep, which normally produces 6.5 lb of wool a year, has found that it produced between 15 lb and 20 lb.

In the U.K. sheep farming is agriculture's most notable example of vulnerability to high and steeply rising costs and falling profits. Gross margins are estimated at £8—£14 an acre compared with £25—£30 earned by cereal growers. Present flocks per acre must be doubled before satisfactory profits can be made but numbers are, at present, limited by winter stock-carrying capacity. A wide range of experiments has been in progress towards radical changes in methods of production and nutrition. The Australian Merino and the Finnish Landrace strains are being introduced to Britain.

Y

YUGOSLAVIA

98,725 sq. m. Pop. 19.9m. Yugoslavia became the first Communist country, late in 1966, to approve industry's attempt to attract foreign capital investment. Under new laws a foreign firm is allowed to enter into partnership with a Yugoslav company by investing up to a maximum of 49% of total funds. At least 20% of the profits must be deposited in Yugoslavia or re-invested and a 35% profits tax is payable. Companies from West Germany, Sweden and Italy had, by early 1968, bought into Yugoslavian business. Earnings from tourism now total £50m and remittances from workers abroad, mostly in the EEC, the U.S.A. and Australia, provide much more foreign money. Agriculture lacks capital, although mechanization is increasing and the government has been buying small tractors and agricultural equipment for issue to poorer farmers.

Z

ZAMBIA

290,587 sq. m. Pop. 3.8m. The country is a crossroads of racial bitterness. Black-nationalist guerrillas use it as a base for raids on the neighbouring white supremacist regimes in Rhodesia and South-West Africa. Zambians resent the white minority of 65,000 many of whom are Rhodesian and South African citizens who still hold the managerial positions and own much of Zambia's small business. The Zambians themselves are divided into 72 tribes whose rivalries are often exploited by politicians. Because the government joined the U.N. sanctions against Rhodesia, from which Zambia bought almost all its imports, the government has to impose rationing, buy its goods in more expensive markets and ship by air and truck routes the bulk of the copper that once moved so cheaply over Rhodesia's railways to ports in Mozambique. Because of this Zambia has had to curtail the 1966-70 development plan. Again, the threat of nationalization—early in 1968 about 25 foreign companies were nationalized—has deterred foreign investors. A major Japanese company, Mitsubishi, was to lend large sums to develop the copper industry and was to buy copper for ten years, but fears of nationalization have forced the Japanese to reconsider the plan. Were it not for exceptional factors such as the Vietnam War which have increased copper prices dramatically Zambia's economy would be in a parlous state, for the sanctions against Rhodesia have harmed Zambia much more. Large-scale ranching and commercial farming is beginning to develop as a means of reducing the nation's precarious dependence on copper.

APPENDIX

TABLE OF PAR RATES OF EXCHANGE FOR STERLING

Australia	2.14
Austria	62.40
Canada	2.59
Denmark	18.00
Finland	10.07
France	11.84
Greece	72.00
India	18.00
Israel	8.40
Italy	1500.00
Japan	864.00
Netherlands	8.68
New Zealand	2.14
Norway	17.14
Pakistan	11.42
Portugal	69.00
South Africa	1.71
Spain	168.00
Sweden	12.41
United Arab Republic	.83
United States of America	2.40
West Germany	9.60

INDEX

Abu Dhabi, 30
Aden, 63
Afghanistan, 17, 80, 134
Agriculture, 18, 33, 78, 111, 115, 116, 129, 157, 166, 172, 173, 176, 178, 181
  Barley, 18, 33, 207
  Chicle, 49
  Cocoa, 18, 61, 97, 147, 177
  Coffee, 18, 44, 47, 61, 62, 73, 83, 130, 147, 155, 177, 196
  Cotton, 44, 58, 65, 73, 83, 147, 176, 196, 197, 215
  Fruit:
    Apples, 83
    Bananas, 50, 65, 78, 99, 118, 155, 177
    Citrus, 66, 83, 99, 115
  Maize, 33, 53, 147, 184, 228
  Oats, 207
  Olives, 152
  Palm oil, 44, 131
  Rice, 20, 33, 37, 38, 52, 56, 73, 100, 112, 141, 144, 147, 177, 228, 229
  Rubber, 53, 130, 165, 229
  Sisal, 121
  Sugar, 49, 50, 53, 66, 100, 118, 121, 130, 132, 163, 176, 177, 178, 194, 228, 229
  Sugar beet, 215
  Tea, 56, 110, 111, 121, 130, 182
  Tobacco, 53, 130, 165, 177
  Wheat, 21, 31, 33, 54, 57, 153, 154, 166, 177, 207, 215, 224
Agronomy, 20–21
Aid, 21, 23, 24, 25, 47, 63, 113, 122
Aid Ceylon Consortium, 23
Airports, 41
Ajman, 30
Alaska, 26, 54
Albania, 76
Alberta, 54
Algeria, 22, 26, 109, 234
Amazon, 47
Andean Development Corporation, 63
Ankole, kingdom of, 196
Antarctic, 29
Antwerp, 43
Aquaculture, 29
Arabia, 30
Argentina, 23, 26, 30, 110, 156, 234
Artificial foods, 31–32
Asian Development Bank, 23
Aswan Dam, 114, 197
Atomic energy, 33–35
Australia, 35, 38, 42, 65, 68, 134, 175, 181, 234, 236

Austria, 38
Avalanches, 39
Aviation, 39

Bahrain, 30
Baltic, 48
Beef, 36, 42, 48, 57, 176
Belgium, 43, 134
Bhutan, 68
Biafra, 44
Biology, Industrial, 44
Bolivia, 23, 45, 80
Botswana, 46, 124
Brazil, 23, 26, 47, 62, 69, 80, 89, 105
Bridges, 48
Bristol, 200
British Colombia, 54, 55
British Honduras, 49
British West Indies, 50
Buganda, 196
Bulgaria, 51, 165
Bunyoro, kingdom of, 196

California, 217
Cambodia, 52, 69, 110
Canada, 23, 27, 53-55, 58, 69, 89, 118, 136, 185, 207
Canals, 55, 116, 155, 209, 233
Cattle, 82, 145
Central America, 56
Central American Common Market, 56, 99, 125
Ceylon, 23, 56, 165, 182
Chile, 33, 57, 63, 64, 73, 134
China, 25, 57, 130, 154
China clay, 202
Chinese trade, 58
Cities, 58-59
Coal, 39, 47, 59-61, 78, 94, 103, 137, 212, 232

Cochin China, 228
Colombia, 23, 55, 60, 62, 63, 76, 150
Colonies, 63
Commonwealth Scientific and Industrial Research Organization, 164
Computers, 217
Congo-Brazzaville, 211
Congo, 64, 73, 110
Continental drift, 76
Conurbations, 59, 223
Co-operative for American Relief Everywhere, 87
Cornwall, 200-202
Costa Rica, 56, 65
Council for Mutual Economic Assistance, 78, 166
Crabs, 90
Crete, 99, 187
Cuba, 65
Cumberland, 203
Currents, 149, 221
Cyprus, 66, 211
Czechoslovakia, 23, 53, 66, 112

Dahomey, 68, 110
Dams, 68
Dead Sea, 71
Denmark, 24, 71, 101, 167, 207
Desert cultivation, 34
Diamonds, 97, 115, 139, 212
Disease, 73, 82
Drought, 73
Dubai, 30

Earthquakes, 74
East African Community, 77, 174
Ecuador, 23, 63, 79, 110
Education, 80
Egypt, 44, 109, 114, 150

Index

Eire, 80
Electronics, 102
El Salvador, 24, 33, 56, 82
Emigration, 49, 81, 118, 172
Emsland, 233
Ethiopia, 69, 83, 110
Euratom, 84
European Coal and Steel Community, 84
European Economic Community, 18, 19, 38, 51, 60, 72, 83–84, 85, 99, 124, 126, 144, 158, 167, 176, 179, 189, 193, 194, 197, 236
European Free Trade Association, 38, 85, 89, 158, 163, 167, 176, 179, 185, 186, 189

Falkland Islands, 87
Famine, 87
Faroe Islands, 89
Fertilizers, 58, 65, 111, 121, 122, 154, 157, 158, 166, 172, 178, 184, 196, 197, 213, 228
Fiji, 63, 124
Finland, 33, 48, 89, 167, 215
Fish canning, 194
Fishing, 26, 88, 89, 90–92, 109, 155, 173, 175, 201, 225
Food, 93
Food and Agricultural Organization, 46, 68, 88, 93, 173
Forest Conservation, 218
Forestry (*see Timber*)
France, 21, 24, 48, 57, 58, 69, 76, 93, 141, 185, 211, 234
Fujairah, 30

Gabon, 211
Gambia, 211
General Agreement for Tariffs and Trade, 21, 158, 189

Geology, 95
Geophysics, 95
Germany (West), 18, 21, 24, 25, 58, 66, 78, 95, 103, 135, 156, 159, 163, 166, 171, 185, 217, 232–233, 234, 236
 (East), 79, 171, 197
Ghana, 23, 72, 97, 114
Gibraltar, 63, 97
Glaciers, 29, 97, 108
Grangemouth, 204
Greece, 77, 98, 187, 234
Guatemala, 49, 56, 99
Guyana, 100, 211

Hamburg, 37, 233
Hawaii, 101, 106
Heating, 101
Honduras, 24, 56, 102
Hong Kong, 58, 63, 102, 161, 173
Horticulture, 51, 109
Hungary, 103
Hunger, 31, 104
Hurricanes, 105, 135
Hydro-electric Power, 28, 31, 39, 48, 54, 68, 69, 71, 78, 100, 109, 112, 120, 121, 127, 145, 173, 181, 184, 195, 212, 225
Hydrology, 33, 106
Hydroponics, 123

Ice Ages, 108
Iceland, 109, 211
Illiteracy, 109
India, 17, 22, 24, 69, 77, 80, 105, 109, 110, 114, 182
Indian Ocean, 111
Indonesia, 41, 77, 111, 114
Indus Waters Development, 153
Institute of Nutrition for Central America and Panama, 32

243

Inter-American Development Bank, 23, 24, 25
International Atomic Energy Authority, 33, 221
International Development Association, 22, 23
International Monetary Fund, 23, 25, 26
Iran, 24, 77, 110, 112
Iraq, 24, 110, 113
Irrigation and dams, 17, 34, 46, 58, 69, 70, 112, 113, 114, 135, 141, 147, 153, 156, 177, 178, 180, 184, 195
Israel, 21, 41, 71, 115, 132, 150, 231
Italy, 31, 41, 66, 89, 116, 185, 234, 236

Jamaica, 118
Japan, 22, 23, 24, 25, 29, 31, 35, 36, 37, 38, 57, 58, 76, 82, 105, 112, 118, 122, 130, 163, 171, 173, 181, 197, 213, 214, 219, 234, 237
Jordan, 71, 119
Jute, 110, 111

Kennedy Round, 22, 189
Kenya, 77, 121
Kirovsk, Siberia, 213
Korea (South), 25, 33, 110, 121, 161, 181, 185
Krasnoyarsk, Siberia, 212

Labour, 124
Land resources and development, 124
Laos, 110
Latin America, 125
Latin American Common Market, 125

Lebanon, 24, 126
Leeward Islands, 127
Lesotho, 124, 127
Libya, 110, 114, 129
Linen industry, 205
Los Angeles, 223
Luxembourg, 211

Malawi, 124, 130
Malaysia, 22, 24, 105, 130, 166
Malta, 131, 211
Maps, 131
Mauritania, 110
Mauritius, 63, 131
Metals and minerals:
  Aluminium, 27, 145, 147, 157, 175, 206, 212
  Asbestos, 178
  Bauxite, 28, 36, 60, 100, 118
  Bromine, 71
  Calcium, 71
  Chlorine, 71
  Chromite, 139
  Cobalt, 139
  Copper, 47, 57, 64, 112, 139, 140, 157, 214, 237
  Gold, 46, 97, 98, 139, 174
  Iron ore, 36, 47, 51, 53, 119, 139, 157, 179, 197, 212, 225
  Lead, 45, 81, 157
  Lithium, 36
  Magnesium, 71
  Manganese, 97, 139
  Methane, 36, 53, 59, 103, 129, 132, 136, 139, 144, 176, 181, 196, 212, 214
  Nickel, 112, 139, 157
  Phosphates, 141, 143, 157, 177, 194, 214
  Platinum, 139
  Potash, 53
  Potassium, 71

Index

Potassium–salt, 214
Rutile, 173
Salt, 47
Silver, 81
Sodium, 71
Steel, 53, 57, 116, 119, 122, 135, 157, 163, 173, 194, 195, 212, 217, 219, 225, 228, 232
Sulphur, 71, 113, 225
Tin, 45, 46, 130, 139, 202
Zinc, 45, 81, 157, 211
Meteorology, 132
Mexico, 24, 33, 115, 135
Micronesia, 136
Mining, 136–140
  Deep sea mining, 139
  Nuclear mining, 139
  Strip mining, 137
Morocco, 24, 140
Mosquito control, 141
Mozambique, 69
Muscat and Oman, 142

Nagaland, 143
Nauru, 143
Nepal, 69, 144
Netherlands, 23, 25, 41, 144, 207, 210
New Guinea, 64, 65, 145
New towns, 224
New Valley Scheme, Egypt, 197
New Zealand, 70, 145, 234
Nicaragua, 56, 147
Nigeria, 88, 124, 147
Nirilsk, Siberia, 213
Nomads, 17
Norway, 148, 167
Novosibirsk, Siberia, 212
Nuclear power, 33, 60, 179, 194, 217, 221, 232

Oceanauts, 149
Oceanography, 149

Oil, 26, 27, 35, 37, 44, 46, 47, 53, 58, 60, 63, 78, 88, 111, 112, 113, 116, 129, 139, 142, 144, 147, 149, 193
Oil pipelines, 116, 117, 147, 150–152, 180, 182, 214
Oxfam, 87

Pakistan, 17, 22, 24, 33, 41, 44, 70, 80, 105, 114, 153
Paleontology, 154
Panama, 25, 56, 154
Paraguay, 25, 155
Patagonia, 73
Peat, 81
Peru, 25, 33, 63, 64, 73, 156
Petro-chemicals, 117, 176, 196
Philippines, 19, 33, 156
Pigs, 72
Plastics, 157
Poland, 66, 158, 197
Pollution, 159
Population, 32, 104, 111, 140, 157, 161, 193, 194, 195, 223, 228
Ports, 53, 109, 115, 117, 123, 131, 144, 156, 191, 202, 209–210
Portugal, 105, 114, 163, 234
Poverty, 218
Prawns, 37, 92
Puerto Rico, 161

Qatar, 30, 109

Rainmaking, 164
Ras al Khaimah, 30
Reclamation, 210
Red River delta, 228
Refugees, 164
Rhodesia, 41, 114, 165, 237
Rotterdam, 233
Rubies, 182

245

Ruhr, 159, 232
Rumania, 66, 112, 165, 166
Saar, 55
Saudi Arabia, 194
Scandinavia, 167
Scotland, 203–204
Seaweed, 149
Selenology, 167
Senegal, 109
Seychelles, 41, 63
Sharjah, 30
Sheep, 82, 127
Shipbuilding, 37, 119, 169-172
Shipping, 37, 148
Shipyards, 177
Siberia, 212
Sicily, 172
Sierra Leone, 25, 173
Singapore, 22, 161, 173
Slovakia, 67
Soil erosion, 27, 137
Somalia, 174
South Africa, 64, 70, 114, 165, 174-175, 234
South-East England, 204
South Yemen, 175
Spain, 24, 66, 70, 97, 115, 175, 185, 234
Spanish Africa, 177
Steppes, 213
Sudan, 25, 177
Swaziland, 63, 178
Sweden, 24, 49, 89, 167, 171, 179, 236
Switzerland, 23, 49, 97, 179
Syria, 180

Taiwan, 161, 181
Tanzania, 25, 77, 124, 182, 184
Telegraphic communications, 183

Textiles, 65, 82, 103, 126, 144, 155, 163, 181, 182, 183, 195, 203, 232
Thailand, 25, 33, 70, 90
Timber, 37, 89, 97, 100, 102, 131, 145, 179, 185, 201, 212
Togliatti, Volga, 125
Toro, kingdom of, 196
Tourism, 18, 39, 47, 50, 51, 57, 66, 82, 94, 97, 101, 116, 117, 121, 126, 127, 135, 141, 144, 145, 163, 176, 182, 184, 185, 194, 195, 202, 206, 211, 213, 236
Trade, 188
Transport, 189–193
 Air, 39–41, 189
 Containers, 190, 205, 210, 233
 Freight services, 192
 Rail, 47, 192–193, 213, 220
 Roads, 36, 144, 155, 193
 U.S. transport, 220–221
Trinidad-Tobago, 193, 211
Tunisia, 33, 194
Turkey, 33, 70, 77, 165, 195, 234

Uganda, 77, 196
Ulster, 205
Umm al Qaiwainn, 30
United Arab Republic, 196–197
United Kingdom, 19, 21, 24, 46, 57, 66, 72, 78, 82, 101, 112, 113, 115, 118, 119, 121, 134, 135, 144, 158, 161, 163, 166, 173, 175, 185, 194, 197–211, 217, 223, 224, 225, 233, 234
United Nations, 211–212, 237
United Nations Children's Fund, 88
United Nations Conference on Trade and Development, 18, 21

Index

United Nations Development Programme, 24
United Nations Educational, Scientific and Cultural Organization, 33, 80, 109, 110, 149, 229
United Soviet Socialist Republic, 17, 18, 24, 27, 29, 51, 64, 66, 70, 76, 78, 89, 111, 112, 115, 130, 131, 134, 154, 166, 172, 180, 185, 197, 211, 212–215, 234
United States of America, 18, 21, 24, 25, 33, 35, 43, 54, 64, 70, 76, 105, 112, 113, 115, 118, 122, 126, 136, 144, 154, 156, 158, 159, 163, 173, 181, 185, 194, 197, 211, 215–221, 223, 234, 236
Uranium, 221
Urban development, 222–224
Uruguay, 25, 224, 234

Venezuela, 49, 70, 77, 109, 135, 194, 225
Vietnam (North), 228
Vietnam (South), 228-229
Volcanoes, 95, 229

Wales, 206
Water, 38, 46, 54, 66, 71, 116, 127, 153, 209, 210, 231
Weather, 231
Whaling, 148
Wine, 27, 234
Wool, 145, 174, 194, 224, 234
World Bank, 23, 24, 25, 48, 145
World Food Programme, 93
World Health Organization, 73, 88, 222

Yugoslavia, 25, 26, 27, 234, 236

Zambia, 41, 64, 71, 165, 237